By JAY HALEY
(as author, co-author, editor)

STRATEGIES OF PSYCHOTHERAPY

FAMILY THERAPY AND RESEARCH: A BIBLIOGRAPHY

ADVANCED TECHNIQUES OF HYPNOSIS AND
    THERAPY: SELECTED PAPERS OF
    MILTON H. ERICKSON, M.D.

TECHNIQUES OF FAMILY THERAPY

CHANGING FAMILIES: A FAMILY THERAPY READER

THE POWER TACTICS OF JESUS CHRIST AND
    OTHER ESSAYS, 2nd edition

UNCOMMON THERAPY: THE PSYCHIATRIC
    TECHNIQUES OF MILTON H. ERICKSON, M.D.

REFLECTIONS ON THERAPY

PROBLEM-SOLVING THERAPY: NEW STRATEGIES FOR
    EFFECTIVE FAMILY THERAPY, 1st edition

LEAVING HOME: THE THERAPY OF DISTURBED YOUNG
    PEOPLE

ORDEAL THERAPY: UNUSUAL WAYS TO CHANGE BEHAVIOR

CONVERSATIONS WITH MILTON H. ERICKSON, M.D.
    Volume 1: Changing Individuals
    Volume 2: Changing Couples
    Volume 3: Changing Children and Families

Problem-Solving Therapy

Jay Haley

Problem-Solving Therapy

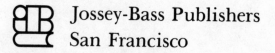

SECOND EDITION

Jossey-Bass Publishers
San Francisco

PROBLEM-SOLVING THERAPY
by Jay Haley

Copyright © 1987 by: Jossey-Bass Inc., Publishers
350 Sansome Street
San Francisco, California 94104

Jay Haley
Family Therapy Institute of Washington, D.C.
5850 Hubbard Drive
Rockville, Maryland 20852

Library of Congress Cataloging-in-Publication Data

Haley, Jay.
    Problem-solving therapy.

    (Jossey-Bass social and behavioral science series)
    Includes index.
    1. Problem-solving therapy. I. Title. II. Series.
RC488.5.H32 1987   616.89'15   87-45413
ISBN 1-55542-058-3
ISBN-1-55542-362-0 (paperback)

TCF Manufactured in the United States of America on Lyons Falls
Pathfinder Tradebook. This paper is acid-free and 100 percent
totally chlorine-free.

JACKET DESIGN BY WILLI BAUM
COVER DESIGN BY VARGAS/WILLIAMS/DESIGN

SECOND EDITION

HB printing: 10 9 8 7 6 5
PB Printing 10 9 8 7 6 5

Code 8728
Code 9188 (paperback)

The Jossey-Bass
Social and Behavioral Science Series

Contents

ix

To Kathleen, Andrew, and Gregory Haley

Preface
to the Second Edition

Preface to the Second Edition

A number of changes in this second edition reflect changes in the therapy field in the decade since this work was first published. Nothing has been removed, but there have been a number of minor amendments and several major additions.

Previously this text offered a guide through the first interview in an average case. Now it also contains an approach to a first interview with clients who are in crisis or who have been ordered to participate in therapy by a court. Recently we have seen an increasing emphasis placed on social control in the therapy field. In response to social conflicts and sexual and physical abuse, more power is being given to government agencies, such as protective services, to intervene in people's lives. The use of custody and medication for difficult and violent people is also increasing. Therapists are asked to cooperate in these social control procedures and must take a personal position on many social issues. Therapy is occurring less and less in isolation, and more therapists are entangled with colleagues in complex ways.

When a court orders a client to participate in therapy, the therapist not only becomes involved with court personnel, but must confront the problem of how to do "compulsory therapy." Here I discuss ways to begin therapy when the client has not sought out the therapist's help as in traditional voluntary therapy.

xi

A related addition in this text is a discussion of how to begin therapy with a family in crisis or when a member is severely disturbed and recently released from custody. Therapists these days are expected to deal with every kind of client, including substance abusers, violent youths, and psychotic individuals. Skill in interviewing in extreme situations is becoming a necessity.

Other changes here reflect the fact that therapy, particularly family-oriented therapy, is old enough now to recognize biases and distortions that were part of its early development. Sometimes an assumption made about the nature of a family is actually a result of the therapist's intervention in that family. For example, the idea that a marital problem always exists when there is a problem with a child might be a result of the way the therapist organized the family's therapy. In this work, I discuss different ways one can enter a family and the consequences for the family of different approaches.

Because most therapists are expected to be able to conduct marital therapy these days, that section has been expanded in this edition. Dealing with marital problems—and resolving individuals' symptoms by focusing on the marriage—has become part of the routine of therapy. Added here is a verbatim example of a first interview with a couple.

Apparently a number of therapists and teachers have found this text helpful as a guide to learning and improving therapy skills. I hope that this new edition will be even more useful.

Rockville, Maryland   Jay Haley
August 1987

Preface
to the First Edition

For the ideas presented here about therapy and the teaching of therapists I owe much to colleagues and students at the Philadelphia Child Guidance Center and at the Family Therapy Institute in Washington, D.C. The communication ideas are largely derived from Gregory Bateson. I participated in Bateson's research project for ten years, and from him I not only learned but also learned how to learn. *Strategies of Psychotherapy* (Grune & Stratton, 1963) expressed my version of the communication ideas of that research group.* At that time I was

*See J. Haley, "A History of a Research Project," in C. Sluzki and D. Ransome (eds.), *The Double Bind* (Orlando, Fla.: Grune & Stratton, 1976). A note to clarify a misunderstanding is appropriate here. One often hears references to the "Palo Alto Group" and its communication point of view, but in fact there were two groups in Palo Alto, with quite different ideas. There was the project directed by Gregory Bateson, which developed the double-bind theory. Bateson's project existed in Palo Alto (actually in Menlo Park) from 1952 to 1962. The full-time members of that project were Gregory Bateson, John Weakland, and I. There were also Don D. Jackson, M.D., and William F. Fry, M.D., part-time psychiatric consultants. The group stayed together for a decade and published over seventy articles and books, especially in the fields of schizophrenia, hypnosis, and therapy. The central focus of the group was on paradox in communication.

At the time the Bateson project was ending, Dr. Jackson formed the Mental Research Institute in Palo Alto with a different group of people who had only a social connection with the Bateson double-bind project. Although the two groups have been confused with each other, in actuality Mr. Bateson declined to be a member of the Mental Research Institute and did not like his project to be confused with that group.

attempting to shift from a focus on the individual to a more social view, proposing that the unit of research and therapy should be at least a dyad. *Strategies* was an examination of different therapy approaches from a dyadic point of view. The present book differs by offering an approach to therapy that defines the unit as at least a triad.

For the general approach to therapy here, I am indebted to Milton H. Erickson; see *Uncommon Therapy: The Psychiatric Techniques of Milton H. Erickson, M.D.* (Norton, 1973). The directive style of therapy and, more specifically, the chapter on directives in this work are derived directly from his teaching. I learned this approach in consultation with Erickson over many years.

For the general orientation to the family expressed here, as well as for many ideas about family interviewing, I am indebted to many colleagues in the field of therapy. The specific approach to families in this work was greatly influenced by my work in Philadelphia. I went there in 1967, commuting daily in a car with Salvador Minuchin, the director of the Philadelphia Child Guidance Clinic, and Braulio Montalvo. Those informal seminars, as well as many other conversations, influenced the views expressed in this work. Equally important was Minuchin's willingness to shelter controversial approaches to therapy and to the training of therapists within his clinic. Although Minuchin's book *Families and Family Therapy* (Harvard University Press, 1974) has a different emphasis from this book, it reflects many similar ideas developed during the years we associated with Montalvo and with each other.

I am particularly indebted to Braulio Montalvo for ideas in this work. He shared with me the teaching of therapy as well as the making of training films on therapy. Over the years, we had many hundreds of hours of conversation about the nature of therapeutic change and the ethics of the therapy situation. He also kindly read the manuscript and suggested improvements as the book developed.

I am indebted to Cloé Madanes for her contribution to this work both in ideas and in critical comments on the manuscript. Many of the ideas about training were developed with her, since we shared teaching positions in both Philadelphia and Washington, D.C.

I was involved in two training programs that evolved many of the ideas about training therapists presented here. The first, the Institute of Family Counseling, trained people from the community to be therapists. The faculty of that project jointly produced many training procedures and included Minuchin and Montalvo as well as Jerome Ford, Mariano Barragan, Lydia Lynan-Gervacio, Cloé Madanes, Carter Umbarger, Rae Wiener, and Marianne Walters. The students also contributed many ideas, particularly those who later became faculty members in the program, including Barbara Bryant, Gerald Hawthorne, Barbara Penn, Edna Smalls, and Peter Urquhart.

The second training program that contributed many ideas was the Institute of Teachers of Family Therapy. In this program, teachers were sent out to various agencies to train staff in family therapy. Along with Minuchin and Montalvo, I was a teacher of teachers in that program. The director of that institute was Kal Flomenhaft and, later, Steve Greenstein. The teachers were Mariano Barragan, Ross Carter, Neal Daniels, David Heard, Gus Kratsa, Gary Lande, Barbara Lewin, Jamshed Morenas, Bernard Raxlen, Samuel Scott, Muriel Shapp, and William Silver.

In recent years I have been directing a program of therapy training at the Family Therapy Institute in Washington, D.C. With my fellow teacher Cloé Madanes and the students there, we have been developing the ideas emphasized in the training section of this work.

Two chapters in this work appeared in somewhat different form in two journals. Chapter Three, "Communication as Bits and Metaphor," appeared in the *American Journal of Psychotherapy*, 1971, *25*, 214–227. Chapter Five, "Examples of Therapy in Stages," was published in different form in the *Journal of the American Academy of Child Psychiatry*, where it was called "Strategic Therapy When a Child Is Presented as the Problem," 1973, *12*, 641–659.

Philadelphia, Pennsylvania   Jay Haley
July 1976

Problem-Solving Therapy

Introduction:
Problem-Solving Therapy

This book is for therapists who wish to develop specific techniques for solving human dilemmas and for teachers of therapy who wish to teach specific skills. The therapy approach focuses on solving a client's presenting problems within the framework of the family. The emphasis is not on a method but on approaching each problem with special techniques for the specific situation. The therapist's task is to formulate a presenting symptom clearly and to design an intervention in the client's social situation to change that presenting symptom. Although the book focuses on problems, the approach here differs from other symptom-oriented therapies in that it emphasizes the social context of human problems.

Defining a Problem

In recent years there has been a debate between therapists who prefer to define a symptom in precise behavioral terms, such as a specific avoidance behavior, and those who use a more general category like "anxiety" or a "feeling of helplessness." Some therapists prefer to formulate symptoms in ways that can be counted as acts, while others prefer to formulate a problem as a state of mind or as a character disorder. The approach in

1

this work differs from both such approaches insofar as the emphasis is not on an individual. Even though this approach assumes that the therapist has failed if he or she does not solve the presenting problem, and even though the symptom is defined in operational terms that are as precise as possible, the therapy focus is on the social situation rather than on the person. It is possible to define a "problem" in different social units. In this book a problem is defined as a type of behavior that is part of a sequence of acts among several persons. The repeating sequence of behavior is the focus of therapy. A symptom is a label for, a crystallization of, a sequence in a social organization. Thinking of such symptoms as "depression" or "phobia" as a contract between people and therefore as adaptive to relationships leads to a new way of thinking about therapy.

One of the contributions of the family approach when it was developed in the 1950s was the discovery that symptoms could be viewed as appropriate and adaptive behavior. Rather than assume a symptom was irrational and based on misperceptions carried over from the past, it was argued that a symptom was a way of adapting to the current social situation. It followed logically that therapy should focus on changing the social situation if a symptom was to be changed.

Shifting one's thinking from the individual unit to a social unit of two or more persons has certain consequences for a therapist. The therapist not only must think in different ways about human dilemmas but also must consider himself or herself as a member of the social unit that contains the problem. The therapist must be considered as part of the social dilemma of the client, and this can be a disturbing idea. Twenty years ago it was a new step to recognize that a family rather than an individual was the therapeutic unit. In time that family unit was expanded to include the extended kin and also the peer group. Now it is becoming uncomfortably evident that a presenting problem includes the professional world in which the problem appears, and the larger society as well.

Diagnosis as Part of the Problem. When a therapeutic problem is defined as the social relationships of clients, a therapist must include himself in the issue, since he helps define the problem. To label a child as "delinquent" or as suffering from "minimal brain disfunction" or to label an adult as an "alcoholic" or a "schizophrenic" means that one is participating in the creation of a problem in such a way that change may be made more difficult. A therapist who describes a family situation as characterized by "a dominating mother and a passive father" or "a symbiotic relationship between mother and daughter" has created problems, although the therapist might think he is merely identifying the problems put before him. The way one labels a human dilemma can crystallize a problem and make it chronic.

Colleagues as Part of the Problem. The issue of professionally created problems becomes more evident when we examine the ways in which clinicians may become part of the presenting problem. If a therapist accepts in therapy a young adult who is defined as schizophrenic and who is in a mental hospital, how does one define the problem? Therapists have assumed for years that the social unit in such a case is the young adult and his family. This does not necessarily imply that the family unit is the "cause" of the schizophrenia, but it does assume that the expression of the problem is in the family and that the family is the best source of help for the young adult. That is where he will go when he comes out of custody.

Besides the family being the social unit in such a case, it also has become increasingly evident that the problem includes the psychiatric staff who have authority over custody and medication. The therapist cannot pretend that the therapy problem is only the young person and his family when decision for discharge is in the hands of other people and when the young person may be drugged at any time without the therapist's permission. Similarly, to do therapy with a man or woman on probation requires defining the problem to include the probation officer and court as well as family and friends. When social control is an issue, the professional milieu is part of the presenting problem. In more routine cases, the dissension among professionals involved in a family may be the therapy problem. If different therapists are seeing different family members, they may be in a territorial struggle over who is right and wrong in the family.

The social unit for the therapist is thus not merely the family but also the professional colleagues.

A Wider Social Unit

The issues are disturbing if one views fellow clinicians as part of the problems, but there are larger issues as well. When a boy refuses to attend school, his behavior can be defined as a therapeutic problem. His therapist is expected to intervene in family and school and to get the youth to function appropriately. Such a problem is usually routine. Yet suppose the school is in a slum and is such a bad school that the therapist can only sympathize with the young person for avoiding it as a waste of time. The problem is thus not simply a child's truancy but also a problem school. If one includes the school, the line between therapy and social or political action becomes obscure.

Adopting a social view of the problem makes it difficult for a therapist to limit his or her thinking to either child or school wihout including the economic system and social issues in which such a school is embedded. A boy who will not go to school may be responding to a bad school or to a problem family. But neither issue is separable from the fact that the father may be chronically unemployed because of the nature of the economic system and the mother may be involved in a welfare situation that may distort the organization of the family. Is the therapist's problem not only the individual family, gang, and school but also the larger society? Although such issues are evident with the poor, they are also present when therapists deal with the upper class. A depressed woman may be defined as the problem, or the therapist may include the fact that she is the wife of a harried corporation executive who is driven constantly to move his family from place to place as part of the competitive struggle of his career.

Whither the Therapist?

A therapist can attempt to deal with the social issue by going to extremes. One may define the problem as really a mat-

ter of misperception by the client and one may concern oneself
with the client's fantasies about his or her social situation. Such
a narrow view no longer seems palatable. The therapist can go
to the opposite extreme and define all problems as economic
and cultural. But then he or she must become a revolutionary
to solve each problem. Such an approach does not seem practical. Not only must the therapist have evidence that a revolution would create a society that would solve the problem, but
furthermore, the client must wait in distress while the therapist
organizes the revolution.

The issue of radicalism became prominent in the 1960s
when therapists were placed in mental health clinics in slums
full of poor black people. Such therapists were caught up in
arguments of polar extremes. If a therapist helped a poor family
deal with a problem, he was accused by radicals of wasting his
time, since the problem was a racist society and unemployment.
Those therapists who shifted to a more radical objective and
attempted to do something about racism and the economic system were open to the criticism that they were only indulging
in rhetoric and not helping even one family in distress.

The task for the therapist has no easy solution. Whatever
radical position he takes as a citizen, his obligation as a therapist
is to define the social unit that he can change to solve the presenting problem of a client. To war with mental hospitals, courts,
and welfare agencies does not usually achieve the goal of the
therapy, although sometimes it may be necessary. The effectiveness of the therapist is evaluated in terms of the outcome of his
therapy, not in terms of the moral stance he takes or his justi-
fiable indignation at the society that is contributing to the problems he is trying to solve. The most useful point of view for
the therapist is the idea that there is sufficient variety in any
situation so that some better arrangement can be made. Rather
than simply condemn a bad school, a therapist must visit the
school and find within it a more suitable place for the child he
is attempting to get back into school.

When one accepts the idea that the problems of a client
include the social milieu, including the therapist, the therapist
must always consider the coalitions he is involved in when he

acts. Not only must he consider whether he is acting as a social
control agent of society whose job is to quiet troublemakers, but
he must also think of this function in social frameworks smaller
than that of society as a whole. Problem solving from this point
of view is not as simple as some behavior modifiers would suggest. Behavior therapy has emphasized problems and has brought
more precision to the field, as well as a concern with results.
Yet there is also a tendency for behavior therapists to define
the problem without including the therapist in the social situation. For example, if a child has temper tantrums and the therapist subscribes to a conditioning theory, she will focus on the
problem of tantrums and use conditioning procedures to extin-
guish the problem behavior. Yet whose agent is the therapist
in such a case? With whom is she in coalition against whom?
A therapist who thinks in terms of the social context will be concerned about the child's temper tantrums as a response to the
child's current relationships. She will also consider the hierarchy
in the situation and decide whether she wants to be employed
by parents to shape a child in the ways they wish. In actuality,
the therapist might decide to focus on the temper tantrum problem, but if she thinks in terms of sequences in relationships,
she will also be aware that she is acting as much in relation to
mother and father as to child. The same concern applies to any
coalition of a therapist and a family member when the context
is ignored. A therapist who habitually rescues wives from subservient positions in relation to their husbands may have good intentions without being aware of the consequences for the whole
family. Whether naively rescuing a child or a wife or a husband, the therapist can confuse a personal moral posture with
therapy and can cause harm to a family.

A more evident dilemma for the therapist appears when
she becomes aware that she is part of the problem in a social
control situation. From a narrow view, a therapist on an inpatient unit may be solving behavior problems of patients on the
ward when she sets up a "token economy" or uses similar procedures. Yet from an organizational point of view, she is joining
the establishment to shape patients into behaving like better
patients for the convenience of the staff. Years ago a report

described a mental patient who collected towels in her room on a mental hospital ward. A therapist solved the problem by paradoxically imposing towels on the woman until her room was so full she could not get into it. This intervention is typically described without clarifying whether it caused the woman to behave better on the ward or helped her to go out into the community into a normal life. Once a therapist thinks in organizational terms, she must think of herself as a part of the social system that is the client's problem.

Besides dealing with the consequences of thinking about his or her place in the social system, a therapist who takes a problem point of view has difficulty finding a place in which to be trained to do therapy. A few settings offer training in problem solving through behavioral techniques. Other, quite different settings offer training in family-oriented therapy. It is difficult to find a place where one can learn a problem orientation while also learning to think about problems within a social framework. It is the purpose of this book to provide ways to formulate problems and ways to intervene in human relationships to solve these problems.

This book is designed for therapists and should not be misunderstood as an attempt to map how society and the human family are in actuality or how they should be if all were well. What is offered is simplistic formulations of social situations that can help a therapist recognize typical interchanges and determine what to do.

1

Conducting the First Interview

If successful therapy is defined as solving the problems of a client, the therapist must know how to formulate a problem and how to solve it. And if he or she is to solve a variety of problems, the therapist must not take a rigid and stereotyped approach to therapy. Any standardized method of therapy, no matter how effective with certain problems, cannot deal successfully with the wide range that is typically offered to a therapist. Flexibility and spontaneity are necessary. Yet any therapist must also learn from experience and repeat what was successful before. A combination of familiar procedures and innovative techniques increases the probability of success.

If therapy is to end properly, it must begin properly—by negotiating a solvable problem and discovering the social situation that makes the problem necessary. The act of therapy begins with the way the problem is examined. The act of intervening brings out problems and the relationship patterns that are to be changed.

A skillful therapist will approach each new person with the idea that a unique procedure might be necessary for this particular person and social situation. The variables are many, but most fall into the categories of time, place, fee, number of persons involved, and the special directives necessary to begin.

8

A therapist who had total freedom might find it best for a particular situation to work in the office, in the home, in the place of business, on the street, or, for a school problem, at the school. The first interview could go on for an hour, or half an hour, or several hours. The therapist could immediately move for a change or perhaps be leisurely and not request action at once. In one case a standard fee may be appropriate; in another the client may be asked to pay what he thinks the therapist deserves; and in yet another he should pay if he does not improve. The therapist may interview one person or several on the first visit and may include only family members or may include friends and other professionals. For one ethnic group the approach may need to be formal, and for another a casual attitude might be more effective. There are many different ways a master therapist might begin, but what will be offered here is a preferred way for the average therapist to begin a first encounter.

Today it is assumed that to begin therapy by interviewing one person is to begin with a handicap. When it was thought that a therapeutic problem was a one-person phenomenon, then it seemed reasonable to interview only one person. Symptoms, or problems, were considered to be maladaptive and inappropriate. Therefore there was no reason to bring in more than one person who was being maladaptive. If a wife had anxiety attacks, these were not considered adaptive to her marriage, but were thought to be irrational. Therefore, her husband was not considered to be relevant except as a stress factor for the woman, who was the "real" problem.

It is, of course, possible to change a marriage or a family by seeing only one person, but it can be a slow and difficult procedure and often fails, as therapy outcome studies have shown. It is much more sensible to interview the natural group where the problem is expressed and so to proceed immediately toward the solution.

If it is obvious that one should interview both husband and wife in a marriage, it should be even more obvious that when the problem is an adolescent who must be helped to disengage from his or her family, then the whole family must be immediately involved. The therapist must bring people together to help them individuate, and it is more sensible to begin that individuation process at once with the first interview.

If one thinks of a problem in its context, the past dichotomy between "individual" and "family" therapy becomes irrelevant. To interview an individual is one way to intervene in a family. By interviewing a man, woman, or child without seeing the others in the family, one forms a coalition in the dark without knowing what kind of organization one is entering. Although after therapy has begun the therapist might want to interview family members one at a time for a particular purpose, in the beginning it is better to see everyone who lives in a household so that the therapist can quickly grasp the problem and the social situation that is maintaining it.

Moreover, it is generally accepted that people cannot report properly about their own social situations. Even a trained participant observer gives a biased report, because of her position in her personal social network. A trained anthropologist cannot adequately report the sequences in his own family. In the 1950s, doubt about self-report led to family interviews and also caused therapy supervisors to prefer to watch a therapist at work through a one-way mirror or on videotape. The supervisors learned that a therapist's description of an interview was not adequate when compared with a recording. When patients were seen privately without being recorded, therapists also were seen privately in supervisory sessions, and no one knew what was actually happening in therapy. A wife would report that her husband did something, without mentioning her part in the sequence that led up to the act. For example, she might report that her husband had struck her "out of the blue." The therapist would report this reported event to his supervisor without describing how he encouraged the wife to tell him about this incident. The therapist would not mention that he was joining, perhaps outside awareness, with the wife against the husband and encouraging her to condemn him. The supervisor had to guess what might have happened from the reports of a wife as reported by a therapist. Both reports would be biased. It is more sensible to see husband and wife together with a supervisor observing the action when that is possible. With this kind of observation, the therapeutic situation changes from "individual" versus "family" to doing therapy in the dark or in the light.

Part of the difficulty in beginning therapy properly has been the confusion between diagnosis for institutional reasons and diagnosis for therapy purposes. For an institution and for medical insurance reasons, it was necessary to see a person alone and to classify him or her as a diagnostic type, according to some scheme, such as the *DSM*. That procedure was irrelevant to therapy and could even handicap the therapist in thinking about how to solve the problem. Now it is known that the best diagnosis *for therapy* is one that allows the social group to respond to attempts to bring about change. A therapist must intervene with a therapeutic act to gather diagnostic information for therapy, and so it is best to begin with everyone involved because change will involve everyone.

There are, of course, times when only one person is available to be interviewed and so the initial session must be one-to-one. If the person is in jail or a mental hospital, naturally the therapist would expect the family to be present at a first interview, in order to plan the future outside. If the person is a college student thousands of miles from home who asks for therapy, it may be necessary to see him or her alone for a first interview. Later there can be letters, telephone calls, visits from parents, and other forms of getting together, but in the beginning the single person must be interviewed. This special and unusual situation requires a therapist who can estimate from talking to one person what his situation is and what the consequences of change will be for people who are not there. It is possible to change a person by seeing him alone, but the skill required is often too much to ask of the average therapist.

For the usual first interview, particularly with child problems, the therapist should expect everyone involved to attend. If the problem involves school, it is often best to have the first interview at the school with the teacher, counselor, child, and parents. These persons make up the social group involved, and time can be saved if therapy is begun with all members of the group present. (The way of doing a first interview to be described here applies to such a group.) For most problems, the intimate network should be invited. Everyone who lives in the household is a member of the proper unit, although if the therapist knows about a grandmother who lives around the corner, he should ask that she come too.

This emphasis on having everyone at a first interview does not mean that therapy cannot be done if total participation is not arranged. It simply means that bringing everyone in is the easiest way to work. The way to conduct a first interview described here will help a therapist begin properly. The procedure outlined can be used with most problems; of course, there are always unique situations that require special handling.

For example, when a young person is in a mental hospital, this kind of exploratory interview is not appropriate. In such a case, the therapist knows in advance that the problem is the hospitalization. The strategy in such a case is to emphasize authority and family hierarchy, since it is a time of crisis. It is not a time to explore.*

There are other times when this type of first interview is not the correct procedure to follow. At times a family is referred in error because of a misunderstanding with the referral source, or the interview is for a "check-up" or a consultation and there is no interest in beginning therapy. Some families merely want a child tested and so do not arrive with a purpose of having therapy. (Even if only testing is to be done, the family can be involved. Some clinics now arrange that a child be tested while the parents observe from behind a one-way mirror so they can see their child's responses. Afterward, when tester and parents discuss the results, the parents have a basis for judging the tester's conclusions and do not merely receive a summary report.)

There are also "compulsory" referrals that require special handling in the first encounter. When the family is referred by a court or a school, the mother or father may be angry and require special courtesy. Whenever a therapist finds a client confusing or apparently behaving in an inappropriate way, he or

---

*For a discussion at length of the therapy of seriously disturbed young adults, see J. Haley, *Leaving Home* (New York: McGraw-Hill, 1980).

she should assume it is the context that is confusing, not merely a peculiar person.

Another special situation is a demonstration interview, in which a therapist must interview a family before a group. If the family therapist does this, he must take care that the family does not expose more than it should before a group of strangers. A therapist should never interview a family before a group if he is not going to see that family again. A demonstration interview of a family by a visiting therapist is an exploitation of the family, and the family members do not receive compensation for their exposure (unless they are paid a fee). Such a one-time demonstration also has nothing to do with therapy. It is simply a demonstration of how to use a family to communicate to an audience, and a student therapist should never assume that he should do a therapy interview in that way.

One further comment on getting everyone in for a first interview. Often a young person, either living with parents or not, would prefer not to have the family involved in the therapy. Sometimes such a young person has had years of individual therapy and prefers that method. A therapist should not let a client decide how therapy should be done, particularly a client who has had previous therapy that was not successful and who wants to continue with the same pattern. Sometimes, too, an adult does not want a spouse brought in. A person may be living alone and the family living in the same area, but the person may not consider family members relevant to his or her problem. Therapy is more effective and more rapid when more people are involved in the interviews. At times one can start with a person alone if he or she insists, but to continue that way makes therapy much more difficult, as outcome results have indicated. Sometimes one can make a bargain that if improvement does not rapidly occur, the family can be brought in. However, seeing a person alone in the beginning can make it more difficult to get the relevant people involved later. Some therapists, learning from Carl Whitaker, argue that the battle over who will be involved in the therapy can determine the outcome of the therapy.

Stages of a First Interview

An interview begins with the first contact made concerning a problem. Usually someone calls asking for an appointment, and some information is gathered on the telephone. To help plan the first interview, at least the following information is helpful. The names, addresses, and telephone numbers of the relevant persons should be obtained for callbacks. There should be a listing of who lives in the household and these persons' ages. The kind of employment should be asked, and whether anyone has had previous therapy. Who referred the family is important. There should also be a one- or two-sentence statement of the presenting problem. This should be asked for in a matter-of-fact way. When the therapist calls later to make the first appointment, he or she should ask that everyone in the household come in for the first interview.

When the family arrives, the following stages occur in the interview: (1) a social stage in which the family members are greeted and made comfortable, (2) a problem stage in which the inquiry is about the presenting problem, (3) an interaction stage in which the family members are asked to talk with each other, (4) a goal-setting stage where the family are asked to specify just what changes they seek, and (5) a task-setting stage where they are given a directive. The interview ends by setting an appointment for the next time, with the whole family or with some part of it.

The Social Stage

At every stage of the interview *all* family members should be involved in the action, and particularly during the greeting stage. When the family enter the interview room, they should seat themselves as they wish. After introducing himself, the therapist should speak to each family member and obtain his or her name.* It is important to get a response from each person,

---

*In this therapy it is expected that the therapist will work alone. The use of a cotherapist is usually for the security of the clinician and not for the value to the client. Outcome studies do not indicate that cotherapy does better, and the cost

in order to define the situation as one in which everyone is involved and important. During this social stage the therapist can also find out who lives in the home and should therefore have been present. If one person starts to talk about the problem, the therapist should stop him until some social response is obtained from each person. The model for this stage is the courtesy behavior one would use with guests in the home. Everyone is greeted and made comfortable.

While the family is being seated, the therapist has an opportunity for observation to guide himself in how to begin the next stage.

Most families who come in with a problem feel defensive about it no matter how agreeable the members may seem. It is embarrassing to have to bring a personal problem to someone. Most families have tried all kinds of remedies that have not worked, and therefore asking for help can mean to them that they have failed. Often the family members have not been in agreement about the problem or about coming in, and some members have been dragged in when they would rather be elsewhere. They may feel they are going to be blamed.

The therapist should note the mood of the family, since he must know their mood in order to get their cooperation in changing. They may be pretending to be more cheerful than they are. They may be unhappy or angry. The family members may have the attitude that bringing the problem person in is a punishment they are carrying out after threatening him with this action for some time. Or they may be desperate. They may also be coming in as a duty because some authority, such as the school or court, told them to come. As the therapist greets the family members, their mood will be communicated to him and he should attempt to match it.

The therapist should note the parent/child relations as the

---

is twice as much. As for training, cotherapy with a more experienced person teaches the student to sit back and not take the responsibility for the case, which he or she must ultimately learn how to do. A therapist working alone can develop and carry out ideas without having to delay to consult with a colleague. If the therapist needs assistance, a supervisor (or even a fellow therapist) behind the one-way mirror can provide it.

family members organize themselves to come to the room. The parents may be too severe with the children, or they may be too easy, just hoping the children will come with them. The children may spontaneously cooperate in the hallway or they may have to be instructed by the parents. The ways in which parents discipline the children can be observed as parts of the process of getting to the room and getting seated. The therapist should keep in mind that the parents are not merely dealing with the children but *showing* how they deal with the children. For example, they might usually smack a child if he misbehaves, but if they are concerned about what they show the therapist, they may behave differently. The children will also be demonstrating how they and their parents behave. The therapist is not necessarily getting the facts from them but, rather, an illustration.

The therapist should note the relationship between the parents or other adults who bring the children (such as mother and grandmother). If there is a child problem in a family, the adults are usually in disagreement about how to deal with the child. Sometimes they show this disagreement immediately and sometimes they present a united front in the beginning. If they seem very much in agreement and too amiable with each other, this situation is different from a situation in which they are showing they have different positions on the child issue. The therapist should also note whether one of the adults is indicating he or she has come reluctantly.

How do the family members deal with the therapist? The behavior of the children will give some indication of what the parents have told them about the place if therapy is being conducted outside the home or school. If the child seems afraid of the therapist, the fear may indicate that he thinks he is there as punishment or that he thinks he will be left there. If the children seem amiable and curious, they may have been told that the place is a pleasant one to visit. In particular, the therapist should note who in the family attempts to engage the therapist on his or her side, even at this greeting stage. If one parent attaches himself or herself too quickly, the therapist can expect a problem in keeping out of a coalition with that person during the session. If a parent is too distant, it may be necessary to work more to get that person involved. If the parents look at the child and then at the therapist with that "sharing exasperation look," they may be bidding to join him against the problem child.

When the family members seat themselves, sometimes the organization of the family is clarified. For example, the mother may be seated among the children and the father at the edge of the group. Or the parents and children may seat themselves in two camps. Or parents and an older child may sit together, isolating the problem child. Perhaps the males seat themselves together and the females together, which gives information about the importance of sex differentiation in the family. Whether or not the problem child is seated between mother and father may suggest his function in their marriage.

It is important to gather information, but it is also important to *keep conclusions tentative*. The therapist may be misled, and therefore ideas should not be too firm. Observation gives information that can be tested as the session continues. A therapist who gets too set in one idea is not free to consider other ideas.

It is also important that the therapist *not share his observations with the family*. If the problem child is sitting between mother and father, the therapist may make a tentative hypothesis that the child's problem serves a function in their marriage. But that hypothesis should not be taken too seriously without further data, and the therapist should *never* comment to the family about the child's position. Not only might the therapist be wrong, but if he is right, he is pointing out to the family what the members already know. To point out something like a seating arrangement is asking the family to concede something they might prefer not to concede, and thus that action could arouse defensiveness and cause unnecessary difficulties in the therapy.

It should be noted that the therapy room is a special place and not the usual social situation. People are there to tell a therapist about their problems and will do so with words and body movement. Typically these are implicit messages that they would rather not put into words at a particular time in the interview.

If the therapist makes such messages explicit—for example, by pointing out the meaning of body movement—it is discourteous. The family will begin to conceal information for fear the therapist will cause trouble by pointing it out explicitly. If the therapist errs by making such interpretations, emotions will come out but change is less probable.

The Problem Stage

Up to this point in the interview, there has been a social interchange with the family that may be quite brief or may last a few minutes. From this stage it is necessary to shift to the therapy stage where the situation is no longer defined as social but as purposeful. It is an unusual situation when a family come for help to someone whose job it is to do something for them. There are no standard rules for this kind of situation, and so therapist and family must work out what kind of situation it is.

The most common procedure is for the therapist to inquire why the family is there or what the problem is. This inquiry changes the situation from a social to a therapy situation. It is the "getting down to business" message. There are many ways to make this inquiry, and each way has its advantages and disadvantages. The inquiry has two aspects: how the therapist makes it and to whom in the family the therapist speaks.

When the family members arrive, they often do not know why the whole family has been asked to come in. Often what they have sought was help for a particular child or adult, and to be asked to come in as a family may puzzle everyone, even if no one asks about it. Therefore, it is often a good idea for the therapist to begin by clarifying his position in the situation. He can say what he already knows and why he asked everyone to come in. When he has clarified his position, it is easier for the family members to state their positions.

One way for the therapist to begin is to say something like "I heard what was said on the telephone, so I have some idea what the problem is. But I asked the whole family to come in so I could get everyone's ideas about it." He can then ask more directly about the problem.

Another way to begin is for the therapist to say, "I wanted everyone in the family to come in today so that I could get all your opinions about the situation." Some variation on this phrasing gives at least a partial explanation of why they are all there and creates a readiness on the part of the family members to contribute their opinions.

How the introduction of the therapist's position is phrased depends on the educational level of the family, since he should state his position in a way that is understandable to everyone. If the therapist has the feeling that it is a secretive family, he should particularly emphasize that he already has some information from the telephone call setting up the appointment. Then it is clear to everyone that someone (usually the mother) has already stated the problem and the therapist has heard that version.

When the therapist asks for more specific opinions about the problem, the way he phrases his inquiry can determine how the interview will develop. Several ways that are commonly used include the following.

The therapist can ask, "What is your problem?" This question defines the situation as one in which problems will be talked about. Usually the authority on the problem, typically the mother of the family, has anticipated this question and is ready with a statement about the difficulties with the child. Often a mother is ready to give a historical review of when the problem developed. To ask the question in this way fits with the mother's expectations.

The therapist can make the situation more personal by asking, "What is it you want from me?" This kind of question reduces the possibilities of the family's report. They not only must think about the problem but also must think in terms of what the therapist may be able to do about it. Such an inquiry by the therapist makes the situation less professional and more personal, which may make some therapists uneasy.

Instead of asking what the problem is, the therapist can ask, "What changes do you want?" By putting the question in this way, the framework of the therapy situation is set as one of change. The parent must then state the problem in terms of how the child should change rather than in terms of what is wrong with him. Even if the discussion later shifts to a problem orientation again, this framework allows the therapist to shift back to what the family would like changed.

Another way to phrase the inquiry is to say, "Why are you here?" This phrasing allows the family the opportunity to focus on the problem or on change. Some members of the family will say, "Because of Johnny," and others will say, "To get something done about Johnny."

As a rule, the more general and ambiguous the inquiry of the therapist is, the more room there is for the family members to display their point of view. They may emphasize the problem or the change or even describe it as a family problem rather than as a child problem. The more specific the therapist is, the more the family is focused on one area in the discussion.

Who Should Be Asked About the Problem. When the therapist shifts from the social to the therapy situation, he or she must speak to the group as a whole or to one person. It is at this point that the personal involvements and biases of the therapist can become an issue. A therapist who considers children to be victims of parents may tend to side with children in the ways she inquires about the problem. Such a therapist may ask the problem child what the problem is, implying that she thinks the child is probably misunderstood. If the therapist sharply divides the world into male and female, the issue of whom to ask about the problem becomes a sexist issue. To speak to a male first could imply that the female was inadequate. If a therapist is older and a grandparent, in a family interview with grandparents, he or she may consider the grandparents the ones to speak to about the problem because they are undoubtedly wiser. A family interview, unlike an interview with an individual, forces a selection on the therapist the moment she begins to explore the problem.

The issue has several relevant dimensions. First, there is the person who tends to be the one sufficiently concerned about the problem to bring the family in for the interview. Usually there is someone else who disagrees that there is that much of a problem and who comes reluctantly. This is a typical conflict in a family with a problem.

A second dimension is one of hierarchy. In any organization, the members are not equal. The therapist must respect the hierarchy in a family in order to gain cooperation. Unfortunately, a therapist's bias can cause him or her to be unclear about who has authority. If grandparents are in a room, many therapists would consider them higher in the hierarchy than parents and so would ask them about the problem. Other therapists would not consider the grandparents as authorities, and so they would address the parents about the problem and politely ignore the grandparents. Similarly, some therapists will observe that a father is withdrawn and marginal from the family and will address him first and treat him as if he were the head of the household. This is not necessarily done because the therapist believes the father holds that position but because if he is addressed in this way the father will respond by becoming more involved and assuming more responsibility in the situation. These therapists will make use of the stereotype about fathers being the head of the household, whether they believe it or not, to solve the family's problem. In the same way, if a therapist believes that a mother should be bolstered in her position in order to solve the presenting problem, he will address her first and treat her as if she were the head of the household. But this decision should be made in relation to the presenting problem, not to the therapist's idea about the proper status position of either sex, which is not the issue of therapy.

Yet another dimension is more of an issue in therapy than in other situations. The therapist has a task to get done, and he or she needs to keep the family involved in order to do it. Often there is one person in the family who can bring the family back, and that person should be treated more respectfully for that reason. For example, one might listen to a grandfather with special respect and find that in actuality he does not think there is a problem worth coming to therapy for and that even if he did think so, the rest of the family would not come at his request. So a therapist treating him with excessive respect may be dealing with the least powerful person in the family.

As an example of the adroitness necessary by a therapist, there may be a family in which mother has the power to bring the family in and father does not. Yet the therapist must emphasize father's status to increase his involvement when that appears necessary as part of a therapeutic plan. Therefore the therapist must treat father as an authority on the problem of the child, while indicating to mother that this is being done as part of the therapy and not because the therapist does not understand father's usual marginal stance in the family.

If the therapist could merely treat all members of the family as equals and behave as if who was asked about the problem were a random choice, the solution would be simpler. That is how one might behave in an artificial group in group therapy. Yet it is in the nature of natural groups that the therapist must deal with the issue of hierarchy and cannot avoid it.

It is recommended here that the adult who seems less involved with the problem be spoken to first, and the person with the most power to bring the family back be treated with the most concern and respect. Usually the most concerned person is the one most burdened with the problem. In a clinic, the most typical arrangement with a child problem in an intact family is a mother quite concerned about the child and a father who is more peripheral. In that situation, it is best to ask father about the problem first because one wishes to define him as involved in the therapy and also to find out how much responsibility he will be willing to take when action is requested.

A certain percentage of families will have a father who is the one excessively concerned about the child while the mother is more peripheral. Sometimes the involvement would seem to be determined by who takes on most of the child-caring functions at home and is therefore more aware of the problems. There is another aspect of the situation that is often overlooked by therapists caught up in the issue of sex roles rather than family organization. Quite often, which parent is more involved and concerned about the child is determined by that parent's involvement with parents or in-laws. That is, a mother who is competitive with her mother about child rearing will be excessively concerned about her child's behavior because it is part of an issue in the older generation. Similarly, a father who is proving to his father how a son should be raised may be the one the therapist notices as more involved in the child problem. Any one relationship is part of another, and it is naive to think of this issue as merely a male or female one. In fact, the same issue of who is overinvolved with the child and who is peripheral is present when the adults involved are of the same sex. A mother and grandmother can express this issue, as can a father and grandfather, or a homosexual pair can be in conflict over whether the child has a problem and who is the authority on it.

In this chapter, a stereotyped view is risked by describing a typical arrangement in which two parents bring in a child with a problem. However, the same interview approach can be taken if it is parent and grandparent or sister and brother or any other relations. The problem may be daughter or son, older or younger child, or it may be one of the parents with symptoms being presented as the problem. The different stages of the initial interview apply whatever the composition of the group.

The issue of whom to address about the problem may be thought to be partly determined by the sex of the therapist, but this appears to be a minor issue in a first interview except in some unusual situations. The competence of the therapist is far more important than his or her sex. If the father seems to behave as if he were feeling left out when mother and female therapist are discussing the problem, the therapist must make special efforts to include him. However, this same coalition issue arises when a male therapist talks with the father about the problem. An awareness of explicit and implicit coalitions on the basis of sex must be assumed by any competent therapist. If a female therapist suspects that her gender is an issue adversely affecting the therapy, it is sometimes helpful for her to become more professional in her manner. In this way the issue of being female is minimized and the posture of an expert is emphasized. Male therapists can do the same.

Generally, it is not a good idea to start with the problem child and ask him why the family is there. He will feel that he is too much on the spot, and it may look as if the therapist were blaming him for everyone's being there. It is better to deal with him later. Every therapist must watch out for a tendency to turn to, or on, the problem person in a benevolent way when the therapist is anxious and under stress. It is the function of problem people to get attention when their intimates are nervous and upset, and therapists typically follow the pattern of giving such attention, too. It is usually better for the nervous therapist to deal directly with the parents at nervous moments.

Another consideration is that the problem child is sometimes sullen and quiet because of a misunderstanding about the context and the reason for the interview. As a rule, a therapist should always state her own position and understanding of the situation whenever she sees anyone worried about the situation. A child may be afraid he is going to be locked up in the place or may believe that he is there because people think he is crazy. It is helpful if the therapist states what she knows about why everyone is there at that point and, if she can, normalizes the situation by emphasizing that it is a usual context for problems.

Some therapists sometimes like to start with the least involved child and ask him why the family is there.* By "least involved" is meant the child sitting farthest out of the group and seeming most detached. Often this is quite a young child, and if he is spoken to, the therapist is making it clear that everyone is going to participate in this session. The therapist is pointing out that it is not a situation where adults only talk about children who only listen. Young children may also say perceptive things, since they have not been taught clearly what should be said and what should not be said in public.

By asking a child why he is there, one sometimes finds out that none of the children has been told why the parents have brought them. This discovery provides the therapist with information about secrecy in the family and what sort of splits there may be between adults and children, or among adults and problem child and the remainder of the children.

Sometimes the therapist can look at the floor or the ceiling, not addressing any particular person, and say, "Can someone tell me what the problem is?" This approach will usually draw out the spokesperson for the family. It also provides information about the father's position in the family, since if he

---

*Beginning with the least involved child is a procedure I first observed used by Frank Pittman.

responds by stating the problem it is more likely that he is a willing participant in family issues. However, addressing the room generally tends to make the situation more unpredictable, and some therapists prefer to address a particular person so that what is said comes out in an orderly manner and in the way he or she would like it to come out.

Sometimes the therapist may "slide" from the greeting stage to the therapy stage without making an issue of the shift. He or she may chat with the children during the greeting—ask them about school or some other activity. This conversation can lead to a discussion by the family without any inquiry about why they are there or what the problem is. Sometimes, by sliding into the problem this way, the therapist can bypass a parent's speech and prevent the child from being labeled as the problem, because by the time the issue comes up in the middle of the interview it is clear that there are a number of problems or else that all the children are pretty much alike.

There are two basic errors in confusing the greeting and problem stages of a first interview. The first applies to any approach to therapy, and the second is relevant to the approach offered in this book. First, the family may begin to be puzzled if the therapist does not focus on the problem, because they are not sure whether this is a therapy situation or a social situation. The therapist loses the opportunity to clarify how this situation is different from a conversation among friends. Sometimes, too, failure to focus on the problem magnifies the problem by making it seem unmentionable. At some point, the therapist must clarify the situation.

Following the approach of this book, what the therapist wants is a clear focus on a problem so that family relationships can be changed by using that problem as the lever. The therapist does not want the problem child to be minimized as no different from the other children, or the problem to be minimized. Nor does the therapist want a discussion of relationships before having the problem stated. This is not a therapy where relationships are changed by talking about relationships; rather, relationships are changed by requiring new behavior to solve a problem. For example, a thirteen-year-old girl was brought in by

Problem-Solving Therapy

her parents because she was stealing money from a neighbor's house. The mother told the therapist about this on the telephone and said she had recently married, so the girl now had a new stepfather. When the family was interviewed, everyone was reluctant to state the problem. The therapist chatted with the family, and father talked about his problem being a stepfather and not knowing how to discipline children in a way that pleased his wife. Finally the therapist was telephoned by the supervisor, who required her to ask what the problem was that brought the family to therapy. When the therapist inquired, the girl began to cry and the parents talked about the integration of the stepfather into the family in a quite different way. It was not a conversation about relationships but about why the girl stole and what was to be done.

Listening to the Problem. The family may describe the problem as something unusual or as something routine. As the therapist listens, he or she should do certain things and not do others.

First, the therapist should not make any interpretation or comment to help the person see the problem differently. He should just accept what is said. If something is not clear, it can be asked about. If the therapist needs to rephrase something to see whether he understands it, he should do so—but he should not rephrase anything to help the other person "discover" something. The procedure here is the safest one for the inexperienced therapist or one inexperienced with family interviews. An extremely skilled clinician with a great deal of experience can reframe and change the problem in a positive way so that it becomes a different problem, or no problem, during the interview. However, that is not giving "insight" into why the family has the problem, which is the type of interpretation that causes resistance and difficulty.

Second, the therapist should not offer advice at this stage, even if asked for it. He should use a phrase such as "I need to know more about the situation before I can say what might be done."

Third, he should not ask how someone feels about something, but should only gather facts and opinions.

Fourth, the therapist's attitude should be one of helpful interest. He should not be diverted to what is really outside the question of why the family is there.

While listening, the therapist should encourage the person to talk. Some people talk at great length, and others find it hard to talk. Talking should be made as easy as possible.

If someone interrupts, the therapist should let the interruption happen to observe it briefly and then should intervene and return to the person first talking. The person interrupting can be told he will get his turn.

Everyone must have a turn. After a statement of the problem from one person, all the others should be asked what they think about it. The therapist should not sound as if he wants a disagreement between two persons or wants to put anyone down. He is only after each person's opinions. When there are disagreements, an issue should not be made of them, but the disagreement can be returned to later. Moreover, one person should not talk too long. If the others get restless, it is too long. Everyone should be asked to pay attention if he or she is not doing so.

Making sure each person takes a turn should happen naturally, if possible. What someone says about someone else may naturally lead the therapist to speak to that other person. However, at this stage the therapist should not return to a previous speaker, but should go on to a third. A dialogue between two persons is not recommended at this stage.

The therapist wishes to join the universe of the family and so understand them, but at the same time he wishes to make enough changes in their behavior so that the interview can proceed in an orderly fashion. If the family is slow, the therapist should move slowly; if rapid, he should join it at that speed. If a parent keeps interrupting, the therapist must intervene so that everyone can express a view. Not only should everyone speak, but also the therapist should take charge of what is happening. If the family takes charge, it will go on as it has in the past, and there will be no change.

If the therapist only listens to one parent and lets him or her take over each time another person speaks, the therapist is saying by his actions that only that parent's words are important. He must persuade other people to have their say and give them equal respect. By preventing an overtalkative parent from being the only one who talks, the therapist is actually helping him or her, because he must save the family from going on doing what has always failed before.

It should be evident that this is not a free-association type of interview (and is not based on the theory of repression). It is organized and controlled by the therapist to achieve the particular goals of bringing out the problems and resolving them. To have family members say anything that comes to mind and upset one another needlessly simply makes therapy difficult.

Sometimes the problem child may be reluctant to talk, particularly after her parents have described her misbehavior. To draw her out, the therapist should be persuasive and may need to move his chair near the child. Usually it is better to talk to the problem child last. After her brothers and sisters have said something, she usually becomes more willing to give her views.

For small children, it is always best to have toys and puppets in the room so that the child is given the opportunity to communicate in a "play" form. The estimate of the child's ability to play may be important, as well as the parents' ability to play with the child when they are asked to by the therapist. Toys and play activities allow action in the room rather than merely conversation about action so the therapist can observe the family members dealing with one another.

Therapist's Observation. When asking about the problem and encouraging people to talk, the therapist should observe how all family members act as well as what they say. He *should not* share his observations with the family.

As someone talks about the problem, the therapist should notice such things as whether the person is acting politely but really feels angry; whether the person is talking about a child as if he were a thing instead of a person; whether the person is worried about what the child or others will think about what he or she says; and so on. The therapist should notice particularly whether the person talks about the problem as if he or she has said the same thing many times before or whether he or she is describing it for the first time. (Sometimes the family has had previous treatment, and this is important information.) By the way the participants talk, they will also be showing whether they feel the therapist can do something or whether they feel the whole thing is hopeless and they are simply participating as a duty.

The therapist should notice who is given responsibility for the problem. The situation if the mother blames the child is different from a situation in which she blames herself or in which she blames other people, such as relatives who are not present, or the school. Ultimately, the therapist might want to have the whole family take responsibility for solving the problem, and so he will want to note how easily the members accept responsibility for it.

While one person is speaking, the therapist should observe the reactions of the others. They will show with their behavior whether they agree or disagree, have heard all this before and are bored with it, are pleased to see a child getting blamed, and so on. Watching their reactions helps the therapist decide how to talk to them. The therapist should particularly notice how the child who is the problem is responding: if she is upset, or too casual or bored, and so on. The therapist should also notice the father when the mother is talking and the mother when the father is talking, because the therapist will be working with their disagreements.

The more responsive and involved the listeners are, and the more angry and upset at what is said, the more likely it is that the family is in a state of crisis and is therefore unstable. The more calm and detached they are, the more likely it is that the situation is reasonably stable and so may be difficult to change.

When listening to people talk about the problem, the therapist should keep in mind that they not only are telling him facts and opinions but also are saying things indirectly that cannot be said directly. These indirect messages are particularly evident when a mother and father describe a child's problem.

A therapist may listen to the mother's talk about the child in two ways: as statements about the child, but also as statements about her husband and the marriage. For example, if the mother says her son is obstinate, the odds are that she is also telling you her husband is obstinate. If the father says the child is threatening to run away all the time, it is possible that mother is threatening to leave him.

It is useful to assume that a child problem reflects, or is a performance of, a family problem. One can get information about that problem in advance by listening to the ways the parents talk about the child. The therapist can think about the data tentatively and check them out later, but it is important to keep such information to himself. *The therapist should not verbalize any interpretations to connect the child's problems with the marital situation.* He should just encourage the participants to talk and listen to the different meanings in what they say. Many things cannot be said directly, or there would probably not be a problem.

There are actually three different ways of receiving the problem, and all three should be used at different times in the interview. In the first inquiry, the therapist should be general and should allow the problem to be expressed metaphorically. Specificity focuses the problem too much on the child and limits metaphor. Later in the interview, after the interaction stage, one wants a more specific and detailed statement of the problem and the goals so that one can eventually use the statement to check outcome and determine whether the therapy has been successful. This statement should have a "how many times a day" and "for how long" sort of specificity, with base-rate information. Finally, related to the specific description of the problem is the therapist's request, toward the end of the interview, for a summary defining what changes are wanted. Specifically, what are the goals the family would like to reach? All of these three ways of dealing with the problem are necessary and will provide different information.

At this stage of encouraging a metaphorical discussion of the problem, the therapist not only should avoid being too specific and more concrete but should also attempt to communicate at the more general level. If the father is complaining that his daughter is difficult to understand, the therapist can respond that women are often hard for men to understand. Such a statement connects wife and daughter at a more general level without making an issue of it. If the mother says the boy is too aggressive and hits her, or hits girls, the therapist can say that it is too bad when males learn to treat women that way. The mother will recognize that he is hearing her complaint about her husband but is not going to force it out explicitly so that there is more trouble. When the therapist responds at the metaphoric level, he will be given more information, because the family members will know he is not going to be discourteous enough to point out what is "really" being said.

It is particularly important not to comment on indirect information directly. For example, if the mother says her husband is helpful, while covering her mouth with her hand, she could be saying that there are some things about him she would rather not say right now. The therapist should never point out to her that there are some things she is not saying or explain her movement to her. She already knows and will consider his comment rude. The therapist should just listen and encourage her to talk more. If he does so, communication will become more understandable, partly because she will know it is safe to talk and give hints as well as direct opinions.

Content of the Problem Presented. When the family members talk about a problem, they will usually describe a person. They will say what is wrong with him or her. This is, however, only one of many ways to think about a problem. For example, the mother may say, "she just never minds." In this way, the daughter is said to be the problem. However, the mother may say, "I don't know how to make my daughter mind." By putting it this way, she is still saying that one person is the problem, but she is saying it is her and not her daughter. It would also be possible to think of the problem as not just one person, but two or more. For example, the mother could say, "My daughter and I deal with each other in a way that makes us both helpless and we can't get anything done." Then the problem is not one person but two. Another way to put it would be for the mother to say, "My husband and I can't agree on how to deal with our daughter, and so she doesn't mind." If said that way, then three persons are defined as the problem.

The important point is that any statement about what is wrong could be put in terms of one person or two persons or three or more. The same behavior by one person looks different in terms of what is wrong and what can be done if one thinks about the problem in terms of different numbers of persons. Usually family members say that one person is the problem. The therapist's job is to think of the problem in terms of more than one person. By thinking that way, he is most able to bring about change. Therefore he will be thinking about the problem in a different way from the way the family members think about it, but he does not have to persuade them to think about it his way. He should accept what they say and seem to go along with it, but in his own mind he can be thinking about the problem differently.

In a child clinic, the parent will say the person is a problem and will say what the person does wrong. Usually the family says that the child does not behave himself or mind his parents. Sometimes the family members will say he does not behave or mind his teacher in school. There are at least three ways a child "does not mind": (1) he may be openly rebellious and defiant; (2) he may not do what he is told, but he does not defy anybody, he "just doesn't mind"; or (3) he "doesn't mind" but may show he cannot help himself by being too anxious or afraid, too nervous, getting sick or having pains, or by generally being too clinging and helpless to do what he is asked. In most cases, a parent will say the boy does not mind and the boy will sit there sullenly. Sometimes the parent will first say the child is anxious and fearful and only later will the parent say that he just does not do anything he is asked and that no one likes to push him because he gets so upset.

When a parent says the problem is at school and the teacher is complaining that the boy will not mind or is not doing well, there are three possibilities. One is that the problem is at the school; another is that the boy is responding in school to trouble at home; and yet another is that there is trouble between the parents and the school and the boy is caught between them and is responding to that situation.

When a parent lists the things the child does wrong, it may be that he never does what he is told to do, lies, cheats, steals, wets the bed, fights with his brothers and sisters, and so on. By giving this list, the parent is also saying that he or she is not competent in dealing with the problem. That is why the parent has come for help. The parent is unable to deal with him, and nobody else in the family can help in such a way that the family can handle the problem by itself. Often parents prefer to say that it is not their fault at all, it is all the child's fault. They like to think that there is something inside the child that is making him misbehave. Thinking about the problem in this way has not been helpful to the parents, and if the therapist thinks that way, he will not do much better than they have done. It is the situation that needs changing so the child can behave more normally. When listening to the report about the child's misbehavior, the therapist should think about what is happening in the total situation of the child that is causing him to behave as he does.

For example, a mother may say that her nine-year-old son is afraid to go outside the house and clings to her all the time. In the room the therapist may see that he sits beside her and holds onto her. She also may say that he lies and will not do anything around the house but that the problem is mostly that he is afraid and never leaves her side. He even sleeps with her, so that the father has to sleep on the living-room couch. The other children do not behave this way, but seem normal.

This information from the mother does not tell the therapist what the problem is or what to do about it. He has only her version that the problem is inside the child and no one else has anything to do with it. To get more information and begin to make a change is the purpose of skillful family interviewing. After the mother has stated the problem, the therapist needs to listen to the father and his views. Then he needs to listen to the brothers and sisters and what they say about it. After speaking to each one, he will see disagreements appearing. For example, he will notice that the father does not quite agree with the mother and thinks she is taking care of the child too much and not letting him be on his own enough. He also does not like to be moved out of his own bed, he may say, although he is willing if it will keep the child from being afraid. Perhaps mother argues that father neglects the child. When mother and father talk about their disagreements, information may appear about how much the child is an issue between them.

During this stage of the interview, it will probably become clearer how to think about this problem in terms of more than the child. The therapist may think of it as a peculiar relationship between mother and son; she has as much difficulty leaving him as he has leaving her. He may also be able to think in terms of three persons and consider the possibility that the child is helping mother and father. If they cannot get together without fighting, particularly in bed, then the child is helping them by acting so fearful that they are kept more separate. They can then say it is the child who is the problem, not bad feelings between them.

When gathering information, the therapist should learn whether part of the reason the child stays at home may be a bad neighborhood or real danger on the street. Is his staying at home related to the situation outside the family as well as within the family? All these factors should be considered as the therapist formulates ideas about what to do to bring about change. The interviewing itself, and the way it is done, is a way of bringing about change as a first step. For example, if the therapist asks the child to sit over by his father, the therapist is beginning to move him out of a too close attachment to his mother. The therapist is also learning how movable the child and his mother are as well as how receptive the father is.

Each family is unique, and so the therapist must fit what he does to a particular family. Yet what happens in each family is familiar because one sees it in family after family. With experience, a therapist learns to expect certain family patterns of behavior. For example, one parent typically accuses the other of being too hard on the child, while the other says that the first person is too soft on the child. The therapist's task is to think about what he sees in the family in a way that helps him devise an idea to change the family. He must also think about how to get these particular family members to cooperate in bringing that change about.

The Interaction Stage

There are two steps to asking about the problem. The first step is getting everyone's comments. In this step, the therapist needs to take charge directly. The second step is getting the family members to talk to each other about the problem. At this point the therapist should stop being the center of the conversation. Instead of being the person each family member talks to, he should turn them more and more to speak to each other. This shift tends to occur naturally, since when they have stated their opinions about the problem there will be disagreements. The therapist should continue to be in charge of what is happening, but he must now begin the interaction stage, in which he sits back and encourages the family members to talk to each other about these disagreements. If the family members try to continue to talk to the therapist, he must turn them back on each other. It may be helpful to move them physically next to each other to talk.

Sometimes a therapist will find that he has started the family members talking to each other before he has finished the stage in which each family member expresses his or her opinion. For example, the mother may say how the boy misbehaves and the boy may start to argue with her about it. If the therapist encourages them to talk to each other, while neglecting the other family members, he will reach a point where mother and son lock with each other and where it is hard to do anything with them. If this happens, the therapist should stop what is happening and go back and finish the first step. For example, the therapist can say, "Well, before you go further with that, let's get some ideas from the others about this situation." Then he should talk to the father or to a brother or sister and later go on to the interaction stage in which family members talk with each other.

It cannot be overemphasized how important it is to have the family members interact with each other rather than with the therapist at this interaction stage. No matter how hard the family members try to involve him, it is necessary to turn them to talk to each other.

When any two persons are talking, the therapist should always be ready to introduce a third person into that conversation. Ultimately, everyone should talk to everyone else. For example, if a mother and son are talking and are getting locked in a struggle, it is appropriate to say to the father something like "They don't seem able to get this straight; could you help them?" In this way the father is brought in and the therapist can observe how much he can oppose either mother or son and how much he cannot. This approach yields information about how to best intervene later when helping the family solve their problems.

Although the emphasis has so far been on talking, the therapist should prefer action to words as a source of information. There is less consequence, and less result, with talk. Rather than only have a *conversation* about a problem, he should try at this stage to bring the problem *action* into the room. For example, if a child deliberately bangs his head, he can be asked to do so. The family will show how it responds. If a child sets fires, he can set one (in a metal ashtray) so that the knowledge he has of how to handle matches as well as the response of everyone is clarified. With toys in the room, problem situations can be performed. If a wife complains and is depressed, she may be asked to behave that way and then all the others can show how they respond. However, these more active procedures should be attempted only when a therapist has learned to give directives effectively (see Chapter Two).

Family Organization. The family members cannot tell a therapist about their sequences and patterns of behavior because they do not know what these are. Only observing how they behave with each other can yield this information. Having the family members talk to each other allows the therapist to observe what kind of sequence there is in the family.

A family is a very complex organization, and each family is unique. Yet for practical purposes one can think about a family in an oversimplified way. This way of presenting types of family sequences is a guideline and does not deal with all the complex behaviors that the adults typically are employing to "save" the child from each other, as they do in families with problem children. If the interaction stage of the first interview is conducted correctly, the structure of the family will become apparent. When one of the parents is siding with a child against the other parent, this situation will become obvious as they talk. If a grandmother is siding with a child against the mother, the behavior will appear in the interview (if the grandmother is present because she lives in the household; otherwise the behavior must be estimated from what they say about her, and she must be brought to the next interview). If the family organization has a child functioning as a parent to the other children, this situation will become apparent. (For a sequence description, see Chapter Four.)

To describe the organization in another way, one can say that when there is a problem child, one adult in the family has violated a generational boundary by becoming overinvolved and overconcerned with a child. This adult is the authority on the child's problem and is both benevolently concerned and exasperated with her. When the child talks to another adult, the overinvolved one will intrude and side with the child. For example, in a one-parent family a mother will say that it is a mystery to her why her daughter does not mind and why she lies to her. The therapist can say, "I want you to choose one of the lies and talk to your daughter about it." As mother and daughter start to talk, an overinvolved grandmother will intrude and question the daughter herself or object to the way the mother is talking with the girl. The more difficult it is to keep grandmother from intruding, the more set the family is in that pattern. If the therapist can prevent grandmother from intruding and mother and daughter have a talk, the therapist is simultaneously making a diagnosis and beginning a change, which is what happens when a first interview goes well.

At times, a therapist may want to have a child tested for intelligence or given a special psychological test, but much information about the child can be gathered in a family interview. As part of the interaction stage, the therapist can have a parent ask a child to do something at the blackboard, draw a person on a sheet of paper, or make an arithmetical computation. Both the child's ability to perform and the type of family involvement can become evident in such a procedure. For example, if a father who seems on the periphery of the family is asked to tell his nine-year-old daughter, who may be retarded, to write her teacher's name, or something more complicated, on the blackboard, a great deal of information can be gathered in the process. How the father asks the girl to do it, whether or not she does it, how the mother intrudes to help, and so on, is information that is available from such a simple testing situation.

Defining Desired Changes

After the family members have interacted together, many of the issues in the family will have been clarified. At this point it is important to obtain from the family a reasonably clear statement of what changes everyone, including the problem child, wants from the therapy. This process helps everyone focus on the important issues, and it provides the baseline for the goals of the therapy. Essentially, the therapist is making a therapeutic contract. The clearer the contract is, the more organized the therapy will be. If problems and changes desired are left fuzzy and unclear, the family's participation and the therapist's chance of success will be more difficult. For example, if the family members say clearly and definitely that they want to get a child over the problem of bedwetting, among other problems, then when the therapist gives them a task later to cure the problem, they are more obligated to accomplish the task. If the agreement on the changes wanted is not made clear from the start, the family will respond in a less cooperative way.

It cannot be emphasized enough that the problem the therapist settles on must be a problem which the family wants changed but which is put in a form that makes it solvable. The negotiation that takes place should involve how to make the problem operational. For example, if a family should say the problem is that a person is anxious, that is not a solvable problem. The ways in which this anxiety manifests itself and the responses to it are the problem. No traditional diagnostic category is a solvable problem. To say the problem is "schizophrenia" or "mental retardation" is to say nothing related to therapy. "Identity confusion" or "low self-esteem" or "unhappiness" or most of the terminology of psychodynamic language is not useful when one is formulating a problem. A "school phobia" is not a problem one can resolve, but a child who will not go to school is an operational problem.

Problems, whether one calls them "symptoms" or "complaints," should be something one can count, observe, measure, or in some way know one is influencing. The kinds of information a therapist needs about a symptom, depending on the type, are such things as: Is it there all the time, or does it come intermittently? Is it unexpected when it arrives or predictable? Does it go away suddenly or drift away? Is it more intense at some times or at others? Is day or night the most frequent time of occurrence, or the weekday or the weekend? How many times an hour does it occur? If something like bedwetting, does it happen early in the sleep, late, or just before waking up? As with all symptoms, asking what has been tried already clarifies the nature of the problem as well as providing guidance about what to do.

One of the most important reasons for specifying the problem clearly is so that a therapist can know when she has succeeded. Presumably, when treatment terminates and in a follow-up interview afterward, a therapist will want to know definitely whether she has achieved her therapeutic goals. If the contract is cloudy, the outcome evaluation will be unclear.

The problems emphasized here are obviously oversimplified, and many unique situations arise that must be dealt with differently. The procedures suggested are for the average case. There are inevitably exceptions, of which one or two can be mentioned here. Ordinarily, one should define a problem as clearly as possible. Yet at times that may not be the best way to proceed.

Sometimes a family or an individual may present a problem so rigidly defined and circumscribed that it is better to seek ambiguity. With an ambiguous situation, the therapist has more room to maneuver. This problem may be a symptom that the patient repetitiously emphasizes again and again, refusing to deal with anything else. Or the family may repetitiously emphasize a person. In some such instances it is best to *un*clarify the problem in order to work with more alternatives.

One unfortunate idea in family therapy was the notion that a person was a scapegoat and that the family should be educated about what the *real* problem is. Sometimes the therapist would "take the pressure" off the problem child by pointing out the problems that all the siblings have. This is an error. Typically, parents feel they have failed when they come in with a problem child, and this feeling is one of the reasons they attack the child. If they are persuaded that they have also failed with the other children, they may attack the problem child even more because they feel he has forced them to be exposed to such accusations. Generally, the attempt to rescue a problem child activates the family to prove that the therapist does not understand what a dreadful person he is. The family tries to prove this assumption by increasing the attack on him—often at home, after the interview.

In the approach recommended here, it is best to keep the focus on the problem person and to use that focus as leverage to change the situation. Since he is such a problem, therefore more is to be expected from the family to do something about it. Of course, the therapist should bring out the assets of the problem person as well as the defects, but not as a way of proving to the family that it is wrong.

Therapy is more effective if the focus is kept on the symptom and on the problem person. At times, of course, one meets unusual situations and is tempted away from that focus. For example, a crisis situation may require a different approach until the crisis is resolved. Certain presenting situations may seem more important to the therapist than the problem presented. However, if possible, one should always tie the shift in emphasis to the problem focus. For example, a family once came in with a problem with a retarded daughter. The parents had devoted their lives to her. In the interview it was learned that the father was dying of cancer and had only a few months to live. This issue was upsetting everyone. A therapist might have been tempted to shift and deal with the issue of death to help the family past this painful period in a direct way. Instead, the therapist took the approach recommended here. She found that the father was concerned because the retarded daughter gave his wife more trouble than the daughter gave him. He was worried about his wife handling the daughter alone. He also regularly had to drive the daughter to a sheltered workshop because mother did not drive. The therapist focused on the father helping mother learn to drive. She also had the father work with the mother on more effective ways of responding to the daughter. This way, the father could leave the world feeling that his wife was competent to drive the girl where she needed to go and to deal with her more effectively. The issue of mother and father dealing with each other more intimately at this crucial time was achieved by dealing with the presenting problem they brought in. Generally, the therapist can find a way of centering the therapy on the presenting problem while also achieving other goals the therapist thinks are important.

Another special situation is one in which a family presents a problem and the therapist finds out that the problem does not exist. For example, one family offered a young daughter as a problem because she was misbehaving and getting poor grades in school. The therapist checked with the school and found out that the daughter was behaving well and was getting good marks. In such a case, it is sometimes best not to confront the parents with this information. Presumably, the parents are not dumb, they know the daughter is not a problem, and they have some other reason for presenting themselves in this way. It is best to explore the situation tentatively and to learn what is behind it. In the case of this nonproblem daughter, the therapist found that the mother had an older daughter, by a previous marriage, who was due to leave a mental hospital. The mother was concerned about how to deal with her as well as about the problems that were arising in her marriage. By accepting the nonproblem presented, the therapist could resolve the other, pressing problems.

At times, a therapist must simply act as a wise adviser and not as a therapist in the usual sense. For example, some people bring a problem that is really not a problem, but in their inexperience of living they may think it is. For example, one young couple came in with their first child, a normal and cheerful four-year-old. They wished to be sure that their child was "sufficiently prepared intellectually for the academic program" at the nursery school. A first interview seemed to indicate that they were just uncertain young people who, like many couples today, did not have parents or older relatives to advise them in child rearing, and so they came to the experts. They were assured their child was intellectually sound and ready for the nursery school program.

Ending the Interview

The first interview should end with the setting of the next appointment, which may involve several issues. It may have become clear in the interview that some family member who is not present is essential to the therapy. This member may be a grandparent living separately, or it may be a separated or divorced spouse who is still involved deeply in the problem. Arranging for that person to come, and discussing how to get the person to come, is part of the ending process.

Some therapists who are directive in their orientation are skillful enough to have devised a directive by the end of the first session. This directive can be offered as homework for the family between interviews. It may be a simple task or it may be complex, but a simple task is usually better at this stage. If a directive is given, the family remains involved with the therapist between interviews.

In summary, for the average problem in the majority of families who seek therapy, a first interview can be conducted in a way that provides maximum information and begins a change. When a family arrives, the members do not quite know what is wrong, but they usually think it is a particular person with a particular set of problems. Often they assume the problems have a cause in the past rather than in the present situation. The therapist meeting the family also does not know what is wrong, but he or she does know that something in the family situation is making the problem necessary. The first interview should clarify the family structure and provide some agreement between therapist and family about the nature of the problem and the goals of therapy. At this point, the therapist's task is to understand the problem and formulate it in such a way that something can be done with it. If the therapist is to change the family, he or she must join the universe of the family and, from within that universe, bring about change.

The therapist joins the family in the ways he or she makes everyone feel at ease and involved in the social stage, has everyone contribute ideas about the problem in the problem stage, involves everyone with one another at the interaction stage, and includes everyone in specifying just what changes are desired from the therapy. Although some types of families cannot fit this format—such as families with infant problems, families only seeking testing for a child, or families erupting in a state of crisis—for most families the interview can easily go from stage to stage. How the therapist proceeds after the first interview will be determined by the particular problems. One must also expect that in the following interviews new problems may be presented and new goals must be established. The "presenting problem" is not only what is offered in the first interview but also what is offered as therapist and family become more involved with each other.

As the interview ends, usually the family and the therapist can manage a reasonably clear agreement, although sometimes more than one interview is necessary to clarify the issues. Some families would like an estimate of the length of therapy; it is best to respond that therapy will be as brief as possible to solve the problems. If a family is particularly resistant or doubtful about coming back, it is sometimes helpful to set a certain number of interviews. One can say, "Why don't we meet for six times (or three times) and then decide whether more times are necessary."

Special First Interviews

Therapy is typically done with people who voluntarily seek out a therapist and ask for help. However, it is often necessary to do therapy with people who present themselves in a quite different way. Two of these situations are (1) when the family is required to come by a court and (2) when a family member is severely disturbed and coming out of custody or in a crisis.

Compulsory Therapy. When a judge tells someone to go to therapy or suffer something worse, like going to jail, the therapist faces the difficult task of doing therapy with people who do not wish to be there and often are reluctant even to concede they have a problem. Such clients can look upon the therapist as an agent of the state and not on their side. This kind of "involuntary therapy" requires special interviewing techniques. One goal is to change the therapy to a voluntary one in the sense that the clients realize they can resolve their problems and get out of such situations.

Although involuntary therapy seems an extreme and special case, it is a factor in many therapy situations. Often a family member is brought in reluctantly by other family members, and for that particular person the therapy is compulsory and not voluntary. Such an arrangement occurs when adolescents are dragged into therapy by their parents because of their misbehavior. It can also occur when a father comes in because the mother is insisting that something must be done about a child problem, and the father does not think therapy is necessary. Often therapists or agencies require the whole family to come in for the first interview, whatever the problem, and so some members may be coming involuntarily. Not uncommonly a spouse comes to marital therapy reluctantly because the other spouse insists on it.

Besides situations where family members bring in other family members reluctantly, there are compulsory therapy situations that are not clearly defined that way, but still the family enters therapy to avoid something worse. When a teacher or school counselor says, "You must take this child to therapy," the family come in at least partly under duress. They are not in the interview because they choose to be there but because someone else requires it. Such a requirement can also be part of the program of drug rehabilitation agencies or psychiatric facilities.

If a therapist does not know in advance, it is best to find out early in the interview whether a family is there under duress. One way to find out is to explore who referred them and why. Another way is to ask what they expect from therapy to get an idea whether they are there for some positive reason or are just filling time. Sometimes it is useful to inquire who among the family members thought it was a good idea to come. This can bring out who wanted to come and who did not.

When faced with reluctant clients, the therapist should not assume they are resistant or difficult people. Rather, it should be assumed they have not fully understood the situation. The attitude of the therapist should be a positive one: if the family just understand the benefits the therapist has to offer, they will be pleased to be there. There are many reasons that a family can resent coming other than the simple fact that they are compelled to be there. Sometimes a family have been mistreated by previous therapists, and they must be persuaded that this time there will be a different approach. For example, parents have often been blamed by therapists who thought of themselves as saving a child from noxious parents and so taught the parents it was unpleasant to go through therapy. Sometimes there is simply a misunderstanding about what therapy is and what is to be expected.

A first step is for the therapist to clarify his or her position by stating what is known about the situation and what the goals are. For example, one can say, "I understand we are all here because Johnny has a problem and we want to get him over it as quickly as possible." This helps make it clear that the parents are not going to be blamed. Sometimes it is best to define the situation more positively by saying, "I assume you are all here because you want to do what is best for everyone." Therapy is then done in a positive framework and not one of conflict and resentment over having to be there.

When an individual attends reluctantly, it is often best to give that person special attention so he will discuss his reluctance rather than sit silently. If a person is sullen and uncommunicative, it is necessary to have patience and to assume there is, to him, good reason for behaving that way. For example, the father of a heroin addict came reluctantly to the first interview. He was sullen and uncooperative in the first part of the interview. As he talked more later, it came out that his daughter had recently stolen money from him and shot up heroin, after agreeing not to do that anymore. His view was that if he agreed to come to therapy to help her, she would take it as forgiveness for that act. He was still angry and did not want to forgive her. When the therapist gave him a special invitation by calling him personally and asking him to come in for one interview, that allowed him to come without appearing to forgive his daughter. Only when the broader goals of the therapy were defined in the interview did he begin to speak to her.

Sometimes, if it is a family interview, it is best to see the reluctant person alone to hear what will not be said in front of the family. For example, it is often best with a reluctant adolescent to hear the family's view of what is happening and to see him or her alone for part of the interview. The therapist should make it clear that the therapy is for the benefit of the adolescent as well as the parents and in that way indicate that he or she is the agent of the adolescent as well as the family. Sometimes it is helpful to say, "You should make use of me to get what you want." Often it is best to ask the child what change he or she would like and then negotiate with the parents to arrange that. Sometimes it is helpful to ask the adolescent what his or her worries about the parents are, indicating that the adolescent's desire to help the parents is known.

Thinking about a family where someone comes to therapy under duress, one should keep in mind that in most cases there is one person who is the key person in getting the family to come in. One should not side with the reluctant person in such a way that the person who can bring in the family is antagonized. For example, if the mother brings in the family because she is concerned about a child problem, the therapist might pay special attention to the father who has come in reluctantly. However, that should not be done in such a way that the mother is slighted or offended; after all, she was the one who initiated getting everyone there. Similarly, if the adolescent is there under duress, one should not join him in such a way that the parents are put down when they are the ones who came in asking for help. Whenever there is a reluctant attendee in therapy, one must keep in mind that there are one or more others who were not reluctant to come and who must be joined if the therapy is to be successful.

When the whole family, or a single person, comes in under duress as part of a court order, the task of the therapist is to get out from under being an agent of the court. There is nothing more painful, and dull, than to sit with a family and try to gather information to be helpful while they are sullen and unhappy about being there. The problem is how to get on the side of the family, and not of the court, by framing the situation so that is clear.

Sometimes one can join the family in their situation by pointing out that they are there because they have to be, but you also are there because you have to be. Since it is compulsory for all of you, everyone might as well make the best use of the time. At that point one can chat about different things in life before approaching problem issues. Sometimes one can discuss the arrest situation and the court appearance or the rules of probation, sympathizing with what the family has been through.

If one knows in advance that the case is court-ordered, and if one has cooperation from court personnel, the best way to begin is to have a representative of the court at the first interview. For example, a probation officer can be invited to the first interview to describe the court requirements and the rules of probation. The presentation can last about fifteen minutes, and then the probation officer can leave. Several things are accomplished with this collaboration. The family often learns for the first time what the rules of probation actually are and what will happen if they are broken. The therapist also learns the facts of the actual legal situation. It is clear in this arrangement that court and therapist are collaborating and not fighting with each other, because probation officer and therapist are working together. However, when the probation officer leaves, the therapist can join the family by discussing what a difficult situation "all of us" are facing. In that way the agent of the court has left the room, and the therapist is defined as the agent of the family in this problem situation.

When dealing with a court-ordered family, one must keep in mind that there is a special problem. The court essentially replaces the family when it puts a family member on probation. Judge and probation officer can be defined as in charge of the person's behavior. In the case of an adolescent, the parents are being set aside by the court as authorities in the life of their own child. Often the parents retreat and let the court deal with the child, even on such issues as what time he should come in at night. One task of the family therapist is to help the parents take charge of their children so the court will not have to be involved again in the future. That is, the task is to help the family solve their own problems without the community having to take action. However, to achieve this, it is sometimes necessary to persuade the court to let family therapist and parents, rather than court representatives, deal with the child. Often courts will cooperate in this endeavor, since they do not like to have the offender back again and again.

In summary, compulsory therapy requires patience from a therapist who must deal with people who did not seek his or her company. Being assigned the case, therapists can be defined as agents of the state. They must redefine the situation as one in which they are on the side of the family to help them prevent such difficulties from happening again. This is sometimes best done by having someone else, such as a probation officer, represent the state in the interview and then leave. It can also be helpful to see different family members alone to join with them in thinking of ways to solve this problem situation. A special problem for the family-oriented therapist is to work in a situation where the responsibility for a family member has been taken out of the hands of the family and placed outside in the community. It is necessary to put the family back in charge of its members and resolve their difficulties so the family is more tranquil and the community need not be called on again.

The Crisis Interview. A nine-year-old boy was brought to therapy because he had hit his teacher so hard he broke her jaw. After a second violent incident at school, he was referred to therapy. The therapist began the first interview with the family by asking each member what the problem was. The father said the problem was the boy, but they all had problems and he did not want to single the boy out. The mother began to express a similar view that everyone had problems. The supervisor called the therapist and advised her that she should do a crisis interview instead of an exploratory one. This was a boy out of control, and the parents were going to have to take charge of him. An exploratory interview would weaken their parental position and make them hesitate to take charge or act to prevent future damage by the boy. The therapist therefore said to the family, "As I hear about this situation, it seems obvious that this boy is out of control, and you will have to do something about him." She said to the father, "Now just what does the boy do when he has a tantrum, and how have you tried to stop him?" From that point on, the emphasis in the interview was not on what everyone thought about the problem but on what to do to contain the violence. The parents were persuaded to cooperate in a plan, and the boy's temper tantrums and violence were resolved.

This type of interview, in which the emphasis is on putting the parents in charge and making a structured hierarchy in the family, is best used in crises and when a family member is coming out of custody in a mental hospital or juvenile residence for severe behavior problems. It is a quite different first interview from the one described earlier, with the average problem, where everyone in the family is involved in defining the problem and planning what to do. In a crisis interview it is assumed that whoever is at the top of the hierarchy has not been able to establish rules for behavior of a family member, and so the social control representatives in the community have threatened to act or have already acted by hospitalizing the person and establishing rules. In this situation the question is not what the problem is, because the problem is that a person has been crazy or violent or suicidal or on drugs and might be again. If it is an adolescent or young adult who is in trouble, the therapist should begin by siding with the parents to help them take charge of a young person who is harming himself or other people. If the therapist does not join the parents in forming a more solid hierarchy by taking benevolent power over the child, the child is likely to spend his life in trouble, if not in institutions, because the community will act. In such an interview the parents make plans and the problem child is given little voice in what is to be done. After normality is established, the child is given the same rights as anyone in his position. If one begins this kind of interview by talking to everyone about what the problem is, the young person might attack the parents in such a way that they become defensive and become unable to take charge and so must ask the social control people to do so. Instead, the therapist organizes the conversation to achieve the goal of a hierarchy with the parents in charge of their family.

For most severe problems the emphasis on a structured hierarchy is necessary. However, there is an extreme problem where parents' taking charge is not the issue. When there is a threat of suicide or an attempt, the issue needs to be parental concern rather than establishing rules. A young person who attempts suicide has escalated the situation, and the therapist's emphasis should be on family concern with why the person would take such a desperate measure. Something truly serious must be happening in the situation when suicide attempts are the problem. Such attempts are not merely misbehavior, and the therapist must leave the session reassured that a death will not happen. Sometimes this is achieved by hospitalization, sometimes by a "suicide watch" at home in which the family takes responsibility never to leave the young person alone. Whatever is done, the seriousness of the problem is not to be underestimated.

A typical situation with violent and out-of-control youths is when a therapist must deal with a young person who is about to return to the community after being locked up for violent or strange behavior. If nothing is done to prepare the family for trouble in the future, what is likely to happen is that there will be trouble and the young person will go back into custody. This can mean the beginning of a cycle of returning to the hospital again and again over the years so that the situation becomes chronic.

If an adolescent or young adult is confined in a mental hospital, in contrast to a jail or juvenile residence home, the parents think of the problem as medical. The nature of the social control institution often determines how the problem is defined: jail is for bad people and hospitals are for sick people. The family members usually feel they have a right to deal with badness or misbehavior but not sickness. To define their child as sick and then ask them to take charge of him can be like asking them to take out each other's appendixes. Therefore it is necessary to define the young person's behavior as misbehavior rather than an expression of an illness. This can be difficult when the context of custody is a hospital with doctors and nurses. Yet only if the problem is organizational or misbehavior do the parents have a right to deal with it. To justify the parents' disciplining or controlling a violent offspring, the problem needs to be defined as within their domain. This issue arises with different kinds of severe psychological problems, such as psychotic behavior, chemical dependency problems, eating disorders, and depression.

It might be emphasized briefly that today some types of problems are brought to therapists where it is ambiguous whether it is a medical or social control problem or a problem in the province of the therapist. Perhaps because of the success of medicine with miracle drugs in this generation, a hope exists that there will be miracle drugs to cure psychological problems. There is also the temptation to define psychological and emotional problems as physical and therefore medical when there is no evidence of physical causes. If a therapist is dealing with an eating disorder, such as anorexia, obviously a physician should be a consultant to the therapist because starvation is a life-threatening physical problem. However, what if someone is depressed? Need a physician be involved when there is no evidence of a physical cause of the depression? This is a controversial area. A therapist typically assumes that a problem is socially caused and is curable by psychological interventions. Those authorities who prefer medication and hospitalization operate on quite different assumptions. Today many adolescents are hospitalized for misbehavior. This action is encouraged by the availability of insurance that pays for hospitalizing adolescents on psychiatric wards, and such a procedure is profitable. Parents are exposed to advertisements which say that if anyone is having trouble with an adolescent, the private hospital will be happy to take him in for an insurance fee and will be better parents than the failing parents. This step is a drastic one, and many adolescents begin careers as mental patients when a family therapy approach could have resolved the problem.

Even when the problem is severe, as with a psychotic episode, it should be kept in mind that the use of hospitalization and medication is a social control device, not a form of therapy. It might be necessary, but it is done to prevent trouble, not to cause a positive change in the person's life. Often antipsychotic medications cause brain damage and more harm in the long run than the psychotic behavior. The more severe debates in the field are over whether extreme behavior is a psychological problem or is based on an individual physical cause that has not yet been found. The approach that does the least harm to a person is the preferred one.

In summary, there are at least three types of first interviews that routinely occur in therapy. One is the interview with a family with the average problem, where all members are encouraged to express themselves and clarify the problem. Second, there is the first interview with the family compelled to be present by some outside force, such as the court, where so much of the emphasis must be on joining the family and getting out from under being an agent of the state. Finally, there is the situation of the severely disturbed person, where the therapist can assume that the hierarchy in the social situation is in confusion. There is conflict over who is in charge among children, children and parents, parents and grandparents, and the family and professional experts. The therapy must emphasize clarifying the hierarchy in the social situation and supporting the parents in taking loving charge of their children.

Evaluating the Therapist

When observing a videotape of a first interview, one can judge whether or not the therapist properly conducted the interviews outlined here. There are a number of questions that might be asked about a therapist and his or her approach. With proper training and experience in interviewing, one can expect that a therapist will develop confidence. He or she should be able to approach an interview without trepidation, feel reasonably at ease with the family, and be able to talk to schoolteachers or probation officers or whoever is involved in the case. A therapist can be expected to be able to interview families of different social classes or colors. He or she should be able to interview in the office or in the home. One can also expect competence whether interviewing a large family group, a nuclear family, a mother and child, or one person.

When observing a first interview with a family, a supervisor can ask the following questions:

> Does the therapist frame the interview situation so the family knows who he or she is, what the situation is, and why different kinds of questions are being asked?
>
> Has the therapist organized the family in the room well so that business can be conducted—for example, by dealing with obstreperous children or chaotic interchanges?
>
> Is the therapist sufficiently nonmoralistic so the family members are encouraged to talk about their problems?
>
> Has the therapist shown the flexibility to shift to another approach when one way of gathering information is not working?
>
> Does the therapist show a range of behavior from being reflective to being confronting?
>
> Has the therapist avoided pursuing a personal interest that is not relevant to the family problem?
>
> Is the therapist able to assume the posture of an expert *while also* able to express ignorance when appropriate?
>
> Does the therapist avoid offering solutions before the problem is clarified?
>
> Does the therapist seem to know when to encourage dissent among family members and when to soothe them?
>
> Does the therapist avoid inadvertently siding with one family member against another or one faction against another (such as child against parents)?

Does the therapist avoid being too personally involved with the family?

Does the therapist avoid being too professional and detached from the family?

Is the therapist attempting to get *all* family members participating in the interview?

Has the therapist shown an ability to tolerate unpleasant material or strong feelings from the family members?

Is the therapist gathering information about significant other people not present at the interview?

Is the therapist learning whether other social agencies are involved with the family?

Is the therapist motivating the family members to change? Is he or she engendering hope and a willingness to make an effort?

Has the therapist's approach been more positive than negative, in the sense of putting down the family?

Has the therapist shown the family that he or she has something to offer them and can bring about change?

2

Giving Directives

I recall a man in his late twenties who wished to be a great novelist but could not bring himself to sit down at the typewriter and write. He was just unable to produce. The young man was also afraid of women. Although he could associate with prostitutes, he had never had an ordinary date with a woman. He came to therapy asking to solve both problems: he wished to write and he wished to have dates with women. The therapeutic strategy was obvious: when posed with two symptoms, the therapist should use one to cure the other. I asked the young man how many pages per day he should write, and he said he should write one page per day of 250 words. I directed the young man to write six pages per week (he negotiated one day off). If he did not follow the directive, then the following week he had to ask young women for dates until he went out with three women that week. The next week, if he did not write six pages, he must arrange three dates again. Rather than ask a woman for a date, the young man sprang to his typewriter and methodically wrote a minimum of six pages per week. Later the problem of dating young women was resolved. By taking this approach, the therapist inevitably wins: if the patient wrote, he solved one problem, and if he did not write, he had to go out with women and so solved another problem. It is, of course, essential that a therapist know how to give directives so that they are carried out. It is a misfortune that most clinical training has not included this skill. A therapist must largely learn it on his own unless he meets a master therapist, such as Milton H. Erickson, and can receive some instruction. Most of what is said in this chapter on directives is derived from Erickson.*

Purpose of Directives

Giving directives, or tasks, to individuals and families has several purposes. First, the main goal of therapy is to get people to behave differently and so to have different subjective experiences. Directives are a way of making those changes happen.

Second, directives are used to intensify the relationship with the therapist. By telling people what to do, a therapist becomes involved in the action. He or she becomes important because the person must either do or not do what the therapist says. If the directive is something the people are to do during the week, the therapist remains in their lives all week. They are thinking about such things as: What if we don't do it? What if we only halfway do it? What if we change it and do it in our own way? When they come back for the next interview, the therapist is more important than if she had not given a directive.

Third, directives are used to gather information. When a therapist tells people what to do, the ways they respond give information about them and about how they will respond to the changes wanted. Whether they do what the therapist asks, do not do it, forget to do it, or try and fail, the therapist has information she would not otherwise have. In fact, in the preliminary talk about the task, the therapist learns things she would not learn otherwise. For example, if the task is to do something at breakfast time, the therapist learns what happens at breakfast because the people will discuss that as they talk about how to do the task.

*See J. Haley, *Uncommon Therapy: The Psychiatric Techniques of Milton H. Erickson, M.D.* (New York: Norton, 1973), *Advanced Techniques of Hypnosis and Therapy* (New York: Grune & Stratton, 1967), and *Conversations with Milton H. Erickson, M.D.*, 3 vols. (New York: Norton, 1985); E. L. Rossi, *The Collected Papers of Milton H. Erickson, M.D.*, 4 vols. (New York: Irvington, 1980).

What Is the Directive?

Some therapists are uncomfortable about giving directives because they feel perhaps they should not take the responsibility for telling someone what to do. It is important to emphasize that directives can be given directly or they can be given in a conversation implicitly by vocal intonation, body movement, and well-timed silence. Everything done in therapy can be seen as a directive. If an individual or a family in an interview is talking about something and the therapist says, "Tell me more about that," she is giving a directive. If the therapist only nods her head and smiles, encouraging the speaker to continue, that is also a directive. If someone says something the therapist does not like, she can tell the person not to say that anymore—and that is telling him what to do. If the therapist turns her body away from the person and frowns, she is also telling the person that he should not say that sort of thing.

Whatever a therapist does is a message for the other person to do something, and in that sense she is giving a directive. If someone says, "I feel unhappy," and the therapist replies, "I understand, you feel unhappy," the reply does not look like a directive. But it can be defined as one, since the therapist is indicating that she is interested in such statements and the person should say that sort of thing or that it is all right to say that sort of thing. Since the therapist may not have responded to something else the person said but has responded to this statement, her response tells the person that this statement is important. The therapist's response also implies there should be more talk about such important things. Once a therapist faces the fact that whatever she says or does not say is telling a person to do something, or is telling him to stop doing something, then she will find it easier to accept the idea of giving directives. In fact, even when a therapist tries to avoid giving directives by pointing out to the client that the client is trying to get the therapist to direct him what to do, the therapist is directing the client how to behave.

There may be times when a therapist does not want the responsibility of directing someone's behavior. For example, someone might ask, "Should I quit my job?" or "Should I

divorce my wife?'' Here, it might be best to respond by saying, "That is something you have to decide yourself." However,
if you have any opinions about that decision, those opinions
are going to be communicated to the person by what you say
or imply, by the tone you say it in, by the way you move. But
you can still put the responsibility for the decision on the client
if you do not want to take it yourself.

The question of who is responsible for what in therapy
is a complex one. A therapist may believe that she herself decided
on a directive and was responsible for a course of action, but
closer examination of the interchange may indicate that the
client led the therapist into that directive. Often, too, the responsibility taken by the therapist is given by the client in more
direct ways. A mother may ask that a therapist bring up a
sensitive subject so that she and her children can discuss it,
and the therapist may choose to cooperate by taking the responsibility for bringing up that subject. At times, one may want
to relieve the client of responsibility, and at yet other times
one may want to have the client feel that one is accepting responsibility when in fact one is not. This chapter does not deal
with the intricacies of who actually determines a course of
action in a therapist/client encounter but, rather, with how to
give directives when the therapist assumes that she herself is
initiating what happens.

Some people are comfortable in giving a task. In fact,
some therapists rush in and give a task prematurely before they
understand the situation. However, many therapists experience
an inertia when they try to do an active, directive therapy.
Sometimes this is because their training was in nondirective
therapy, and it was instilled into them that they should only
interpret and reflect, not direct people what to do. Sometimes
therapists seem to feel that telling someone what to do takes too
much responsibility for a person's life, and sometimes they
simply believe they have not had sufficient training and therefore
they should continue to say only, "Tell me more about that."
More than these practical reasons, there seems to be a natural
inertia about intruding into some stranger's life and telling him
or her how to behave. Overcoming this inertia is part of becoming a directive therapist.

One way to arrange an obligation to give directives occurs when a therapist sets up a situation where he or she *must*
tell someone what to do. For example, one can talk to a family
or an individual about change. "Would you like to change?"
one can ask. The answer is often "Of course, or I wouldn't be
here." But it does not follow that the client is there to change;
clients can be there for many reasons. One can also ask, "Would
you rather change slowly or quickly?" Or a question can be
"Would you rather know what I am doing to change you, or
would you rather just find out you changed and not know why?"
Some people certainly want to know everything you are doing,
and others do not really care. You can also say, "Are you willing to make a sacrifice to have a change?" Often the answer
is "What sort of sacrifice?" The reply can be "Any sacrifice
that is necessary to get over the problem." In the process of
talking about change in this way, two things are happening.
One, the idea that the client is going to change is being accepted—
the only question is how. (This is like saying to a hypnotic subject, "Would you rather go into a trance now or later?" and
so setting aside the question *whether* the person is going into the
trance.) The second thing happening is that the client is accepting the idea that you are going to do something to change him.
If he agrees to a sacrifice, for example, he turns to you expecting you to offer one. In this way a therapist can arrange to overcome the inertia about giving directives and proceed to do so.

Types of Directives

There are two general types of directives: (1) straightforward directives, given when the therapist has power to get people to do what he or she says, and (2) indirect directives, given
when the therapist has less authority and must work more indirectly to get the change desired. Another way to put it is that
with straightforward directives the therapist wants people to do
what is asked, as in good advice or coaching. Indirect directives are used when the therapist does not want the client to
do precisely what he says because he wants the change to occur
more "spontaneously," as when the therapist uses the indirect
technique of restraining change.

First, we will discuss giving directives when the therapist wants people to do what he says. The emphasis here will be on giving directives to whole families during an interview, but the procedures are essentially the same when interviewing a person alone.

When a therapist wants people to do what he or she says, there are two possible approaches. One can try to change behavior in a family by telling one or more members to stop what they are doing. For example, if a mother intrudes when a father and son try to talk to each other, the therapist can tell the mother not to intrude. Whether the therapist puts it nicely or forcefully, the therapist is asking her to stop what she is doing.

To ask someone to stop doing something is one of the most difficult directives to enforce. It can be done, but it is not easy. Usually one needs high status or a reputation as an expert for someone to stop usual behavior simply because he is told to. With minor problems or educational situations such direction is easier. If someone drinks too much, sometimes it is a good idea to tell him not to drink. He might stop. But if the problem is severe, he is likely to drink more, and a therapist does not usually have the power to enforce the directive. In the same way, some mothers in families with minor problems will stop intruding on father and son if told to stop. But if the family problem is severe, the mother may very well not stop but, rather, may debate the therapist about how he does not understand or appreciate her. A directive to stop needs to be accompanied by other messages. A therapist may have to repeat the directive often or magnify it by standing up and waving his hands at her to stop. Or he may have to put the mother behind a one-way mirror and have her watch father and son talk. Sometimes he needs to get the cooperation of the father and son by asking them to prevent her from interrupting.

If the therapist tells someone to stop usual behavior, he must usually go to an extreme or get other family members to cooperate and change their behavior to support him in this task. Often it is like trying to stop a river from flowing; one can try to block it, but the river will go over and around the block and the therapist will drown.

In telling someone to do something different, the therapist is trying to change behavior in a family by telling the family members to behave in a way that is different from their usual behavior. The therapist is asking them to try new ways. Instead of trying to block the river, the therapist is diverting it into a new pathway.

There are two ways to tell people to do something different: (1) good advice and (2) directives to change the sequence in the family.

Telling people that they should treat each other better is usually not useful to them. For one thing, they have had good advice from other people and have not been able to follow it. For example, if a mother fights with her daughter about what time the daughter comes in at night, good advice to them is usually not helpful. The therapist may say, for example, that they should listen to each other with respect, be nicer to each other, and find some compromise they both like. In most cases the therapist gives this kind of advice when he thinks they have not realized they should do these things. The therapist thinks he is telling them something new. Actually, they know how they ought to behave; their problem is that they cannot behave that way. Every time they try to be nice and respectful they get into a runaway fight.

Unless the therapist is dealing with someone who is quite unintelligent, or unless the problem is a mild, educational kind, good advice is not usually helpful. If the therapist is tempted, he can ask the family a question like this: "If I were to give you some good advice, what would I say?" The family members will then tell the therapist all the good advice that he has considered, that they have been given in the past, and that has not helped.

Giving good advice means the therapist assumes that people have rational control of what they are doing. To be successful in the therapy business, it may be better to drop that idea.

The directives that will be talked about here are ones in which the goal is to change the ways the family members deal with one another by introducing action. There are many ways to accomplish this goal. For example, if a mother and daughter

are in a continual fight about when the daughter is to come in
at night, one can direct the father to take charge of this problem. This directive will change the sequence in the family. Or
one might use many other kinds of directives in this situation.
How to give such directives so that they are followed is a matter of skill and practice.

Motivating a Family to Follow Directives

To motivate someone to do something means to persuade
the person that there is some gain in it for him. When a therapist wishes to motivate family members to carry out a task, it
is necessary to convince them that the task will achieve the ends
they want for themselves individually and for one another and
the family. How to motivate a family will depend on the nature
of the task, the nature of the family, and the kind of relationship the therapist has with the family. But one can talk about
general ways to motivate people.

The direct approach, a common approach for persuading
family members to do a task, is to say to them that you know
they want to solve their problem and that you want the same
thing. When they agree on a goal, the task is offered in that
framework of achieving what they want out of therapy.

When the family members are in conflict over their aims,
it is sometimes necessary to find some gain for each of them
in the task. For example, the therapist can say that the mother
wants to be sure her daughter behaves properly, the daughter
does not want this constant arguing with her mother, and the
father does not want always to be called in as a referee. Therefore
they should do the task.

In the direct approach, the therapist takes what has been
learned about the family members in the session and uses what
seems most evident and matter-of-fact as the basis for persuading
them to do the task.

If it looks as if the family will not easily cooperate in the
task, the therapist can go at the matter more indirectly. Often
this indirect approach can be used first; later one can be more
direct. In the indirect approach, the therapist leads the family

members to talk about their difficulties in such a way that they are ready to listen to someone who can offer something to do. For example, the therapist may ask the members to talk about everything they have tried to do that failed to solve the problem. This discussion yields information about what has been tried, so that the therapist does not ask them to do something that has failed already. Equally important, such a discussion gives the therapist the opportunity to emphasize what has failed before. As each failure is listed, it can be emphasized as a failure by sáying, "And that failed too." After the listing is done, the family members will notice that everything *they* have tried has failed, and so they are more likely to listen to what *the therapist* has to offer.

A similar approach can be used by encouraging the family members to talk about how desperate their situation is. Rather than reassure them it is not so bad, the therapist can agree with them that it is quite bad. If the situation is made to appear desperate enough, they will listen to the therapist and do the task he or she offers. That is, the therapist uses their desperation as a motivation by emphasizing it. One can even project their situation into the future and have them talk about how disastrous the future will be if something is not done.

However, one can take a quite opposite approach if family members are talking about how things have been improving. One can agree with them and go along with that assessment. Then one can ask them to do the task as something that will help them continue to improve even more, so that what one offers is seen as a small addition to help along an improving situation.

It is possible to motivate family members to do a task at home by starting them on small tasks during the interview. For example, if a mother is asked to help her child do something in the room, and this task goes well, then she will be motivated to do what the therapist asks in directing her to help the child at home during the week. Similarly, if the therapist asks a father to intervene and help the mother and daughter while in the room, to ask him to intervene at home during the week can be seen as merely a continuation of that initial intervention. In such situations, the task at home does not seem such a major event because in a smaller way it has already been done during the therapy session.

The therapist must fit the task to the people. While interviewing a family, one will observe what sort of people the members are and can fit the task to the family style. If the family members emphasize doing things in an orderly, logical manner, the task offered to them should be an orderly, logical task—they will be more likely to do it. If they form a casual, disorderly household, a casual framework for the task may be more appropriate. If they are concerned about money, the therapist emphasizes that the task costs nothing. One of the ways to get this kind of information is to ask the family members to do things while in the therapy room, such as move their chairs or talk about certain subjects. The ways they go about doing such tasks will give the therapist information on how to frame the outside task most acceptably for them.

How the therapist describes the size of the task is important. For some families and for some tasks, the therapist may choose to describe the task as small. For families who seem resistant, sometimes it is best to define the task as a small thing being asked of them. Families who enjoy crisis or have a flair for the dramatic can be told that this task is a major thing being asked of them. That is, some families will feel that a large task is too much for them, while others will feel that a small task is beneath them. The needs of both types must be met.

The therapist can exert authority in a number of ways. Generally, in motivating the family, the therapist should use his position as an expert on what should be done. If he acts as if he knows his business, people are more likely to do what he tells them. Usually people in trouble prefer to have a therapist know his business. Sometimes this preference can be used in an extreme way. If a family is the kind that bickers about things and unravels whatever is suggested, the members will continue to do so when the therapist tries to motivate them to do the task. In that situation, the therapist may tell the family, ''I want you to do something, and I have my reasons, but I'd rather not go into them. I just want you to do this in the coming week.'' The therapist can also get many tasks done by getting people to do the task in order to prove to the therapist that he is wrong or that his method will not work.

A variant approach is to say to a family, ''I'm going to ask you to do something that you will think is silly, but I want you to do it anyway.'' Then debate is cut off, because the family cannot say the task is silly after the therapist has already said it is.

Being Precise

After the family is motivated, the therapist should give clear instructions (unless there is a particular reason to be deliberately confusing). The directives should be clearly *given* rather than *suggested*. For example, it is better to say, ''I want you to do such and such,'' than to say, ''I wonder whether you've considered possibly doing such and such.'' To say, ''Why don't you do such and such?'' is really asking a question rather than giving a directive. It is better to be precise and clear and say exactly what one wants done. Observing the family members' responses while giving instructions will usually show whether they are clearly understanding what the therapist is saying. The therapist should not be afraid to repeat himself. Being repetitious is better than not being understood. Sometimes people will think ahead about one part of the instructions and thus not listen to another part. If the therapist has any doubt that someone understands, he or she can ask that person about the instructions and even ask the person to repeat the instructions.

One of the reasons for being precise is not only that the therapist wants the task done but also that if it is not done, he or she will want to be sure it was not left undone simply because the instructions were not clear.

However, in some situations it may not be desirable to be precise and detailed when giving a task. The therapist may want, instead, to drop in an idea so that the family ''spontaneously'' thinks of doing that kind of task. Nevertheless, the therapist still must be precise in his or her casual dropping of the idea.

Involving Everyone

Just as it is important to involve all the family members in an interview, it is also important to give everyone something to do in a task. (For special reasons the therapist may leave someone out, but exclusion should not happen accidentally.) A good task has something for everyone. Even if the therapist specifically asks someone to stay out of the task, this request is still giving the person something to do.

The task should be structured like any other piece of work. Someone is needed to do the job, someone to help, someone to supervise, someone to plan, someone to check to see that it gets done, and so on.

If, for example, the task is that the mother and father are to agree on something during the week, this task should be made quite precise. The time set aside to talk about it should be decided, what each is to bring up should be specified, and the children should be assigned something to do. One child can remind the mother and father that it is time, if that is necessary; another child can interrupt them when it is time to end; and a third can report the agreement to the therapist at the next interview.

The purpose of involving everyone is to put the emphasis on the total family unit, except in special cases where the therapist wants one part of the family to do a task and wants the others to stay out of it. The therapist must also be careful not to confuse hierarchy in the family by involving children in adult tasks. But, just as no one should be left out in the interview, no one should be left out of the action designed to take place in the home.

It is important to involve the siblings in a task for other reasons than just being fair. If a sibling becomes distressed, the case can go badly. For example, there is often a hierarchy confusion among the siblings in a family with a drug addict child. In one particular case, the addict was the younger daughter. Her oldest brother also had problems. The second brother was the pride of the family because of his success in life. This brother proposed a plan for the father and daughter to do something together. It was a good plan, accepted by the therapist. It was important to involve the oldest brother in the task because if he were left out, he might become jealous of his younger brother and increase his own problems. Should that happen, the parents could become distressed, and the daughter might consequently relapse to help her parents. Providing therapy for a particular sibling can often be seen as requiring the therapeutic involvement of other siblings so that everyone does well in the therapy.

Reviewing the Task

In many cases, particularly if the task is very complex, it is a good idea to have the family members review what they are to do. If one member reviews, the others should be brought into the discussion by asking them to specify their particular parts in the task. This review, which can be done quite quickly with most families, is further insurance that the task is fully understood.

The therapist should anticipate difficulties while reviewing the task. When the therapist gives family members a task, while he or she is talking they are sometimes thinking of ways to get out of it. If this situation seems possible, the review should be followed by a discussion of ways they think they might avoid the task. Usually, family members will bring up what they have thought about. If not, a few suggestions may be helpful. For example, the therapist can ask: "What if somebody forgets?" or "Suppose someone gets sick?" Such suggestions are helpful, particularly if family members have indicated that such things often happen. When the therapist does this, the family members have blocked themselves off from getting out of the task and are more fully committed to it.

Examples of Tasks

A few simple examples of tasks may be helpful at this point in the discussion.

1. In an actual case in which the grandmother is siding with her ten-year-old granddaughter against the mother, the

therapist sees mother and grandchild together. The girl is instructed to do something of a minor nature that would irritate grandmother, and the mother is to defend her daughter against the grandmother. This task forces a collaboration between mother and daughter and helps detach daughter from grandmother.

2. In another case, a husband is asked to do something for his wife that she would not expect, and she is asked to receive it graciously. He must not do something routine, which she would expect, and therefore he is encouraged to initiate something new in the marriage. He also must think about his wife carefully to decide on something she would not expect.

3. A father and son are asked to do a minor thing that the mother would not approve of. It will be difficult for the mother to arrange what they do when the thing must be something she does not want.

4. A mother who does not differentiate among children of different ages may be asked to set and enforce a different bedtime for each child, even if the times are only fifteen minutes apart. This task forces her to differentiate on the basis of age.

5. A father who is siding with his small daughter against the wife may be required to wash the sheets when the daughter wets the bed. This task will tend to disengage daughter and father or cure the bedwetting.

6. Among the many tasks that can be done inside the interview room are those that involve changing pathways of communication. Father and mother may be directed to talk without including daughter, or mother and son may be told to talk without father interrupting. A son may be physically moved to sit beside a male therapist while they observe the women in the family making a decision about something, thereby drawing a gender boundary. A family in which everyone constantly interrupts may be told to pass a coat or hat around and only the person holding it may talk. Or a "speaker's chair" may be set and only the person sitting in it may talk. All these tasks shift the pathways of communication.

7. A mother and father who need an excuse to be affectionate with each other may be asked to show affection to each other in an obvious way at set times to "teach their child" how to show affection.

8. A husband and wife with sexual problems may be required to have sexual relations *only* on the living-room floor for a period of time. This task changes the context and so the struggle.

9. When there is an intense triangle between a mother, a teenage daughter, and a father, the father may be asked to take the daughter out to a nice place for lunch to give her experience in behaving well in public. Mother can be asked to dress the daughter for the occasion or choose the place. Such a directive may seemingly involve father and daughter more intimately but actually draws a generation line in the result.

10. A man who is afraid to apply for a job may be asked to go for a job interview at a place where he would not take the job if he got it, thereby practicing in a safe way.

11. Among the many tasks a supervisor may give to a therapist is one to help him disengage from a family. The supervisor can have the therapist tell a couple near termination of therapy that they will probably have a major disagreement. The couple will be inclined not to want such a fight, and they will pull together against the therapist to avoid it, thereby extruding him.

12. When a mother is behaving helplessly with the children and so keeping the father involved but exasperated, the father may be instructed to educate the mother in how to deal with the children (beginning by practicing in the room). To get the husband off her back, the mother will become more effective with the children, and the couple are then likely to begin quarreling more openly.

13. An individual or family may be told that during the coming week they will spontaneously get an idea that will improve their situation. They may be told they are at a stage where they are responsive now to ideas from within themselves. This task helps patients initiate changes.

14. To get more distance and objectivity between a mother and child, the mother may be asked to hide something where the child will take no more than ten minutes and no less than five minutes to find it. She must repeatedly attempt this task until she succeeds. The mother must think through just how her child thinks, and how he thinks differently from her, to succeed.

15. Some tasks involve compromises that satisfy everyone. For example, one husband was always concerned about his health, and he regularly took his temperature, even walking about the house with a thermometer in his mouth. His wife became angry every time he did this, and they would fight about it. They could not resolve the issue. The therapist agreed that the husband should be able to take his temperature when he felt it necessary. His wife should also not be provoked by her husband's "forgetting" and walking through the living room with a thermometer in his mouth. The directive was that they break the oral thermometer that same day and purchase a rectal thermometer for his use.

16. When a husband and wife, or parent and grandparent, are at an impasse over who is correct in the way the child should be dealt with, a therapist can provide a behavior modification program. One person may be excluded by this arrangement, or they may be brought together. For example, the parent can say to the grandparent that this is a new procedure being learned at the clinic and so from now on parent and not grandparent is to be the authority on what to do with the child with this new procedure. Or parents who have fought over different ways of dealing with the child can reach agreement on this new way and so resolve a parental conflict that has been maintaining a child problem.

17. With a depressed person, the therapist can require a series of tasks that require the person to activate. The more trivial the tasks, the more angry and less depressed the person will be. To change the organization maintaining the depression, the therapist can require the family members to initiate and enforce the tasks to activate the person.

18. A task can be used to prevent something happening that a therapist does not want. For example, a mother who felt she was unable to control a twelve-year-old boy said that she was reluctantly going to put him in military boarding school, because there was nothing else she could do. The therapist suggested that the boy did not really know what a military school would be like, and in fairness the mother should teach him about one before sending him away. The mother agreed, and under the therapist's direction she began to teach the boy to stand at at-

tention, be polite, and make his bed every morning after rising early. It became a kind of game between mother and son to have her be the sergeant and him be the private. In two weeks he was behaving well enough so that mother did not think it was necessary to send him off to military school. Mother had found a way to deal with the son, and he had found a way to do what she asked.

The Task Report

After giving a task, the therapist should always ask for a report at some time in the next interview. Generally there are three possible results: the task has been done, it has not been done, or it has been partially done.

If the family members have done the task, congratulations are in order and the interview goes on from there. If they have partially done it, an exploration is necessary of why they have not completed it. Sometimes there are practical reasons and they just could not complete it. At other times they just did not get it all done and have no good excuse.

When people have only partially done what the therapist asked, he or she should not excuse them easily. If they are let off, it is saying that what they were asked to do is not important. This message makes the therapist less important and also makes it less likely that they will do the next task asked of them. Once the therapist has given a task, he or she has started something that must be finished.

When family members have not done a task and have no valid excuse, there are two extreme ways to deal with the situation. One is the nice way, and the other is the not-so-nice way. The nice way is for the therapist to apologize. One should say, "I must have misunderstood you or your situation to ask that of you—otherwise you would have done it." That is, the therapist takes on the burden of not having acted correctly. Out of such a discussion can come a somewhat different task which they will do.

With the not-so-nice response, the therapist should have the attitude that the family has failed. It is not that they have failed the therapist, but they have failed themselves. That is, the therapist condemns them for unfortunately having missed an opportunity. One way to express this approach is to tell the family members that the task was very important and that for their sakes it is too bad they did not do it. The therapist can tell them that now they cannot know how beneficial it would have been to them. If they say they did not think the task would do any good, the therapist can say they can never know that now, because they did not do it. Throughout the interview, when they bring up problems, the therapist can point out that naturally they have those problems because they did not do the task. His or her goal is to get them to say they would like to have the opportunity to try again and do the task. If they do say this, the therapist can tell them that that opportunity is gone and can never come again—they cannot do the task now. In this way, the therapist sets up the situation so that the next time he or she asks them to do a task, they will do it.

Generally, a therapist should not easily forgive people who have not done what was asked. Sometimes it is best to be hard on people for not doing a task and then later in the interview find a way to excuse them. But failure to do what a therapist asks, or only partly doing it, should never be treated lightly.

It should be emphasized, however, that the therapist should not anticipate resistance from a family when setting up a task. If the focus is on what is important to the family, the presenting problem, and if the therapist offers a reasonable explanation why a task is necessary, cooperation will be obtained. Most typically the family will simply agree and do the task asked of them.

Metaphoric Tasks: The Use of Analogies

The metaphoric way of directing someone is important because it is not always appropriate to make explicit what the therapist wants to happen in a family or what the therapist wants the members to do. Sometimes people will be more willing to follow a directive if they do not have to concede that they have received one. Talking in metaphor is one way to give such a directive.

A metaphor is a statement about one thing that resembles something else. It relies on the analogous relationship of one thing to another. We say "high as a kite," meaning the way the person is "high" resembles the way a kite goes "high." Or we say, "The way his father talked to him, it's like he was run over by a train." A play on the stage is a metaphor about life because what happens there resembles what happens in life. Often when a therapist wants family members to behave in a certain way, he or she gets them to behave in some other way that resembles the one the therapist wants. Then they will "spontaneously" behave the way the therapist wants them to.

As an example, in one case where a boy was reported to be afraid of dogs, the therapist learned that the boy had been adopted as an infant. The boy ostensibly did not know he had been adopted, and the parents did not wish to tell him. The therapist assumed the boy did know. The therapist wanted to get the family to take a dog into the home and also wanted to deal with the adoption issue. He therefore talked to the boy about "adopting" a dog who had a problem of being frightened. He then discussed with the boy various issues, such as the possibility that the dog might become ill and have to be taken to the doctor (which situation paralleled the adopted boy being taken to the doctor). When the boy said the family might have to get rid of the dog if he became ill and cost doctor bills, the therapist insisted that, once the dog was adopted, the family was committed to him and would have to keep him and pay his doctor bills no matter what. Various concerns the boy might have had about himself as well as the parents' concerns about him were discussed in metaphoric terms in relation to the proposed adoption of the puppy.

Metaphors are not only words but actions. The ways in which a therapist deals with the children in a room can influence the ways the parents will deal with the children even if he does not point anything out to them. By how he operates, the therapist is showing them how to operate without making an issue of it. This approach is showing something metaphorically; the therapist is saying something in action that resembles something else he wants to have happen.

Another example can illustrate this approach. Suppose that a therapist wants a married couple to enjoy sexual relations more than they do. She wants husband and wife to behave differently together and to have a more pleasant mood during sex. She sees that there is bad feeling and a sense of contest around sexual relations, and she also sees that they (or she herself) have difficulty talking directly about their sexual activities.

If the therapist decides not to approach the problem directly, then she begins to think of what other situations a married couple go through together that have some processes resembling sexual activity, something that is permissible to talk about. One possibility might be for them to have a date together as they did in their courtship days. The therapist can talk about what is to take place on their evening out. Or there might be a game they play together. The therapist can talk about the way they should deal with each other during a session of the game.

One of the metaphors Erickson developed to use for this problem is to have the couple talk about eating together. The therapist can discuss how they have dinner together. Is there a time they have dinner without the children present, just the two of them? As the therapist asks the couple about this, she can talk about aspects of eating that resemble sexual relations. She can say, for example, "Sometimes a wife likes to have appetizers before dinner and start slowly, and her husband likes to dive right into the meat and potatoes." Or "Some husbands compliment their wives on how nice everything looks, and other husbands just don't notice and so their wives don't put out any effort." As she talks about these things, if the couple appear to be connecting what she says with sex, she changes to a part of the subject that does not touch so closely on the sexual topic. She does not want them to make the connection consciously. Then she moves back again to talk about how some people like dinner with the lights dim and perhaps with candles, while others like bright lights where they can see everything they want to enjoy.

At the end of such a discussion, the therapist can move naturally toward a task about dinner together. They are to choose a night, and together they are to prepare a pleasant dinner.

They are to show appreciation for each other's differences in taste and are only to bring up pleasant things and not the troubles of the day. The wife is to try to stimulate her husband's appetite, and he is to do what he can to provide what will please her. If the dinner goes well, the odds are that the mood will carry over to sexual relations.

As another example, a family was in therapy with a problem boy who improved. The mother said she would also like to improve her marriage. The father, who also appeared unhappy with aspects of the marriage, said he did not want to deal with his marriage in therapy. He was there for the boy and nothing else. At this point the therapist could choose to focus on the boy and drop the marital issues. Or the therapist could deal with the marriage indirectly so the father would not have to reveal his marital problems or discuss them with the wife in the therapist's presence. That approach was decided on, and the therapist began to talk with the parents about their two boys in a way that was metaphoric to the marriage. Mother had tended to side with the good boy, in general, and the father sided with the problem boy. In that sense the children represented them. The therapist discussed the relationship between the two boys, which paralleled the relationship of the couple. For example, the good boy was embarrassed by the problem boy in public. Mother, too, was sometimes embarrassed by the father in public. A crucial issue was the right of the problem boy to have some time to himself. Father insisted the boy should have some, and he added, "It's like when a man comes home from work, he likes some time to himself with a beer and the newspaper before his wife tells him all the day's problems." In the following week, the couple made the arrangement that father was to have time for himself when he came home, which improved his relationship with his wife. They thought they had "spontaneously" thought of that. The therapist assumed it was a product of the metaphoric conversation. A series of such conversations led to similar changes, without the marriage ever being explicitly discussed.

There is an important aspect of this metaphoric technique that is sometimes not known. Merely discussing something in a metaphoric way does not produce change. It is important that the therapist take a position when talking metaphorically. For example, if the therapist is talking about having dinner as a way of discussing sex, it is necessary to say that enjoying dinner is a good idea. That is, when trying to change A, the therapist should take a position on B. In the case of this couple, it was when the therapist said that the boy should have time for himself that father made an issue of people needing time to themselves. Merely drawing parallels in metaphor does not cause change.

Another important aspect of the metaphoric technique is that it raises ethical problems. The therapist is changing some aspects of a person's life outside the person's awareness, ostensibly, and without an explicit contract that this area is to be changed. It might be that the person is always aware, at some level, or he or she would not participate and be influenced. But still the therapist must approach change through the use of metaphor with a concern that special ethical responsibilities are involved.

In summary, in the metaphoric approach the therapist chooses a goal of achieving some change. The therapist selects an activity that resembles the one he or she wants to change, an activity easier for the family to deal with. A story or a conversation is used to discuss that area in order to gain information and to influence the way they think about it. The therapist takes a position on how things should be in the metaphoric area. Finally, a task might be assigned in the metaphoric area.

Paradoxical Tasks

The directives up to this point have been the kind a therapist gives when he wants the family members to do what he says. There is another kind of directive in which he wants the members to resist him so that they will change. These tasks may seem paradoxical to family members because the therapist has told them he wants to help them change but at the same time he is asking them not to change.

This approach is based on the idea that some families who come for help are resistant to help offered. The members are very good at getting a therapist to try and fail. The therapist is then pulling at the family members to improve, while they are resisting and provoking him to go on pulling. This situation is frustrating for both the therapist and the family.

To some extent it is true of all families that they are resistant to change if they are in a stable state. If they are in a crisis and unstable, with everyone upset, they will often follow directives easily because they are trying to stabilize. But if they are stable and a therapist asks them to change, he is asking for instability and something new, and people may react against that. Yet all families who come for help are unstable enough to have sought assistance. So it is never simply one way or the other.

Usually a family has stabilized around one family member being the problem. When the therapist moves to make a change in the situation of the problem person, he is moving to unstabilize the family, and he will meet resistance in varying degrees. Paradoxical tasks are designed to deal with this problem.

There are two general approaches with a paradoxical task: (1) an approach to the family as a whole and (2) directives that involve only part of the family.

The Approach to the Family as a Whole. An example of an approach to the whole family is the case described in Chapter Five. The therapist expressed his concern about what would happen if the child were properly toilet-trained and became normal. Within a framework of trying to change the family, the therapist restrained the members from getting better. The paradoxical approach always has two levels on which two messages are communicated: "change" and, within the framework of the message, "don't change."

As another example, a family may enter with a problem child who will not go to school. The therapist—within the framework of her job, which is to help the child get back to school— can talk to the family about how perhaps the child should not go to school. She can suggest that it might be better if the child just stayed home and can offer various reasons for this, depending on the particular family. She might say that perhaps the family would get upset if the child went to school like normal children and therefore it would be better if he or she stayed home.

This approach requires skill, because the therapist is communicating a number of different things at the same time. She is saying, ''I want to help you get better,'' and she is saying, ''I am benevolently concerned about you.'' She is saying things to the family that are on the edge of being insulting: she is saying she thinks the family members can really tolerate being normal, but she is also saying perhaps they cannot.

The dangers in this approach come about when the therapist does not communicate all these things at once. If she does not, the family members may feel merely that she thinks they are hopeless. Or they may feel that she is taking advantage of her position to be insulting—or that she does not really care whether they change or not.

When the approach is successful, the family members achieve the goal of the therapy to prove to the therapist that they are as good as other people. They ''spontaneously'' change. The therapist must accept the change when it happens and let the family put her down by proving her wrong. If she wants to ensure that the change will continue, she might say to the members that probably the change is only temporary and they will relapse. Then the family will continue the change to prove to her that it is not temporary. Talking about the change being temporary serves to block off a relapse. The therapist can do the same thing by encouraging a relapse. This approach can ensure that no relapse will occur. One can say to the family, ''I can see you've changed and are over the problem, but I think this has happened too fast. I would like you to have a relapse and this week go back the way you were before.'' Sometimes one can put it, ''I want you to feel as miserable as you did when you first came in.''* To make this directive reasonable to the family members, the therapist might say that too fast a change is upsetting, or that they really need to understand how bad

---

*Milton H. Erickson was, of course, the master at directive therapy, and he had a particularly graceful way of encouraging a relapse. He would say, ''I want you to go back to that time when you felt miserable, feel as you did then, and see whether there is anything from that experience you wish to salvage.'' Since there is usually a nostalgia for lost symptoms and problems, as well as relief, such a suggestion fits particularly well.

they felt before, or whatever else might seem reasonable to them. However, when asked to relapse, they will resist by not relapsing, which is the therapist's goal. (Even if they should relapse, the relapse is under her direction, and so they are following her directives and cooperating with her. In this way she can then get them not to have a relapse again. But such relapses do not happen if the approach is done properly.)

Directives That Involve Part of the Family. Often a therapist will not want to use a paradoxical approach to the whole family, but only with a particular person or a particular pair. The procedure remains the same: one asks people to stay the same, within a framework of helping them change.

For example, a mother may be overprotecting her child and hovering over him so that he has no freedom to make decisions or take responsibility for what he does. If the therapist tries to persuade her to do less for the child, she may respond by doing more, often saying that the therapist really does not understand how handicapped the child really is. One can take a paradoxical approach by asking the mother to spend a week hovering over the child. She is to watch over him, protect him, and do everything for him. A therapist might give different reasons for this directive, depending on the mother. For example, he might say she should do this so she can find out how she really feels in this situation or so that she can observe herself and the child. To use this approach well, the therapist should ask for more extreme behavior than the mother has been showing. For example, she should not only hover over the child but also set aside a definite time to spend a whole hour warning the child about all the dangers in life (an hour is a long time). Or the therapist should take some other aspect of her behavior and make it more extreme. If this approach is done well, the mother will react by rebelling against the therapist and hovering over the child less. She will not like to do what she is doing because someone is telling her to do it. She also will not like to do more of it, particularly when she also feels that too many demands are made on her by the child already. She will begin to emphasize that the child should do more for himself and take more responsibility. That is, she will begin to move to the position the therapist would really like her to go to. Usually it is necessary to pursue this approach. If the mother hovers over the child less, the therapist should not congratulate her but should push her to do more. This approach is one way of disengaging a child from a parent without using another family member.

The same approach can be used with couples who are always fighting in an unproductive way. The therapist can ask them to go home and have a fight at a set time and for a certain period, such as three hours. The goal is to get them to fight less. People do not like to fight or make themselves miserable because someone tells them to do so.

Similarly, if a child is provoking her parents, the therapist can ask her to do that for a full week. If she provokes them, they will react differently because they have heard her asked to do so. If she does not provoke them, the therapist has changed a pattern in the family, which is what he is after.

To use the paradoxical approach, a therapist must develop skill and must practice. He also needs to be able to think about problems in a gamelike or playful way even though he realizes that he is dealing with grim problems and real distress. He also needs to tolerate the emotional reaction of the family toward him, since this approach forces them to deal with him in ways they have never dealt with a helper before.

The design of a therapist's directives in this approach is relatively simple. He observes how the family members deal with each other and directs them to behave in that way. How he gives the directive, how he makes it seem reasonable, and how he reacts to a change and follow-through can require more innovation than the design of the task.

Stages of a Paradoxical Intervention. To summarize the paradoxical approach, the proper stages can be illustrated with a case example. A nine-year-old boy was referred to a clinic for a problem of compulsive masturbation. He masturbated at school and at home in front of his mother and sisters. The problem was so severe that he had worn holes in the crotch of his pants, and his mother reported he had been hospitalized for blood in his urine. The problem had existed since the boy was five years old. A child therapist had worked with the problem for a year and a half with no improvement. He had tried insight into the problem, had tried some rewards and punishments, and had met regularly with the boy's mother. He referred the case hoping that family therapy would help. The family was on welfare, and the father had been dead for several years. There were three older daughters in the family, two of them living outside the home. The twenty-year-old daughter had two small children who were also in the home.

The stages of the paradoxical approach can be summarized. First, as in all directive therapy, one must establish a relationship defined as one to bring about change. This definition is usually implicit in the framework when someone asks for therapy, but it can be emphasized. Second, one must define the problem clearly. In this case the problem was defined as public masturbation. Third, one must set the goals clearly.

The goal was not to stop the boy from masturbating but from masturbating in public and without pleasure. Setting goals clearly is particularly important if one is using an effective therapeutic technique.

Fourth, one must offer a plan. It is helpful to offer a rationale to make a paradoxical directive reasonable, although one can also leave the plan implicit and merely give the directive. In this case the first step in the plan involved the mother and other family members, and the second step involved the boy. The therapist asked the mother to let him deal with the problem with the boy privately, although he also wished to see the whole family together at times. The mother agreed. In this way the therapist attached the boy to himself and made the problem an issue between two males. Later, when he saw the boy alone, he offered the rationale that his paradoxical request for an increase in the masturbation was to prevent the boy from doing it on days when he did not enjoy it.

Fifth, one must gracefully disqualify the current authority on the problem. The authority on the problem may be a spouse or a mother or some other family member. Usually someone is trying to help the person solve the problem, and that someone must be defined as not doing the right thing.

In this case, the mother had taken the boy from doctor

to doctor for years to solve the problem. The therapist suggested that she would become upset when the boy improved. The mother did not like that idea. The therapist asked her what she might do with herself when the boy was over the problem. She thought she could find something else to do with herself. A purpose in dealing this way with the mother is to encourage her to prove that she will not get upset when the boy improves. The only way she can prove this is to help the boy become normal and show she is not upset. Therefore she is working at home to improve the boy while the therapist is working in the office to improve him, and they are working together. In the therapy the mother was also seen alone to interest her in school and work so she would have more in her life than this problem son (and an even more problematic daughter).

Sixth, the therapist must give the paradoxical directive. As part of defining the problem, the therapist asked the boy to make a baseline chart on how often he masturbated. The boy came in the following week and reported the number of times. He said that he had enjoyed it most on Sunday. The therapist gave the paradoxical directive that the boy do it more on Sunday, when he enjoyed it, and not on the other days, when he enjoyed it less. He was asked to do it eight times on Sunday, twice as often, perhaps getting up early to get it done.

Seventh, the therapist should observe the response and continue with encouragement of usual behavior. The therapist should not relent for rebellious improvement or if the person is upset but should reemphasize the rationale and the plan. If the person improves and does less, the therapist should define that as not cooperating, because the request was for more problem behavior.

In this case the boy had done his masturbating on Sunday, but he had also done it on Monday, when he was not supposed to. To punish himself, he was asked to do it twelve times on the next Sunday. Masturbation was also made more of an ordeal by requiring him to undress completely, fold up his clothes, and so on.

The next week the boy came in without the baseline paper, had joined a hockey team, and was more cheerful. The therapist insisted on more masturbation. By the fifth interview, the boy had rebelled and masturbated less than required on Sunday. The therapist condemned him for not cooperating and, as punishment, required him to masturbate once each day in the living room in the presence of his mother and sisters. It had taken five weeks to arrange that the boy do as a punishment exactly what he had been doing as a presenting problem. (Some clinicians would have difficulty being this punishing, but given the severity of the problem and the fact that the boy was only being asked to do what he was already doing, this therapist did not find it difficult.)

Eighth, as change continues, the therapist should avoid credit for it. Accepting credit means that relapses occur in relation to the therapist. Although a therapist might want to "share" with a client and explain what he is really doing, the risk is a relapse caused by the therapist's need for comfort. A way to avoid credit is to be puzzled by the improvement.

In this case, the therapist recessed for two weeks. The first week he required the masturbation program. The second week he left unclear what the boy was to do. This omission allowed the therapist to judge the amount of spontaneous change (rather than a methodical extinguishing of the behavior). If the boy gave up the public masturbation, the therapist would drop the issue. If he did not, the procedures would be reinstituted.

In two weeks the boy reported that he had done little or no masturbating the second week and seemed to have lost interest in it. The therapist dropped the matter and talked to the boy about going to camp (which had not been previously allowed by mother).

The therapist continued the therapy focused on the mother and daughter problem, with the boy present but not involved around the issue of his symptom. A few weeks later the masturbation was inquired about, and the mother said at times the boy provoked her by putting his hands in his pants while watching television. This action was not made an issue, and in a follow-up a few weeks later the problem was gone.

The mother was allowed to show that she did not get upset when the boy improved, and the boy's general manner became more mature in a matter of a few weeks. He even made some trouble with a friend at school, which he had never done before because he was a quiet boy and a good student. The therapist and mother defined this kind of trouble as normal for a boy that age. The teacher confirmed that he was changing.

It should be emphasized that in this case the paradoxical maneuver was used within a family context. The therapist dealt with the boy about other issues, such as sports and girlfriends. He also dealt with the mother about other interests in her life. When the boy improved and became less obedient, the mother showed that she did not get too upset about the change. The shift to the daughter's problems allowed the mother to be less focused on the boy. All these aspects were part of the therapy and not merely the paradoxical maneuver. There were also stages to the therapy and not merely an encouragement of the symptom and a backing off when improvement occurred. It was necessary to follow through in a systematic way.

Designing Tasks

When a therapist first gives tasks to families, designing tasks may seem difficult. With practice and experience design becomes easier.* A few guidelines can be offered.

Whatever the task, it should be simple enough so that the family can do it (unless the therapist has a special reason for wanting them to fail). The therapist wants successful achievement, and so he or she should only ask people to do what is possible for them to do in their situation. The therapist should be able to say with confidence, "This is something you can easily do." The task should also be adapted to the financial and time situation of the family.

Although the goal is to design a task the family can do, getting the task done can be less important than the negotiations around the task. For example, if the therapist says she will not assign a task until all the family is present, she is setting up

*For a discussion of designing strategies, see C. Madanes, *Behind the One-Way Mirror: Advances in the Practice of Strategic Therapy* (San Francisco: Jossey-Bass, 1984), chap. 5.

the task properly, but she is also using the task to get the family to organize itself in a new way by the members taking charge of getting everyone to the session. Sometimes the arrangements to do the task, when accomplished, solve an organizational problem without requiring the task. Sometimes, too, a threat of a task will force changes. With the directive approach, the directive becomes something for the family to talk about instead of about their problems or their past. It provides an issue for therapist and family for discussion.

A task can be a simple one if the primary goal at that stage is to intensify the relationship with the therapist. Asking family members to make a list of problems, or to observe certain behavior during the week, or to talk together at a set time all will serve the purpose of getting families involved with the therapist.

When the primary goal is to bring about an organizational change, the task to be given requires more thought. The best task is one that uses the presenting problem to make a structural change in the family. For example, if the therapist wants mother and problem child more involved and wants a parental child excluded, and the problem child is a fire setter, the therapist can ask the mother to teach him how to set a safe fire with matches for a certain period each day. If a child is afraid of dogs and the therapist wants to disengage mother and child and have the father intervene, father and child can be asked to select a particular kind of puppy.

With this approach, the focus is on respecting and utilizing what the family considers important, the presenting problem, and what the therapist thinks is important, an organizational change.

The steps in designing a task are to think about the presenting problem in terms of the sequence in the family and to find a directive that changes both. For example, a common problem is a child who declines to go to school. The families differ in many ways, but the most typical sequence is the following.

The child refuses to go to school. The father insists the child go and in the morning pushes the child to go. The child manifests anxiety, illness, or vomiting or runs away. The mother steps in and insists the father is too hard on the child, and the father backs off. After a while the parents agree the chld must go to school. The father insists the child go, the child manifests involuntary behavior, the mother intervenes, and the father stops insisting.

There are many variations to this sequence. It may be the mother who insists the child go and the father who becomes upset. It may also be that some physical problem overwhelms the mother as child and father get into altercations over the school issue. The explanations for why the child stays home vary, but (unless the problem is at school) they usually include the idea that the child is necessary at home for some function in the life of one or both parents. Of course, it is necessary to be sure that the problem is not that the school situation is unsafe or for some other reason the child should not go there.

To get the mother and father to work together, it is necessary to motivate them by having them agree that the child must go to school and is falling behind. Drawing them out about a child's future if the child does not attend school is also helpful. Usually parents agree that something must be done; that is why they are there. It is best to review with them all the ways they have tried to get the child to go that have failed. An important part of this motivating stage is to join the parents within their difficult problem. It is very important to avoid interpretations about why they have failed or what might be "really" behind the problem.

The directive designed must take the usual sequence into account. Various directives are possible. The responsibility might be put on the father to take the child to school, or it might be put on the mother. Or the therapist may say that mother must see that the father does it. Or it could be appropriate, if logistically possible, that both parents escort the child to class.

In a straightforward task such as this, the crucial issue is anticipating what will happen. The therapist must review with the father how he will take child to school. The parents are then asked to discuss how the child will behave—temper, upset stomach, anxiety, vomiting, or whatever might happen. The mother is asked what she will do when the child becomes upset. Her concern that the father and child might kill each other can be examined in terms of its validity. The parents should anticipate that the child might be innovative at the moment when success is about to occur and say something like "I won't go to this school, but I will go to some other." How should the parents respond? Generally it is best to agree that the child could finish the term in this school and then perhaps transfer to another, but they should not let the child deflect them from their task.

The therapist should keep in mind, when discussing this task, that the goal is both to get the child into school *and* to resolve the difficulties between the parents to which the child is responding by not going to school. These difficulties need to be defined in terms of the child's problem. For example, if the parents say they get so upset with each other's way of dealing with the child that they think about separating, the therapist should not discuss separation. He should say that separation is an important issue but whether they separate or not, the child must go to school, and they must solve this problem together. Later, when the child is going steadily to school, the parents may bring up separation. At that time it is appropriate to deal with separation, since it is a real issue and not merely part of the previous sequence.*

The therapist may want the parents to review with the child in the therapy interview what is to happen on the morning designated for going to school. Perhaps the therapist will want them to practice the task. He can have the father insist and the child get upset and mother try to rescue the child. If siblings are involved, they should be given something to do in relation to the task.

When the family report what happened, the therapist finds that they have succeeded or not, or they have partially succeeded. Each alternative leads to different results. If the family have succeeded, the therapist should see them for a period to stabilize them with the child in school and deal with the other issues involved. If the family have partially succeeded by getting the child to school but he left school early, or some unanticipated difficulty arose, the task can be repeated.

*For designing a task in relation to the structural organization, see Chapter Five.

If the family have no excusable reason for not having done the task, the therapist must deal with this seriously, mourning this misfortune, and offer an alternative. He can begin, for example, a set of procedures designed to make it more uncomfortable for the child to be at home than at school. For example, the child is to get up at school time, get dressed, and stay in his room reading during school hours—no television or entertainment, and so on. Often the parents will do this task, since they failed at the other. After succeeding at this task, they can again push the child toward school.

This example illustrates designing a task when the problem is serious and organized action must occur. Other examples would include having an anorectic young woman be required by her parents to eat or having a family organize an extreme response to stop the use of drugs. Similarly, a threat of suicide can involve a whole family in a suicide watch, just as there can be a family consequence around preventing drinking when there is an alcoholic problem. In these cases the directive is straightforward: the therapist decides how the situation would be if therapy were successful and gets there as rapidly and directly as possible.

If the therapist does not have the authority to arrange such actions as getting a family to organize an action or getting an individual or a family to follow an ordeal,* then more indirect procedures are necessary, such as paradoxical or restraining techniques. Often a therapist can have alternative plans for backups that can be used if necessary.

When children and young people are the problem, the therapist should keep in mind that he or she is changing a repeating sequence and so is changing the structure between parents and children. Drawing a generation line clarifies parental functions and husband-and-wife issues. When one uses a directive approach, the design of tasks is greatly simplified if a clearly defined presenting problem is negotiated. The better tasks use the presenting problem as leverage for inducing change. As a therapist learns to clarify problems and to set goals, designing directives becomes easier.

*For the design of ordeals, see J. Haley, *Ordeal Therapy: Unusual Ways to Change Behavior* (San Francisco: Jossey-Bass, 1984).

3

Communication as Bits
and Metaphor

The two most important questions in therapy are whether a person has changed after therapy more than he or she would have without it and whether one therapy approach is more effective than another. When investigating such questions, clinicians often do not agree on how to describe the problem in the therapy situation. At one extreme are the behavior modifiers who wish to use a rigorous description and quantitative measurements. They would like to classify the therapy problem as the presence or absence of acts that can be listed as discrete items. Many other clinicians at the opposite extreme object to this approach and argue that no act is independent of another act, because both acts are connected through different meanings. Clinicians at each extreme argue that the other misses the point of the therapy experience. They cannot agree on procedures and results because they have not agreed on the language for describing a therapy problem.

When therapists listen to a complaint in a first interview, or when they investigate their results after therapy, they must classify in some kind of language what is happening. The ways they describe what they hear and observe will be determined by their point of view and by their training. Some therapists classify what people say as symbolic communication. Others

listen for the frequency of some type of behavior. Others will
be hearing what happens as a sequence of interpersonal action
in an organization. To formulate problems and to answer the
question whether therapy has been successful, one must clarify
the different languages in which the problem situation is being
defined.

Suppose that a woman enters therapy reporting that she
washes her hands many times a day and would like to recover
from this affliction. The behavior modifier might describe such
a person by focusing on her behavior and counting the ritual
washing acts performed per hour. Therapy would be defined
as a set of operations to reduce or eliminate the inappropriate
acts. The premise of this approach is that this person's behavior
can be described in terms of "bits" of behavior. A traditional
dynamic clinician might describe the same person by saying she
is expiating guilt with this compulsive washing. The therapeutic
task would be to offer a human encounter that would resolve
the person's guilt and change her perception of the world. The
ritual washing would not be described as a "bit" that could be
counted. It would be a metaphor, an analogy, about her life.

Digital and Analogic Ways of Communicating

The fact that there are two such extreme ways of describing human beings may be based on the fact that the human being
is capable of communicating in two different styles, or languages.
Sometimes people communicate in precise and logical ways, and
sometimes they express themselves in the language of metaphor.
When someone is being logical, his or her behavior can be described in a logical, scientific language just as a scientist might
describe plants or mollusks. Yet when a person is not communicating in terms of logical categories, no descriptive system made
up of logical categories can encompass what he or she is doing.
The "map" is not appropriate for the "territory." Describing
the person in logical categories would be as useful as counting
the words in a poem. Conversely, when someone is communicating in terms of discrete categories, to describe the person in
terms of metaphors is not appropriate.

One way to characterize the two different modes of human communication is as *digital* and *analogic* communication.* Digital communication consists of that class of messages in which each statement has a specific referent and only that referent. Something happens or it does not happen; there is *one* stimulus and *one* response. It is possible to make a computer classification of such communication because each message fits into a specific category. In this mode, behavior appears to be as logical as the object-linguists would like it to be: one cay say "If *A*, and only if *A*, then *Z*, and only *Z*." Each message is about *one* thing and not about something else as well.

It is because human beings can communicate in digital language that they are able to build computers, reshape nature, and function in complex organizations. The use of digital language to describe human behavior appears most appropriate when the subject is the study of a human being dealing with the environment—when a person is building bridges. This language begins to be problematic when it is applied to human beings dealing with one another. To used digital language to describe people talking with one another, we must expect them to communicate in logical, rational ways, speaking words that have specified, previously defined referents. From the digital view, the description of a man pounding a nail and the description of a man fighting with his wife should be synonymous descriptive problems. In both cases it would be a matter of phrasing the description in a precise language of single referents. Yet describing an interchange between husband and wife in digital language may leave out the essence of the interchange. The fight a married couple may have over who is to pick up whose socks does not necessarily have socks as a referent but, rather, what the socks have tended to mean in the context of the relationship. If one tried to program the interchange into a computer, each message in the quarrel could not be placed in a single category but would need to be coded for all its multiple referents.

*G. Bateson and D. D. Jackson, "Some Varieties of Pathogenic Organization," in D. D. Jackson (ed.), *Communication, Family and Marriage* (Palo Alto, Calif.: Science & Behavior Books, 1968), pp. 200–215.

When a message has multiple referents, it is no longer a "bit." It is analogic, in that it deals with the resemblances of one thing to another. In an analogic language each message refers to a context of other messages. There is no single message and single response—there are multiple stimuli and multiple responses, some of them fictional. Analogic communication includes the "as if" categories; each message frames, or is about, other messages. Included in this style of communication are "play" and "ritual," as well as all forms of art. The analogue can be expressed in a verbal statement, as in a simile or verbal metaphor. It can also be expressed in action—the showing of how something is by acting it out. A message in this style cannot be categorized without taking into account the context of other messages in which the message occurs.

If there were a continuum from digital behavior to analogic, the problem could be more easily resolved. But there appears to be a discontinuous change from one style of communication to the other. This change forces a dichotomy. To illustrate the problem of discontinuity, we can take as an example a television picture or a halftone newspaper photograph. Both are comprised of a series of dots, or "bits" of information. Yet the newspaper picture is more than the sum total of the dots that make up the picture. If we build such a picture by adding dots, they continue to be dots until a certain point at which the picture becomes recognizable as a representation of something, such as a scene or a person's face. At the point where the shift takes place from bits to scene, the change from digital to analogic communication is discontinuous. Information theory and the theory of quantification of bits of behavior can easily deal with the dots, but these approaches cannot easily relate the scene of the picture to the original scene or describe what is being communicated to the reader by the photograph. If the picture has a caption, the problem is the same. It is merely a group of letters, or digital bits, but at the point where the bits form a recognizable word, the communication has shifted from digital to metaphoric. The problem is not one of extremes of a continuum but, rather, a dichotomy between two types of communication. Problems of description arise with these two styles of communication when-

ever one is talking about human action, particularly in the field
of therapy and its evaluation.

Therapy and the Use of Analogies

The use of analogies, or metaphors, seems especially central to the procedures of therapy. Quite different schools of therapy have in common a major concern with the use of analogic
communication. It is not simply that the behavior modifiers concern themselves with "bits" and the dynamic clinicians with
analogies. Behaviorists do tend to be digital when describing
problems and when evaluating outcomes, but their actual therapy can be described as both digital and analogic.

Psychoanalysis was a procedure that encouraged patients
to talk in analogic style. The request for "free association" was
a directive to the patient to temporarily abandon the digital style
of communication and say whatever came to mind, no matter
how irrational it seemed. Speaking in this way, patients offered
a series of analogies about their lives. The analyst also requested
dreams, and when the patient was reporting a dream, the style
was again analogic. The analyst's task was to apply analogies of
his or her own by interpretations and to explore the connections
between the various metaphors that the patient was communicating. The dream metaphor was exposed to free association, which
led to a description of an event that was, in turn, discovered
to be a metaphor about other aspects of the patient's life.

Rather than have the patient offer the analogies, some
behavior therapists offer analogies when attempting to change
the same type of patients. The patient is asked for a list of "anxiety" situations, and he ranks them in order from those that
make him least anxious to those that make him most anxious.
Then he is asked to relax while the therapist offers a series of
analogies about those situations. For example, if the person is
afraid of blood, the therapist first describes a scene where there
is a little blood and increasingly emphasizes wounds and bleeding
as the scenes progress. The patient responds only by a digital
indication of whether he is "anxious" or not as he listens to
the metaphor. He does not offer analogies himself, except in

describing his problems and in casual discourse with the therapist, but he has veto power over the analogies offered to him
by the therapist. When the patient indicates he is "anxious,"
either by a word or by a movement, the therapist stops offering
analogies or shifts to a milder kind.*

In an opposite approach, rather than avoid making the
patient anxious by carefully paced metaphors, as in behavior
therapy, Thomas Stampfl developed implosive therapy, a procedure of helping people become less fearful by asking them to
be fearful.† He forces the patient to be "anxious" by building
extreme metaphors. For example, if the patient says she is afraid
of bugs, the therapist will tell her that she is surrounded by bugs,
the bugs are getting bigger and approaching her, they are over-
whelming her, and so on. In this kind of therapy the patient
has no veto power, since becoming anxious only increases the
extreme nature of the metaphor offered. She can "recover" only
by not being anxious, often by laughing as her fears are reduced
to absurdity in the analogies offered by the therapist. Paradoxical intention therapy follows a similar procedure.‡

Verbal conditioning therapy operates in a way opposite
from Wolpe's behavior therapy and from Stampfl's procedures
even though all the approaches are derived from conditioning
theories. Instead of the therapist offering analogies while the
patient responds with digital signs, the patient describes his or
her life in analogic style and the therapist offers digital responses.
From the therapist's view, these responses—nods of the head
or encouraging words—"reinforce" certain parts of the patient's
communication. For example, if the patient says something like
"My life is a drag," the therapist does not respond, but when
the patient says, "My life sometimes looks bright," the therapist
smiles or nods to encourage further metaphors of this kind.

A neglected aspect of research on therapy is the fact that

*J. Wolpe, *Psychotherapy by Reciprocal Inhibition* (Stanford, Calif.: Stanford University Press, 1958).
†P. London, *The Modes and Morals of Psychotherapy* (Orlando, Fla.: Grune & Stratton, 1964).
‡V. E. Frankl, "Paradoxical Intention and Dereflection," *Psychotherapy* 12 (1975):
226–237.

it is not uncommon for therapists to offer analogies about life, often in the form of examples from their own experience or reports about patients' experiences. This use of analogy is not usually considered a focus of the therapy but is done in passing, during informal interchanges with the patient. A surprising number of therapists tell their patients jokes. Some employ a systematic use of anecdotes with patients. Milton Erickson has developed this procedure more fully than most people. He tells the patient a story that is formally parallel to the patient's problem, and he views therapeutic change as related to the shift in the patient's analogies provoked by the analogies the patient is receiving.*

Analogies in Family Interviewing

The procedure of interviewing whole families has made evident a level of analogy that is also implicit in all forms of treatment. Family therapy consists of many approaches by different schools, but usually the whole family is seen together and typically a therapist asks the family members to offer verbal analogies about their problems. Simultaneously, as the family members deal with one another in the interview, they are enacting an analogic portrait of their life together.

The verbal descriptions by the family are examples of what is happening that is analogic to other things happening, and the therapist responds with metaphors about the family or about other families. However, in addition to the verbal exchange, many family therapists actively request changes in behavior of the family members either in the room or outside it. It becomes more evident when one observes this style of therapy that in all therapy the relationship of patient and therapist is analogic to whatever is being communicated in the therapeutic sessions. For example, the therapist may note that a father talks to his

*J. Haley (ed.), *Advanced Techniques of Hypnosis and Therapy: Selected Papers of Milton H. Erickson* (Orlando, Fla.: Grune & Stratton, 1967), pp. 229–312, and *Uncommon Therapy: The Psychiatric Techniques of Milton H. Erickson, M.D.* (New York: Norton, 1973); S. Rosen (ed.), *My Voice Will Go with You: The Teaching Tales of Milton H. Erickson, M.D.* (New York: Norton, 1984).

son only through the mother. The therapist's intervention may be to ask the mother to sit over to one side while father and son move their chairs so that they face each other and have a talk. Sometimes this request is phrased as being necessary "to see how father and son talk to each other." This interchange between father and son is then a metaphor about their relationship with each other, but when the therapist makes this arrangement, he or she is also acting out an analogy about many aspects of the family, including how the mother should remain out of the interchange. Whether the interview is with one person or several, each act by a therapist is also an analogy about how to behave. This relationship analogy or metaphor is *meta,* or "about," the content of the discussion. If therapy were merely a matter of offering digital bits of information to patients to give them understanding, the relationship would not be particularly relevant. However, the change in the behavior of the patient occurs as an aspect of the analogic changes in the relationship with the therapist.

When we recognize the multiple levels of analogic communication that occur in therapy, we can face the complexities in the process of inducing therapeutic change. Each statement by a patient is multiply coded. It refers at least to her previous statements, to her context of interpersonal relationships, and to her current relationship with the therapist. That is, the patient's statement "fits" a complex set of situations by resonating analogically to these multiple facets of her context. The patient appears peculiar—that is, neurotic or psychotic—when her statements are of a deviant kind because they must "fit" a deviant context. For example, if a psychotic patient says to a therapist, "My stomach is full of cement," with no cue that indicates she is speaking in metaphor, the statement is an analogic expression of a complex context. She may be metaphorically speaking about the hospital food and expressing an analogic statement about her relationships in the hospital. By providing no cues to how her statement is to be received, she is indicating her distrust of the therapist. Simultaneously, the statement may also be a metaphoric response to a previous comment by the therapist. When the patient is "cured," she might communicate in a more normal way by saying something like "The food in this place is terrible, and the way I'm treated makes me sick to my stomach anyhow." Then she would be properly labeling her metaphor. She still would be speaking analogically but would be using a more "normal" analogy. Change in the patient would be shown by a shift in the style in which she indicates the kind of situation she is in with the person to whom she is talking.

When we examine the question of how a therapist induces a patient to change her communicative style, it would seem evident that insofar as the patient's communication is adaptive to her context, then that context must be changed for her communication to change. The life situation of the patient, and her relationship with the therapist, must shift if the way she communicates to the therapist is going to shift. The patient's style cannot be changed by "working on her communication," but only by making organizational changes in the situation to which she is adapting.

A Problem as a Metaphor

Let us take an example to illustrate the use of analogy in therapy. A man enters therapy because, he says, he is afraid he is going to die of a heart attack. He has been assured by a number of doctors that his heart is functioning well, but he still fears that his heart will stop at any moment and he will die. The therapist is faced with the task of changing this patient's style of communication.

If the physician takes the patient's analogy as a digital statement about his heart, she is likely to reply with a digital answer: "Your heart is all right." The patient then proceeds to the next doctor even if the physician supports her reassurance with impressive scientific instruments for examining the heart.

Some therapists will receive the patient's communication about his heart as an analogy—a statement that means something about something else. They will ask a series of questions to gather information about aspects of the patient's life that are analogic to his statement about his heart. These questions typically are "Can you tell me more about that?" (to increase the flow of analogies), "How do you feel about that?" (to encourage more specifically analogic material), and "Do you have similar fears about other things?" (to bring out related analogies).

The kind of analogies that interest the therapist will depend on his particular theory about the "cause" of the patient's presentations. The psychodynamic therapist as well as the behavior therapist is interested in metaphors about the past because of an assumption that past traumas lead to present difficulties. For example, should the patient say, "My fear came on about the time my brother died of a heart attack seven years ago," both kinds of therapists will show active interest even though their therapeutic procedures will be different. The psychodynamic therapist will begin to make "interpretations" to help the patient connect the analogies about his own fear of death and his feelings about his brother. The behavior therapist will have found an area of anxiety, the trauma of death, to be deconditioned. He might deal with the present rather than the past in his therapy, but his causal explanation will be oriented toward the past.

A family-oriented directive therapist will have quite a different view: he will assume that the patient's statement about his heart is analogic to his current situation. He will inquire about how the client relates to his wife, about his job, about his children, and so on. The therapist will also want the wife present in a session so that he can examine how they deal with each other and how the complaints about the heart are used in the ongoing interchange between husband and wife. When he interviews husband and wife together, the therapist will take an interest in the wife's response when the husband is feeling better and when he is feeling worse. For example, he might note that she communicates depression when the husband is emphasizing the better aspects of his life and health and that she appears more involved and animated when he discusses his heart problem. The family-oriented therapist will construct a theory that the husband's communication about his heart is a way of stabilizing the marriage. The kinds of data he will seek are those that reveal how the heart analogy is built into the person's ecology, or interpersonal network.

For example, the family and work life of a person with this kind of presenting symptom is organized around this analogy. The children must be quiet or it will upset father, who fears for his heart; trips and recreation are determined by the state of father and his heart; the kind of job he has and his task performance on the job are regulated by his heart. Often the problem is both the focus of fighting and the way of avoiding conflict in the marriage. For example, sexual relations must occur only under circumstances determined by the man who is concerned about overtaxing his heart. Conflicts about sex between the couple can be avoided when the heart is such a convenient issue. One also finds, in such cases, that husband and wife fight in the morning because he says he cannot go to work because he might die if he exerts himself, while his wife insists he must go or he will lose his job. Often one finds that the days the husband stays home because of his heart are those days he is most worried about his wife's state of mind and is afraid to leave her alone.

What Causes Change?

When we turn to how to bring about changes in a person who communicates this kind of analogy, we must make a distinction between how different therapists understand such a problem and what they do about it. All therapists, whatever their schools, are attempting to change a metaphor in such a case—they wish to change the patient's communication that he expects to die of heart failure at any moment. Many therapists would not see it as a problem of changing the patient's communication. They would postulate something inside him that has to be changed, such as a conflict, a fear, an idea, or an incubus. However, the definition of successful change would be that the person no longer communicates a statement about dying of heart failure.

By the nature of their approach, most therapists would not reassure the man that his heart is all right, as many physicians, wife, and friends have done. However, implicit in all their communication to him is the message "There is nothing wrong with your heart, and your statement is an analogy about something else.'' By not responding to him as having a "real" heart problem, their metacommunicative behavior indicates to the patient that his heart is all right. It is important to emphasize that this framework exists, in order to make it clear that even if a therapist should take literally the metaphor about dying of a heart attack, he does so within a framework that indicates there is nothing wrong with the person's heart.

There are two approaches that appear to succeed with this problem more often than they fail. The first approach defines the problem as a one-person situation, and the subsequent therapy attempts a shift in perception. (Actually, there is no such unit as one person. There is at least the client and the therapist, or an observer, making the description of a person who is part of the system. There are also always other people who will respond to what happens in a particular situation where supposedly only one person is involved.) The second approach assumes it is a multiperson problem, and the therapy is family-oriented.

The first approach is a paradoxical intervention that includes taking literally the person's metaphor about dying of a heart attack. Typical exponents of this way of working are Victor Frankl and Stampfl. The procedure is to advise the person that not only is he going to die of a heart attack but he should drop dead right now. If this procedure is used improperly, it merely dissuades the person from returning for another session of such treatment. If it is used properly, it brings about a transformation that includes abandoning the communication that he is going to die of heart failure. The proper approach includes, first, establishing a trusting relationship with the person. This step involves defining the relationship as one in which the therapist is being helpful and is on the client's side. It must also include the communication that there is nothing wrong with the person's heart. In the second step, the person is encouraged to fall dead of a heart attack at that moment. This approach takes the person's metaphor about his heart absolutely literally: since he has a heart that will fail, it should fail now. The person's communication is not received as an analogy about something else but as a digital statement about his heart.

Both aspects of this procedure must be included: the framework of helping the person over the problem with an indication that his heart is all right and the statement that his heart is failing and he should drop dead right now. When the therapist is successful, the patient abandons his analogy about his heart, often laughing at some point in the procedure. The procedure is repeated at every instance of the expression of a fear about the heart.

Although this approach can be successful, it does not take into account the consequences within the person's family of the change when the heart analogy is abandoned. Predictably the wife and other members of the family will be pleased, but they might also become at least temporarily upset. Marital uproar may occur and may lead to a separation. One cannot change this kind of communication without changing, often unpredictably, the organization in which the person lives.

A Family Approach

Milton Erickson has developed a procedure that is similar in that it also takes literally the metaphor about the heart but that also takes the family into account. Rather than himself take the metaphor about the heart literally, Erickson arranges that the wife do so. In such a situation the wife usually believes the doctors who say that her husband's heart is normal, but she also responds to her husband's behavior by fearful concern that he might indeed have something wrong with his heart. Essentially, she oscillates between condemning her husband at one moment for his illusion and sympathizing with him at the next moment for his heart condition. This kind of oscillation is typical of the intimates of people who show various kinds of severe psychiatric symptoms.

Erickson establishes a trusting relationship with both husband and wife, which is essential in this approach. This approach includes assisting the wife with her problems that are avoided by the communication about the heart. When this relationship is set, and the wife is ready to have her husband give up this metaphor, Erickson arranges that the wife encourage the husband to die of his heart attack. He may have her do so in various verbal and nonverbal ways, including having her respond to each complaint as if it were a real heart attack, calling for an ambulance or other proper medical assistance. An even more effective procedure he has used is to have the wife visit various funeral parlors and collect their literature on funerals. Each time the husband expresses his fear of dying of a heart attack, the wife quietly distributes the funeral literature throughout the house. This procedure rapidly resolves the problem.

To say that the problem is "resolved" with such an approach is to say that the metaphor has been blocked and the couple are forced to develop other ways of communicating with each other. In all areas of encounter between husband and wife where the heart metaphor was previously used, other styles of behavior must now develop. The system has been forced into instability. One might think the husband would substitute another incapacitating metaphor, such as a fear of cancer. However, this substitution does not occur in actual practice. The alliance of wife and therapist forcing the change in the heart metaphor also seems to force a change in that *class* of metaphors. Typically, the husband becomes angry and speaks more straightforwardly about various situations with his wife where the metaphor was previously used, such as sex life or recreation. The wife, in turn, expresses herself with another metaphor than depressive behavior, and in the process the two of them work out changes in their behavior with each other and more "normal" marital communication.

This example is similar to other kinds of metaphors which are expressed with bodily sensations and in which the bodily sensations change when a different kind of communication becomes necessary. For example, the wife with a "real" pain in the neck that has no organic cause can be described as a woman expressing analogically her opinion of her intimates. Similarly, the pain in the head, the pain in the stomach, the nausea, and so on can be understood as metaphors about family life and so treated. Some people seem to be able to say, "You give me a headache," and not have the headache. Others must actually develop a headache, using themselves as an analogic tool to express a statement about their system. Often patients who use the headache metaphor can be taught in therapy to say verbally they have a headache when they have not, so that the verbal statement continues to serve the purpose of the metaphor without the pain. Usually this approach leads to the patient's abandoning both the somatic and the verbal metaphors.

Whatever therapeutic approach clinicians use, they are distinguished from other students of human behavior by their particular interest in analogic communication. When social scientists insist clinicians are "soft" in their approach and should deal with facts, the clinician says they misunderstand and are overlooking the importance of metaphoric communication.

Assessment of Therapy

When we turn to the question of change in therapy and how change can be described and evaluated, one problem seems immediately apparent. Most people evaluating therapy have tried to evaluate change by focusing on digital communication. Evaluating a change in a metaphor is a problem with an undeveloped methodology.

Most evaluations of therapy in recent years have attempted to be scientific by comparing factual information gathered before and after therapy with similar information gathered from some contrast group such as prospective patients on a waiting list. The methodology used relies largely on the self-reports of the people involved. Two factors are usually emphasized: Is the problem the patient originally presented still there, or has it been relieved? Has the patient sought assistance from other people after the termination of therapy? The investigator gathers this information by self-report from the patient, the therapist, and perhaps family members and looks for responses that can be coded as "bits" for quantifiable measurement. The responses must be in a "yes or no" form or in the form of a scale involving "no change, some change, great change," and so on. For example, if the patient presents the problem of a fear of dying of a heart attack, some classification of severity is made at the beginning of therapy. At the end he is asked whether he still has the fear, and if so, he is asked to classify its severity. Whether a phobia, a depression, or whatever, the attempt is to make the problem a "thing" that is either present, not present, or partially present.

   Serious questions can be raised about self-report. Clients who have invested a great deal of money in therapy—or who like or dislike their therapists—will report "facts" biased by that context. Similarly, therapists are hardly objective observers of a task in which they have a large personal investment. The supposedly disinterested investigator also has his or her interests and works within a context that influences what happens. For example, a patient may exaggerate the problem to an investigator at the beginning of therapy even though the investigator will not be treating him, because the patient may believe that whether or not he is treated depends on the investigator's opinion. Another problem, besides bias and unreliability, is that self-report is metaphoric as well as digital. Insofar as what patients and therapists say is "biased" by the experience and context of the treatment, they are communicating analogically about that context even if they ostensibly respond in digital form. Communication is a metaphor from the person to the investigator, which not only has as its referent the problem, and whether the problem exists or not, but also carries an analogic statement about the relationship with the therapist, with family members, and with the investigator. The problem thus becomes one of evaluating a metaphor that is cast in digital terms.

   It is also possible to approach the problem of evaluation as one that necessarily involves changes in the patient's analogic style of communication. When symptoms are seen as metaphors, the question is whether the metaphor has changed. One might use projective tests before and after therapy to determine changes in metaphors, but the reliability of these tests is most doubtful. A clinician would not stake his or her reputation on the outcome of a projective test, partly because the test must be interpreted subjectively and partly because the influence of the tester enters into performance. A more self-evident reason is that the projective test produces metaphors that are a communication to the tester—and the patient does not live with the tester but with his or her intimates. For example, a woman is likely to give a different response to an ink blot if she is talking to a tester than if her mother is administering the test. The relationship is different, and so the style of communication is different. What is relevant to change is whether the patient has changed her style with those people with whom she lives (unless the particular symptom involves a problem of relating to strangers).

The importance of doing even digital evaluation of change in therapy is granted. But when there is such a focus by clinicians on analogic communication, it seems evident that evaluation must deal with analogy. Such an evaluation necessarily should include observation and measurement of the way the "patient" communicates with other people, including spouse, children, employer, and therapist. Since analogic communication has multiple functions in an interpersonal network, the network must be examined for change. Self-report about this kind of communication is not adequate. There must be actual observation of how the patient behaves with his or her intimates. For example, after therapy does the man still take his pulse when his wife looks at him amorously? Does he fight with his wife about other matters than his heart? The difficulties of research in this area are being explored with studies of films and with family testing, but the development of rigorous measurement has hardly begun. Without this exploration of change in analogic communication, most clinicians would feel that evaluation of therapy is incomplete and misses the point. (However, the difficulty in evaluation does not mean that therapists should be excused when they avoid evaluating the outcome of their therapy. The difficulties are a matter of degree. Certainly a therapist can keep track of his or her successes in helping clients get over their presenting problems while still accepting the more complex aspects of change.)

From the viewpoint offered here, therapy is an intervention by an outsider into a tightly structured communication system in which symptoms are a style of behavior adaptive to the ongoing behavior of other people in the system. Whether the problem is defined as a phobia, a depression, a character disorder, acting out, or whatever, the communication is functional within the system. The act of intervening, whether it is called "individual therapy" or whether the therapist brings together the intimates of a patient in an interview and so calls it "family therapy," is an intervention into a family system. The therapeutic process may consist of easing the persons out of the metaphors they are using into more appropriate ones, or the metaphors can be blocked so that others must be developed. When therapy is done effectively, the total system in which a person lives undergoes change so that more normal communication is possible from everyone involved. Determining whether the change has happened is a more complex problem than the preliminary therapy evaluation studies would indicate.

To summarize, it is possible to describe symptoms as communicative acts that have a function within an interpersonal network. The symptom is not a "bit" of information but is an analogy that has as its referents multiple aspects of the person's situation, including the relationship with the therapist. From this view, the goal of therapy is to change the communicative behavior of the person—to change his or her metaphor. Insofar as the behavior is a response to the person's situation with intimates, that situation must change if the person's communication is to change. Various forms of therapy can be described as ways of responding to the patient's analogies in such a way that the analogies change. Evaluation of outcome should include not only the presence or absence of a "bit" of behavior by the patient but also an evaluation of the changes in the system to which the patient is adapting by his or her special form of communication.

4

Communication: Sequence and Hierarchy

Research investigators require complex theories; clinicians need simple ones. The researcher must account for and reflect on innumerable variables. The clinician must choose key variables and act. The situation is incredibly complex when several persons deal with one another in organized ways. Researchers who examine slow-motion films to study body movement, linguistics for vocal intonations, and semantics for the meaning of the verbal content find themselves in a world with an almost infinite number of variables. Fortunately, clinicians are more free to simplify; the problem is to choose the important variables most relevant to change.

Power and Organization

When one is observing people who have a history and a future together, one sees that they follow organized ways of behaving with one another. If there is any generalization that applies to humans and other animals, it is that all creatures capable of learning are compelled to organize. To be organized means to follow patterned, redundant ways of behaving and to exist in a hierarchy. Creatures that organize together form a status, or power, ladder in which each creature has a place in the hierarchy, with those above and those below. Although groups will have more than one hierarchy because of different functions, the existence of hierarchy is inevitable because it is in the nature of organization that it be hierarchical. We may dream of a society in which all creatures are equal, but on this earth there are status and precedence and inequality among all creatures. In many societies, one does not even speak the same dialect to a superior as to an inferior, and everywhere the messages that creatures interchange in their repeating ways are messages that define positions in organizational hierarchies. If a group attempts to organize on the basis of equal status among the members, some members become more equal than others as organization develops.*

Before proceeding further with a discussion of hierarchy, it might be best to clear up a misunderstanding that can occur when power and hierarchy are discussed. Although one must accept the *existence* of hierarchy, that does not mean one needs to accept a *particular* structure or a particular family hierarchy. One need not accept the status quo either in the economic structure of society or in a particular unfortunate hierarchy. Everywhere there are hierarchical arrangements that are unjust. One economic class suppresses another. Women are kept in a subordinate position in both family and work groups merely because they are female. People are placed in subordinate positions because of race or religion. Children are oppressed by their parents, in the sense of being restricted and exploited in extreme ways. Obviously, there are many wrongs that need righting that

---

*A possible objection to the concept of hierarchy is that there are alternative ways to describe an organization. The "pecking order" we observe may be a product of our thinking, not of the nature of organization. For example, when horses enter a barn, we note that they assume a certain order and maintain it each time they enter the barn. We may not describe this pattern in terms of one creature being superior and one secondary. What we observe is a pattern in which the animals behave in a sequential order. The description scheme we choose will depend on our purpose in making the description. If our focus is on how to change a malfunctioning organization, then a description should clarify how organizations malfunction and offer ideas about how to produce change. The concept of hierarchy, or levels of status and power, seems most appropriate as a description for therapeutic purposes.

involve hierarchical issues, and any therapist must think through his or her ethical position.

It is crucial that a therapist not confuse the existence of an unjust hierarchy with a strategy for changing it. If one sees a child being oppressed in a family, that does not necessarily mean one should join that child against the parents to "save" her. The result could be an unhappier child as well as unhappier and more restrictive parents. By attacking the parents directly, the therapist may feel morally justified, but the goal of therapy is not the moral justification of the therapist and it is usually the child who pays for such an attack. To attack parents merely because they are the authorities and part of the establishment is naive and can easily lead to the failure of therapy.

Not only do all higher animals form hierarchical organizations, but it is important to note also that the hierarchy is maintained by *all* the participants. Those of higher status enforce their status by their actions, but those of lower status will act to enforce hierarchy if a higher-status creature does not enforce its status. When animals or humans step out of order, the reestablishment of hierarchy is a group effort, with those below as active as those above. (The cooperative behavior of those below has often aroused the despair of revolutionists.)

A family as a hierarchy includes people of different generations, of different incomes, and of different degrees of intelligence and skills. These complex hierarchical lines are related to the many functions of a family. The most elementary hierarchy involves the generation line. Within the family there are intricate involvements of uncles, aunts, cousins, and others in the kinship system. But at the most simple level it is parents who nurture and discipline children, who in turn nurture and discipline children as the generations proceed over time. At any one moment there are, at most, four generations operating. Most commonly there are three: grandparents, parents, and children. These three generations can be simplified into three levels of power, or status. In the traditional family, as still is evident in Asia, the greatest status and power resided with the grandparents; the parents were secondary and the children lowest in status. In the Western world, particularly in this time of rapid social change, the status and power position of the grandparents is less. In the nuclear family living arrangement, the power often resides with the parents, and the grandparents are moved to an advisory, if not superfluous position. Professional experts tend to replace the grandparents as authorities.

Yet whatever the arrangement, every family must deal with the issue of organizing in a hierarchy, and rules must be worked out about who is primary in status and power and who is secondary. When an individual shows symptoms, the organization has a hierarchical arrangement that is confused. It may be confused by being ambiguous so that no one quite knows who is his or her peer and who is a superior. It may also be confused because a member at one level of the hierarchy consistently forms a coalition against a peer with a member at another level, thus violating the basic rules of organization.

When the status positions in a hierarchy are confused, or unclear, there will be a struggle that an observer would characterize as a power struggle. An observer who has a theory of innate aggression or of a need for power may say the participants are satisfying an inner drive by struggling for power. Yet it would seem more useful to characterize such a struggle as an effort to clarify, or work out, the positions in the hierarchy of an organization. When a child has temper tantrums and refuses to do what his mother says, the situation can be described as an unclear hierarchy. In such a case the mother is often indicating that she is in charge while treating her child as a peer, and so the hierarchy is confused. There are various explanations of why a mother would behave in this contradictory way. It is possible to say there is something wrong with the mother's thinking if she offers conflicting messages. For example, if she asks her child how to discipline him, she is taking charge by putting the child in charge. If one thinks in a larger unit than mother and child, it is possible to note that the child is in coalition with some powerful person in the family, such as a father or grandmother, and so the child has more power than the mother. The mother is in charge by the fact of being a parent, but she must ask the child's permission to discipline him because of his power. The inclusion of a wider interpersonal context offers new explanations of why people do what they do.

If there is a fundamental rule of social organization, it is that an organization is in trouble when coalitions occur across levels of a hierarchy, particularly when these coalitions are secret. When an employer plays favorites among her employees, she is forming coalitions across power lines and joining one employee against another. Similarly, if an employee goes over the head of his immediate superior to a higher authority and joins that authority against the superior, there is difficulty. If a manager sides with an employee against a foreman in the middle, trouble will occur. When such a coalition happens occasionally, it is a minor matter. But when sequences of this kind become organized so that they repeat and repeat, the organization is in trouble and the participants will experience subjective distress.

Since therapy includes the art of keeping the kind of relationship ambiguous, it is not surprising that power struggles often appear in a therapy context. For example, when a therapist defines himself as an expert by taking money for his assistance and then declines to be an expert and even asks the patient what he feels should be done, the hierarchy is confused. The patient will try to clarify the relationship. An observer might call the resulting action a "working through" of resistance, but it can also be seen as an organizational problem. To say that a therapist and patient struggle for control in therapy does not imply that they have a "need" for control but that the relationship is ambiguous because of the nature of the therapeutic process.

Sequences

One of the ways we can map out a hierarchy is by observing the sequences that occur in an organization. If we see that Mr. Smith tells Mr. Jones to do something and Mr. Jones does it, that may be an isolated act. If the act occurs again and again, we deduce that Mr. Smith is higher in the hierarchy than Mr. Jones. A structure is composed of repeating acts among people. What has revolutionized the field of therapy is the realization that a goal of therapy is to change the sequences that occur among people in an organized group. When that sequence changes, the individuals in the group undergo change.

A therapeutic change can be defined as a change in the repeating acts of a self-regulating system—preferably a change into a system of greater diversity. It is the rigid, repetitive sequence of a narrow range that defines pathology.

People seem to have a difficulty, in fact a reluctance, to observe and describe repeating patterns in a chain of three or more events. This difficulty is particularly great if we ourselves are involved in those events. For example, a therapist may notice that a wife repeatedly provokes him. Perhaps he will even recognize a sequence of two actions by noticing that she provokes him after he has criticized her husband. Yet, it seems more difficult to notice that the child was rude, the father disciplined the child, the therapist reacted against the father, and then the therapist was provoked by the wife. Our cognitive attention spans seem to have difficulty with such sequences. In fact, it is possible, as Braulio Montalvo has suggested, that we have built into ourselves necessary amnesias for overlooking parts of sequences. It is when we record interactions on videotape that we observe sequences for the first time and think about them in new ways.*

Let me give an example of a way to think about sequences as they have been thought about within the developing child guidance movement. There were progressive stages: first it was assumed that the problem was a child who had something wrong with him. It was hypothesized that he was responding to past experiences that had been interiorized.

Later, the mother was emphasized and it was said the child had a problem of the relationship with his mother. For example, it was said she was helpless and incompetent and the child was adapting to that behavior. To explain why the mother was that way, it was hypothesized that she was responding partly to past experiences and partly to the child.

Later yet, the father was discovered. It was suggested that the mother's behavior was explained by her relationship to the

---

*This idea about the function of amnesia was first suggested to me in a personal communication and is expressed in a videofilm of a therapy session edited by Montalvo: "Constructing a Workable Reality."

father. For example, if the mother behaved competently with the child, the father withdrew from the family; but if she was helpless and incompetent, he was involved. It was also hypothesized that her ineffectiveness with the child was a way of supporting the father when he was under stress and depressed. If the mother was helpless, the father would pull himself together to help her deal with the child.

Finally, it began to be recognized that a system was involved, and all participants behaved in a way to keep the sequence going. The father's state of mind was a product of his relationship with mother and child, who were also as they were because of sequences established with him and with each other.

To clarify a sequence further, a simple description can be made of a repeating cycle. The sequence can be absurdly simplified to three persons, each capable of two "states." There are father, mother, and child, and each of them can be either competent or incompetent (the child can be said to behave or misbehave). Since the sequence repeats in a circle, there is a series of steps each leading to the next and so back to the beginning again. One can start such a description at any point in the circle.

Step 1. *Father—incompetent.* The father behaves in an upset or depressed way, not functioning to his capacity.

Step 2. *Child—misbehaving.* The child begins to get out of control or express symptoms.

Step 3. *Mother—incompetent.* The mother ineffectually tries to deal with the child and cannot, and the father becomes involved.

Step 4. *Father—competent.* The father deals with the child effectively and recovers from his state of incompetency.

Step 5. *Child—behaving.* The child regains his composure and behaves properly or is defined as normal.

Step 6. *Mother—competent.* The mother becomes more capable and deals with the child and father in a more competent way, expecting more from them.

Step 1. *Father—incompetent.* The father behaves in an upset or depressed way, not functioning to his capacity, and the cycle begins again.

The therapeutic task is to change the sequence by intervening in such a way that it cannot continue. Making family members "aware" of the sequence by pointing it out to them does not change it and can raise resistance, causing failure. It would also appear that changing any *one* of the steps, or the behavior of any one of the three persons, is usually not sufficient to bring about change in the sequence. At least two behaviors must be changed.

A way to think about a sequence of this kind is to see it as an example of a malfunctioning hierarchy. Mother and father are not relating as peers with each other in an executive capacity. Their difficulties with each other, including the ways they protect each other, prevent them from defining a clear hierarchy within the family. As a therapist encourages them to deal jointly with the child, the issues between them that prevent their joint action become more evident. It also seems clear that if the therapist joins the child against them by attempting to rescue the child from them, he or she is not changing the sequence and is confusing the hierarchy even more.

A Note on Normality. These descriptions of human interaction are offered as a way of thinking for purposes of therapy. They are not offered as a model for what normal families *should* be like. In examining the context of a symptom, a clinician may find a confusion of hierarchical levels in a family. Such a finding does not mean that to raise normal children, one should not have a confusion of hierarchical levels in a family. It might or might not be so. Where there is a problem child, one can describe a certain organization in the family, but it is an error to deduce from that description how to raise normal children. I have observed over 200 normal, or average, families in research settings, and the patterns are so diverse that to talk about a "normal" family seems naive. How to raise children properly, as a normal family should, remains a mystery that awaits observational longitudinal studies with large samples. How to think about the organization of a family when planning therapy is a different issue. As an analogy, if a child breaks a leg, one can set it straight and put it in a plaster cast. But one should not conclude from such therapy that the way to bring about the normal development of children's legs is to place them in plaster casts. A clinical description that is used to plan for a change and a research description of ordinary situations are not synonymous.

Malfunctioning and the Family. A therapist should be able to think in terms of three steps in a sequence, at least, and three levels of a hierarchy. Once the therapist puts together sequence and hierarchy, he or she is in a position to devise strategies for bringing about change in a rational rather than merely an intuitive way. The simplest goal is to change a sequence by preventing coalitions across generation lines. When one changes a sequence of father consistently joining child against mother, the family will begin to function differently and the individuals in the family will give up their subjective distress. The goal can be presented in this simple way, but achieving that goal requires ingenuity and skill.

Although three levels of a hierarchy do not seem many when describing the complexity of human life, even that number creates sufficient permutations to be awesome. For example, if one thinks in terms of a triangular unit—such as mother and father and child, or mother-in-law and husband and wife—one can calculate how many triangles there are in the average family if we think in terms of three levels of a hierarchy. In a family with two parents, two children, and four grandparents, there are only eight persons, but there are 56 triangles (and this count does not include uncles, aunts, neighbors, employers, or therapists). Each person in the family is involved in 21 family triangles, and every one of the 21 triangles of parents and children carries the possibility of a coalition across generation lines and so the possibility of a malfunctioning structure.

Summarizing the hierarchical idea offered here, there are certain characteristics of a malfunctioning organization if one thinks in terms of three levels and a triangular unit.

First, the three persons responding to one another are not peers but members of different generations. By *generation* is meant a different order in the power hierarchy, such as parent and child or manager and employee.

Second, the member of one generation forms a coalition across generations. In a two-generation conflict one person joins

another against the other's peer. In a three-generation conflict
the person at the top forms a coalition with the person on the
bottom against the person in the middle. The term *coalition* means
a process of joint action *against* a third person (in contrast to
an "alliance," where two persons might share an interest not
shared by the third).

Third, the problem is most severe when the coalition
across generations is denied or concealed.

In this scheme it should be emphasized that an organization is not malfunctioning because cross-generation coalitions
exist but because such coalitions are repeated again and again
as part of the system. A woman must save her child from her
husband at times, but when this act becomes a way of life, the
family organization is in trouble.

Three-Generation Conflicts

Therapists should keep in mind that the "map" in their
heads will never be identical with the "territory" that they are
offered when a case walks in the door. The clients just will not
present their problems in the properly contextual way. For example, a woman might come in complaining about her daughter
being irresponsible, and she will add that her daughter drinks
and leaves the child alone at night. Or a mother might bring
in a twelve-year-old child complaining that he steals from her,
which upsets her and his grandmother who lives around the corner. A noncontextual therapist might see the child as sullen and
deprived, having a poor self-image, and feeling unloved. When
therapists watch their colleagues at work in inpatient institutions, they will observe at times that a patient becomes obstrep-
erous and "acts out." The staff may decide that the patient is
"acting out" an internal conflict and may put him in a group
to express himself. They may also discuss him as spoiled,
rebellious, regressed, and so on.

A therapist must examine such presenting problems in
terms of the hierarchy and the sequence that is being followed
that requires people to behave as they are doing. All these examples of presenting problems can be seen in the following
sequences.

One of the most common problem sequences met by a therapist is the one involving three generations. The classic situation is made up of grandmother, mother, and problem child. That is the typical one-parent family situation among the poor and among the middle class when a mother has divorced and returned to her mother. In the classic example, the grandmother tends to be defined as dominating, the mother as irresponsible, and the child as a behavior problem.* The typical sequence is as follows:

1. Grandmother takes care of grandchild while protesting that mother is irresponsible and does not take care of the child properly. In this way grandmother is siding with the child against the mother in a coalition across generation lines.

2. Mother withdraws, letting grandmother care for the child.

3. The child misbehaves or expresses symptomatic behavior.

4. Grandmother protests that she should not have to take care of the child and discipline him. She has raised her children, and mother should take care of her own child.

5. Mother begins to take care of her own child.

6. Grandmother protests that mother does not know how to take care of the child properly and is being irresponsible. She takes over the care of the grandchild to save the child from mother.

7. Mother withdraws, letting grandmother care for the child.

8. The child misbehaves or expresses symptomatic behavior.

At a certain point, grandmother protests that mother should take care of her own child, and the cycle continues, forever and ever. Included in the cycle, of course, is sufficient

---

*"In this type of family the grandmother is allocated executive power, while the mother and grandchildren function as one vaguely differentiated subgroup." See S. Minuchin and others, *Families of the Slums* (New York: Basic Books, 1967), p. 364. The authors also point out that in some cases a grandmother and mother may struggle in such a way that the child is simply neglected.

misbehavior or distress by the child to provoke the adults to continue the cycle.

When one thinks of generation lines as hierarchical lines of power, it is evident that the classic three-generation conflict can take place with an expert substituting for the grandmother. In long-term child-oriented therapy, the sequence is as follows:

1. The therapist deals with the disturbed child, implying that mother has not raised the child properly and so the expert must take over and free the child from internal conflicts. Insofar as the therapist is an expert, he is higher in the hierarchy than mother, and by attempting to save the child from mother he is forming a coalition with child against mother across generation lines.

2. Mother withdraws, letting the expert take responsibility for the problems of her child, feeling that she has been a failure or this intervention would not be necessary.

3. The therapist runs into difficulty with the child, and he also realizes he cannot adopt the child and so protests that the mother should do more for the child and care for him properly.

4. Mother begins to involve herself more with her child.

5. The therapist protests that the mother is not dealing with the child correctly. Taking over more, the therapist insists the child must be saved from mother.

6. Mother withdraws, letting the therapist take care of the problems of her child.*

This sequence continues until the child becomes an adolescent and graduates to a therapist who treats adolescents.

It is possible for clinicians to have this kind of three-generation conflict in relation to each other and not only to family members. Typically, student clinicians in training have a supervisor above them and a patient below them in the hierarchy. In the class structure of any agency, the same situation applies

*B. Montalvo and J. Haley, "In Defense of Child Therapy," in J. Haley, *Reflections on Therapy* (Washington, D.C.: Family Therapy Institute, 1981).

with clinicians who are not students. For example, a psychiatrist may be supervising a therapist staff member with patients. The typical sequence is as follows:

1. The supervisor disagrees with the way the student or staff therapist is handling a case and wishes to save the patient from the student. Sometimes the patient has come to the supervisor with a complaint, initiating this sequence, and sometimes it is merely apparent in the discussion between supervisor and therapist. As the supervisor insists on a particular way of dealing with the case, disagreeing with the therapist, she is forming a coalition across generation lines by siding with the patient against the student.

2. The student withdraws, either letting the supervisor handle the case or asking for excessive help from the supervisor.

3. The patient misbehaves or makes an extreme demand.

4. The supervisor protests that she cannot treat every case in the clinic and the student should be more autonomous and take responsibility for his own patients.

5. The student begins to deal with the patient in his own way.

6. The supervisor protests that the student is not dealing with the patient properly and takes over, insisting that she must save the patient from the student.

This sequence continues and the patient becomes part of the chronic caseload of the clinic. It is also typical of in-staff conflicts in a mental hospital setting.

The Parental Child. In some families, particularly one-parent families with many children, there is a third generation that is not clearly a "generation." There is a mother and her children, but in between there is an older child who functions as a parent for the younger children. He or she is not of the adult generation but is a child, and yet the child functions as an adult insofar as he or she is taking care of the younger children.*

*The idea of the parental child is described in S. Minuchin and others, *Families of the Slums* (New York: Basic Books, 1967).

The position of this parental child is often quite difficult because he has the responsibility for the younger children but not the power. Therefore, he is caught in the middle between misbehaving children and a mother who does not delegate full power to him. What typically happens is that the mother sides with the children against the parental child when there is trouble. She insists that the parental child be in charge while not giving sufficient autonomy to deal with the situation.

The sequence is very much like the grandmother, mother, and child conflict, but with different personnel. The indicators of this situation are an older child speaking for the younger children in a family session, protecting them, and often dealing with quite serious problems without letting the mother know about them.

In clinical organizations, this hierarchy is evident wherever there are paraprofessionals. Usually, the hierarchy includes a professional in charge, a paraprofessional who actually takes charge, and the clientele. The paraprofessional is not really at the staff level and yet does the actual work with clients and is blamed by the professional if there is trouble. Often there are secrets between client and paraprofessional, just as there are in families with parental children. This hierarchy is also typical in mental hospitals where the aides or attendants function as parental children because they are not professional staff members and yet are not at the level of patients. They have the responsibility but not the power and so must deal with the patients secretly on many issues, including disciplinary issues.

Two-Generation Conflicts

It is arbitrary to differentiate one-generation from two- or three-generation structures, since all situations involve multiple generations. Yet for practical reasons it can be helpful to focus on one set of levels rather than on another. There are two typical patterns that appear as two-generation problems.

The Overwhelmed Mother. In some families with many children there is a mother who is in charge of everyone, with no hierarchy among the children. The center of whatever happens, like the hub of a wheel, the mother has each child go through her to deal with any other child. Such a mother appears overburdened by constant demands from the children. This structure can be seen if one asks the children to do something, such as draw a picture on the blackboard, while the therapist talks to the mother. The children will constantly interrupt to ask the mother something, show her what they have done, ask her to settle arguments, and check with her before doing anything. Such a structure is typical of organizations where an administrator cannot delegate authority and so remains in charge of everyone.

One Parent Against Another. The most typical two-generation problem is where one parent sides with a child against the other parent. The "child" may be two years old or forty years, since the problem is not age but organization. A depressed woman with several children may still be functioning as a child in the relationship with her parents. The sequence can also take place when the parents are separated, if they are still at odds over the child.

The typical sequence in this situation is as follows:

1. One parent, usually the mother, is in an intense relationship with the child. By *intense* is meant a relationship that is both positive and negative and where the responses of each person are exaggeratedly important. The mother attempts to deal with the child with a mixture of affection and exasperation.

2. The child's symptomatic behavior becomes more extreme.

3. The mother, or the child, calls on the father for assistance in resolving their difficulty.

4. The father steps in to take charge and deal with the child.

5. Mother reacts against father, insisting that he is not dealing with the situation properly. Mother can react with an attack or with a threat to break off the relationship with father. The threat to leave may be as indirect as "I want a vacation by myself" or as direct as "I want a divorce."

6. Father withdraws, giving up the attempt to disengage mother and child.

7. Mother and child deal with each other in a mixture of affection and exasperation until they reach a point where they are at an impasse.

This sequence can continue forever and ever as mother (or father) crosses generation lines and sides with the child against the other parent. Another way to describe it is as an intense involvement of one adult and child that regularly includes and excludes the other adult.

The fact that change in the child is followed by the development of a chasm between the parents, or even a threat of separation and divorce, has led to the family theory that a child with symptoms is always holding a problem marriage together. Some therapists who are "insightful" will even tell parents that they must have conflict in their marriage, or they would not have a problem child. Such an oversimplification of the situation is naive. The problem has two aspects.

The fact that when a child improves, the parents in some cases threaten separation does not mean that the child was holding them together by having a problem or that they want the child to have a problem. It merely means that once they are organized around the child as a problem, when the child improves that is a change with instability, which everyone must adapt to. If improvement in a child is followed by a parental threat of separation, that only means that improvement is followed by a parental threat of separation. The second aspect of this situation to be concerned with is the possibility that the reaction of the parents, and the whole family, is a product of the ways the therapist intervened in the family. That is, when a therapist encourages a peripheral parent to take charge, as the problem improves there seems to be more parental conflict than if the therapist encourages the more involved parent to be more involved and take charge.* The possibility that the conclusions we draw about families might be the product of the ways the therapist deals with the family is discussed further in Chapter Five.

*See C. Madanes, *Strategic Family Therapy* (San Francisco: Jossey-Bass, 1981).

As a sequence of this kind continues, the focus on the child becomes a way of dealing with issues that arise in marriage. In that sense it seems justified to say that the symptoms of the child have a function in the marriage. Many problems between a couple that cannot be dealt with directly may be communicated about in terms of—and therefore through—the child. The child becomes the communication intermediary and so stabilizes the marriage. For example, at those moments when mother comments on how the child is threatening to run away, she may be indirectly threatening to leave her husband. By discussing the child, the couple can deal with the marriage issue without making it explicit and therefore without making irreversible decisions.

The two-parent sequence is seen most clearly in a family where one parent is a stepparent. For example, an unmarried woman with several children may marry, partly to have a man's help in raising her children. When the new husband begins to discipline the children, or perhaps show affection to them, the mother may react against him by saying he does not truly understand these children. She may even suggest that the marriage was a mistake. The husband will withdraw, not wanting to upset his marriage. Then the children will have a problem that the mother will have difficulty with. She will call upon her husband again, and the sequence will repeat. Such a situation can continue for many years, since it is independent of time.

The Problem in a Clinical Organization. The situation of a person of the parent generation siding with a child against the other parent is also typical in staff conflicts in agencies and mental hospitals. The situation occurs whenever a therapist is dealing with a patient and a fellow staff member is in charge of that patient and many others on a ward. The typical sequence is as follows:

1. An "intense" relationship, a mixture of affection and exasperation, develops between a therapist and a patient on the ward.

2. At a certain point the patient misbehaves or requests something special, such as some privilege or freedom from discipline for some misbehavior.

3. The ward administrator insists on dealing with the patient as one of many who does not deserve anything special, and he tries to persuade the therapist that this approach is best.

4. The therapist reacts against the ward physician, saying he does not truly understand this patient.

5. The ward physician withdraws, giving up the attempt to intervene between therapist and patient.

6. Therapist and patient continue in their intense relationship, therapist joining patient against ward doctor by attempting to save him from the doctor who does not understand him.

This organizational situation and others like it are inevitable in the nature of mental hospitals. The pattern may explain why so many patients and doctors become chronic members of such institutions.

Variations. The marvelous complexities of human life have been simplified here to three generations and a short sequence, which is rather like describing a human being as a skeleton without flesh. These different sequences have also been presented as if they occurred independently. However, one may also find a two-parent family in which mother and grandmother are in the central struggle over the child and the father is outside the sequence. One may also find a situation in which the grandparents are crossing generation lines, the parents are in conflict over a child, and a parental child is saving the child from the parents. That situation is sometimes called a *psychotic family*. It is probably true that an individual is more disturbed in direct proportion to the number of malfunctioning hierarchies in which he or she is embedded.

The Therapeutic Problem

The goal of any clinical description is that it should lead to ways a therapist can think about what might cause change and what might not. The sequences have been oversimplified here, but even in this form it becomes possible to think about how change may be induced. What would *not* bring about change seems evident. If a person is caught up in a sequence of this kind, expressing his emotions is not likely to cause change.* Similarly, if a person discovers "why" she is behaving as she does, through some explanation in terms of her past history, change is not likely to occur. From this point of view she is behaving as she does because of the ways other people are behaving, not because she was programmed by her past. Whether in terms of catharsis or insight into the person's unconscious, the theory of repression is a handicap if one is thinking about how to change sequences.

It is tempting to believe that if a person only "discovers" she is part of a sequence, she can change—that if a mother could only "learn" that she is regularly including and excluding her husband from caring for their child, she would be able to stop such a sequence. However, the evidence indicates that such learning, or discovery, does not usually lead to change but, rather, becomes a rationale for continuing the sequence. When such insight is offered by a therapist, the mother may "discover" that the therapist is just like her husband and does not truly understand her special child. She may exclude the therapist as she does her husband, only to bring the therapist back again when she has difficulty with her child. The therapist may develop a theory of resistance to explain why his insightful approach is not producing change.

If expressing emotions or having insight does not produce change, what does? A few general ideas guide this new way of thinking about the therapeutic problem. The first and primary

*When a person expresses his emotions in a different way, it means that he is communicating in a different way. In doing so, he forces a different kind of communication from the person responding to him, and this change, in turn, requires yet a different way of responding back. When this shift occurs, a system changes because of the change in communication sequence, but this fact has nothing to do with expressing or releasing emotions in the sense of catharsis. For example, if a man gets red in the face and is silent every time his wife criticizes him, the therapist may arrange for the man to express his anger in words instead of by changing the color of his face. If the man does so, the wife must respond differently, and a new system is being generated. Asking "How do you feel?" about something is the least likely way to bring out emotion; the client simulates it in words. It is better to provoke him to more anger, perhaps by sympathizing with him, to shift the way he is communicating.

idea is that change occurs when the therapist joins the ongoing
system and changes it by the ways he or she participates within
it. When dealing with a governed, homeostatic system that is
maintained by repeating sequences of behavior, the therapist
changes those sequences by shifting the ways people respond
to each other because of the ways they must respond to the
therapist.

At the most general level, therapists should not side consistently with anyone in the family against anyone else. But that
does not mean they should not temporarily side with one against
another, because that is in fact the only way therapists can induce change. If they only place their "weight" in coalitions
equally, they will continue the sequence as it was. In the same
way, if they only join one person against another, they may
maintain the system as it was by simply becoming part of the
deadlocked struggle. That task is more complex: the therapist
must temporarily join in different coalitions while ultimately
not siding with anyone against anyone.

With situations in which a family has a severely disturbed
member, it is necessary for the therapist to join in multiple coalitions simultaneously. One must, for example, side with the parents in their executive function in relationship to a disturbed
young person while at the same time siding with the young person toward the ultimate goal of helping the young person out
of that disturbing situation. With skill gained by experience,
one can learn to skate among coalitions, being partially involved
at one moment and firm at another. It is necessary to retain
the freedom to join in whatever coalition is appropriate at any
particular time.

It is also necessary at times to cause a crisis in a situation
by siding only with one person for an apparently indefinite
period. When a husband and wife are stable and miserable, the
therapist can induce instability by joining one or the other and
saying that person is completely right. This temporary firm coalition can later be balanced by shifting to a coalition with the other
person, but at any moment in time the coalition can appear
permanent.

The most typical way to proceed when balancing within

different temporary coalitions is to proceed in steps. The first step is to determine what type of sequence is maintaining the presenting problem. The second step is to specify a goal. If grandmother is joining child against mother, the goal is to have the mother in charge of her child and the grandmother in an advisory position to the mother. If mother or father is too intensively involved with a child in a coalition against the other parent, the goal is to have the parents involved with each other and the child more interested in associating with peers than with parents. The goal in all cases is to draw a generation line and prevent consistent coalitions across it. By the ways the therapist forms coalitions from his or her higher status as an expert, the therapist prevents the family from forming coalitions across generation lines. The third step involves a new idea. It is improbable, if not impossible, that a system will go from "abnormal" to "normal" in one step. Change must occur in stages, and the first step should be to create a different form of abnormality.

The idea that therapy has stages is relatively new. Possibly the first clinician to introduce stages systematically was Joseph Wolpe with his reciprocal inhibition technique.* Another early designer of stages was Murray Bowen. He reports, in a personal communication, that the way he once began family therapy was by seeing an individual alone and asking that person to take a stance in relation to his or her family that he had always wished to take but had not taken. As the person takes that stance, stages follow: first the family members attack that person as disloyal, and second they threaten to divorce or expel the person. If the person holds out against them, then the third stage is Bowen interviewing the whole family together.

Although specific stages for most therapy methods have not usually been worked out, a variety of therapeutic approaches do assume that the therapeutic process is such that one cannot go *directly* from the problem at the beginning to the cure at the end. The process takes different forms. There is a class of therapeutic situations in which the problem presented must be

---

*See J. Wolpe, *Psychotherapy by Reciprocal Inhibition* (Stanford, Calif.: Stanford University Press, 1958).

redefined as another problem before it is resolved, because the kind of abnormality has been redefined as another kind. Sometimes this shift occurs routinely as part of the initial negotiations to select a solvable problem and sometimes it occurs later.

For example, a case of "mental illness" may be redefined as one of bad behavior. The family of a psychotic might be asked to put him in jail rather than in a mental hospital. "Crazy" and "bad" should not be confused as one category if the therapist is thinking of shifting from one to the other. Similarly, criminal behavior is sometimes solvable if it is redefined as an "illness" problem. (This approach has nothing to do with the philosophical issue of whether crazy people are bad or criminals are mentally ill. It is a tactical therapeutic issue.)

In more minor form, it is not unusual for a clinician to define the psychiatric or medical problem of a child or an adult as a misbehavior problem. For example, anxiety attacks might be redefined as manipulative and so misbehavior. In the case of a child starving herself, her not eating can be redefined as not minding. The problem shifts from a child who is ill to parents who should pull together to make her mind.*

In all forms of therapy there has been a tendency to take whatever the patient says as something that needs to be redefined as a different problem. The patient who is too emotional needs more cognition, and the overly intellectual patient needs more emotion. The patient who concentrates on details needs to generalize, and the one who consistently generalizes needs to be more concrete. The client who talks about her "misbehavior" needs to have that behavior redefined as something she cannot help and therefore an "illness." The "ill" psychiatric patient needs to take responsibility for his actions, and therefore his "illness" is redefined as "misbehavior."

Whenever the therapist prescribes a symptom and so offers a paradoxical directive, he or she is requesting a different abnormal situation by exaggerating the presenting abnormal

---

*S. Minuchin, "The Use of an Ecological Framework in Child Psychiatry," in J. E. Anthony and C. Koupernick (eds.), *The Child in His Family* (New York: Wiley, 1970).

situation. This approach is clearest with the procedure of "flooding" someone. An abnormal situation is made into a parody of that abnormal situation, and so into a new one, when someone who is afraid of bugs is forced to think about bugs crawling about everywhere. In most of the behavior therapies, the presenting problem is redefined as a different one. Some behavior therapists translate the presenting problem into a frequency count of certain behavior, and this new definition of abnormality is then resolved. Wolpe transforms a presenting problem into a list of anxiety situations that are items which he can set up a procedure to cure.

When we turn to the schema of pathological systems outlined here, it becomes evident that one way to think about designing a strategy and planning the stages of therapy is to think about shifting from the presenting system to a different abnormal one. This different abnormal system may be the presenting system of some other family. The following examples serve to present this idea (further examples are given in Chapter Five).

A mother may be too central to her children, so that there is no hierarchy in the family and all the children function through her as if she were the hub of a wheel. In such a case it may be appropriate to create a system where an older child relieves the mother by taking charge. Essentially, this change creates a parental child hierarchy. From this new abnormal state, it is possible to shift to a more reasonable hierarchy in the family so that all children can participate with different responsibilities.

Conversely, if the family comes in with a parental child system, one possibility is to make the mother overly central as the first stage. This change frees the parental child, and from this new abnormal hierarchy it is possible to go to a more normal one.

If the sequence involves a grandmother who is crossing generation lines and siding with the child against the mother, one can follow the procedure suggested in Chapter Five in which full responsibility is given to the grandmother. One can then go from this abnormal stage to another abnormal one in which all responsibility is given to the mother and the grandmother must not discipline the child at all. From this abnormal state one can go to the more normal one.

If mother and child are in an overly intense relationship and the father is peripheral, the first stage can be one where the father takes total control of the child and the mother is excluded. This is an abnormal system, and from it one can move to a more normal one. It might also be possible to use an older sibling as a parental child to disengage mother and child, thereby introducing a parental child system as the first stage. Similarly, one might introduce the grandmother and create that hierarchy as a first stage.

In summary, one of the reasons some therapies have failed has been that they assume one can go from an abnormal state directly to a normal state. It is more productive to think in terms of stages between abnormality and normality. Faced with a malfunctioning system, one can think of how to transform that into another malfunctioning system that can then be shifted to normal.

Sequence and Hierarchy

It is in the ways that repetitive sequences define hierarchies that systems theory and hierarchy come together. The hierarchy is shaped by the behavior of the people involved, and insofar as the behavior is repetitive and redundant, it is a governed system that is error-activated in that deviance activates a governing process. If the person deviates from the repeating behavior and so defines a different hierarchy, the others react against that deviation and shape the behavior back into the habitual pattern.

Pathological behavior appears when the repeating sequence simultaneously defines two opposite hierarchies or when the hierarchy is unstable because the behavior indicates different shapes at different times. For example, if the parents at one point take charge of a child and at another point accept the child as the authority in the family, the hierarchy is confused.

A parallel can be drawn here between levels of communication and levels of hierarchy. The "double bind" was a concept derived from the paradoxes that occur when messages are on multiple levels and are conflicting.* For a therapist to ask another person to disobey him, or to direct someone to behave spontaneously, is to produce a paradox. The person cannot behave spontaneously if she has been *instructed* to behave in that way.† In the organizational description offered here, the same principle applies to a larger unit. To direct someone to disobey is to define the hierarchy in two incompatible ways. The person directed is lower in the hierarchy, since she is being told what to do, but she is also equal or higher in the hierarchy, since she is being expected to disobey or to behave spontaneously. Two incompatible definitions of the hierarchy are offered simultaneously by communicating paradoxical messages. Just as one cannot *not* communicate with other people—even trying to avoid someone is communication‡—so must one always deal with the issue of hierarchical position in relation to the other person. When a therapist indicates he is not superior to a patient (by being "human" with her or even asking her what might be done) while accepting an expert's fee from the patient, he is offering incompatible positions in a hierarchy: he is a paid expert and therefore higher in the hierarchy, since he is a helper paid to help the other, but he is also asking the other's advice on what to do. Quite possibly the nature of therapeutic change centers in the ways the hierarchical issues are kept unstable in the therapeutic relationship, either by being ambiguous and confused or by being defined in shifting and incompatible ways.

A changing definition of a hierarchy may develop as part of a sequence. For example, when a mother asks her husband's assistance with a child, she is defining the hierarchy as one in which two parents are joint authorities over a child. When the

---

*G. Bateson, D. D. Jackson, J. Haley, and J. Weakland, "Toward a Theory of Schizophrenia," *Behavioral Science* 1 (1956): 251–264.
†J. Haley, *Strategies of Psychotherapy* (Orlando, Fla.: Grune & Stratton, 1963).
‡It should be emphasized that most of the ideas about communication in this book derive ultimately from Gregory Bateson. I participated in his research project for ten years, along with John Weakland, Don D. Jackson, and William F. Fry. An idea such as the one that people cannot not communicate predates that project: it was published by Bateson with Jurgen Ruesch in *Communication, the Social Matrix of Psychiatry* (New York: Norton, 1951). For a collection of Bateson's writings, see *Steps to an Ecology of Mind* (New York: Ballantine, 1972).

husband responds by dealing with the child, and the mother reacts and condemns him for not understanding the child and joins the child against him, the definition of the hierarchy has shifted. She is now defining it as one in which she and the child have the authority over father's behavior.

It is the task of therapists to change the sequence and so change the hierarchy of the family. It is also their task not to be caught up in a sequence in such a way that they are perpetuating the problem they are supposed to resolve. If the goals therapists have are clear to them, they are less likely to be caught up helplessly in the ongoing process.

Certain consequences of a theory of systems as a model for therapy are sometimes not thought through by members of the profession. If we assume that a family is a system, we must accept the premise that behavior will repeat and also the premise that movements toward change will activate the governing processes that have been keeping the system stable. Granting these premises, once therapy has begun and the therapist has become part of the system, we must assume that when change occurs he or she will react to keep the system as it was during therapy. That is, we must assume that the therapist, the change agent, will resist change once the therapy is an ongoing process. Some professionals are willing to accept the idea that treatment institutions, like mental hospitals, resist change, but they do not think through the fact that this idea must apply also to the therapist. Given this view of the therapeutic situation, the supervisor, who operates more on the periphery of the system than the therapist does, has the function of helping the therapist move past change as well as helping the therapist disengage from the family. (The supervisor too is part of the system but is less involved in terms of the immediate feedback processes exchanged by therapist and family.)

To put the matter another way, therapy involves changes in relationship between the therapist and the clients. If a therapist and a family accept a helping contract, they are agreeing that the therapist should help and that the family should receive the help. All messages are in that framework and define the relationship in that way. Yet it is impossible to cure a family by helping them if the cure involves arranging that they no longer need help. The more help the therapist offers, the more he or she is defining the family as needing help. The more the family accept help, the more they define the relationship as a helping one. The goal of the therapy is to have the therapist and the family achieve a relationship as peers in the sense that the family do not need any more help than the therapist does. Once the helping relationship is established, if either party moves toward changing the relationship, the other will react to stabilize the relationship they have.* Not only does the patient resist change in a relationship, but so does the therapist. The art of therapy includes shifting from one type of relationship to another while being part of a stabilized system. The supervisor can help in this situation by the use of a variety of techniques, including the use of recesses in the therapy, such as meeting in a month rather than next week, and even the encouragement of controlled relapses.

Once it was thought that clarifying communication in families would not only bring about togetherness and harmony but also cause basic change in family structure. But such clarification, when it means pointing out to family members how they are communicating, seems to produce little change. At the opposite extreme was the idea that the therapist should individuate family members from one another and so provide more autonomy and less togetherness. With experience it has become more clear that the autonomy of a person is dependent on how other people behave. Even the definition of autonomy can only be in relation to other people. Of course, at times both the effort to clarify communication and the emphasis on achieving autonomy can inadvertently break up habitual sequences in families and so produce change. It has merely become more evident in recent years that the therapist can focus directly on changing those sequences and so more quickly and efficiently produce change.

The particular strategy of a therapist will vary with the unique family and the context of therapy, and it will also be influenced by the stage of development of the family, since fam-

*J. Haley, *Strategies of Psychotherapy* (Orlando, Fla.: Grune & Stratton, 1963).

ilies change over time.* As children mature and parents and grandparents age, sequences and hierarchies change. In the family life cycle, there is an extraordinary reversal of hierarchical structure. Children shift from being taken care of by their parents to becoming peers of parents as fellow adults to taking care of parents in their old age. It is now being assumed that "spontaneous" change is related to developmental processes in families. Sometimes therapy is given credit for a change when a natural process has accomplished it. Yet often families do not develop and change over time, but remain fixated in a problem sequence. The therapist must intervene to make a change and cannot depend on a natural process to do his or her job.

*J. Haley, *Uncommon Therapy: The Psychiatric Techniques of Milton H. Erickson, M.D.* (New York: Norton, 1973).

5

Therapy in Stages

The first obligation of a therapist is to change the presenting problem offered. If that is not accomplished, the therapy is a failure. Therapists should not let themselves be distracted into other matters so that they forget this primary goal. Moreover, by focusing on the symptoms, the therapist gains the most leverage and has the most opportunity for bringing about change. It is the presenting problem that most interests the client; by working with that, the therapist can gain great cooperation. If a person with symptoms is offered as a problem, the therapist may believe that changes must take place in the family system before that person can change. Yet he or she should not try to convince the family that the *real* problem lies in the family and not in the person. Such a distinction is artificial. The therapist who engages in pointless debate with the family about the cause of the problem, attempts to educate them about family communication, or tries to persuade them to accept "family therapy" may fail to achieve his or her ends. The goal is not to teach the family about their malfunctioning system but to change the family sequences so that the presenting problems are resolved.

In dealing with a symptom, the approach must vary depending on whether it is a one-parent or two-parent family, the class and ethnic background of the family, and the age of the children involved. A wealthy middle-class family must not be dealt with the same way as a lower-class family on welfare, just as one must adjust one's approach to accommodate an Italian Catholic working-class family or a German Lutheran farm family. How the therapist approaches the family will be determined by many factors; the emphasis here will be on a schematized structure that can apply to many families.

When a child, whether small or adolescent, is brought to a clinic by a family, he is a problem or the family would not have taken the trouble to come. (At times a family present a child as a supposed problem when actually he is not and they really have other purposes in coming, but the emphasis here is on the usual situation.) From the family's standpoint, the child is the problem, and they may even be puzzled when the therapist asks the whole family to come for the first interview. It is not necessary to convince the family that they have family problems, but they do need to be persuaded to cooperate in doing what the therapist asks to help them get over the problem they present.

If the therapist is thinking in terms of dyads, or two-person units, he or she is considering the child's symptoms as a response to one other person who is making the symptoms necessary. The therapist might think of how to change the child's symptomatic behavior or how to change the reciprocal responses of the other person so that the child's symptomatic behavior cannot continue. (If the therapist includes himself or herself in the plan to change the reciprocal behavior of two persons, it is actually triadic thinking although the theory might be dyadic. For example, if the therapist helps a mother deal differently with her child, it may offend a father who has previously been helping mother and does not like to be replaced.)

A therapist who is thinking in terms of triads will seek out the triangle involved in the problem and the sequence that requires the symptomatic behavior. The therapist will assume that when a child has symptoms, at least two adults are involved in the problem and that the child is both a participant and a communication vehicle between them. If there is only one parent in the family, the therapist inquires into the relationship with some other adult, such as a grandmother or a divorced or separated parent. If there is no other adult at the parental level who seems to be important and a grandparent is involved, the problem will be seen as a three-generational one. (Sometimes, of course, the problem may not even be in the family but in the school or neighborhood or in the relationship between the family and some other institution. The emphasis here is on problems within the family.)

Whether to think of a psychological problem in terms of the individual, the dyad, or the triad should be based on what unit gives the therapist the most ideas about what might be done to solve a problem. It is not a question of what is true, since any problem or situation can be described in a number of different units. When thinking of the unit as the individual, one must think about changing emotions or perceptions or ideas or individual behavior. With a unit of two persons, there are twice as many possibilities, since twice as many people are involved. With three persons as the unit, the possible interventions go up geometrically. Therefore the therapist who thinks in terms of three persons can demonstrate more variety in therapeutic interventions and strategies (as well as consider the coalitions involved, since coalitions appear with a minimum unit of three).

Case Examples

When the therapist has conducted the first interview properly and so has learned the sequence of the family problem, he or she then seeks out the most appropriate strategy for bringing about change. It is best to assume that change should occur in stages and that one cannot jump from the problem stage to the cure stage in a single leap but must have other stages in between. Usually one must go from a problem stage to a new problem stage before going toward the normal systems. Some case examples will be offered here to indicate the kinds of stages that can be used.

The Intrusive Grandmother. One family presented the problem of a ten-year-old boy who was generally misbehaving as well as wetting his bed. In the family interview, the grandmother reported that the mother mishandled the child and did not appreciate him. The mother reported that whenever she attempted to discipline the child, the grandmother intruded and protected him. The therapist had mother and grandmother agree that the goal was to have the boy mind properly and stop wetting the bed, so that the destination of the treatment was clear.

In the approach to be described here, only the key moves in the therapy are emphasized. The work on relationships is taken for granted. For example, it is assumed that the therapist explores the boy's ideas about the problem and that he develops an understanding relationship with both mother and grandmother.

Since grandmother and mother explicitly stated that they disagreed about how to handle the boy, it was possible to persuade them to experiment with a new approach for a short period of time. The grandmother was asked to take full responsibility for the boy for two weeks. She was to deal with all matters of discipline and with the bedwetting, including the washing of the sheets. The mother was not to discipline the boy but simply to enjoy him. If he misbehaved, she was to report that misbehavior to the grandmother, who would take care of it. All negative communication between boy and mother was to go through the grandmother, who would be central. The family agreed to this two-week experiment.

Essentially, this stage is the creation of a malfunctioning structure. It is not appropriate that a grandmother have full charge of a child and that the mother be peripheral.

The family was interviewed during the first two-week period, and the grandmother's difficulties and exasperations were discussed. The mother was warned to continue to leave everything to the grandmother. At the end of two weeks, the therapist required the family to reverse itself. The mother was to take full charge of the boy, and the grandmother was merely to enjoy him. All communication of a negative kind between grandmother and boy was to go through the mother.

This stage too creates an abnormal arrangement insofar as grandmother is completely shut out of the boy's problems, even to the point of not being allowed to offer advice to mother about what to do with him. Having the grandmother in charge first makes it easier for her to stay out of it when the mother is put in charge.

By the end of the second two weeks, it is possible to have a session discussing which arrangement proved best. In most cases the grandmother prefers that the mother take charge of the work of the boy, since the grandmother is older and has already raised her children. She will also agree to communicate through the mother to the boy rather than side with the boy against his mother. She agrees partly because she is threatened with having full care of the boy if she intrudes. The child's symptoms usually disappear when the hierarchy is correct. In some cases the family can decide that the grandmother should continue to be the one in full charge of the child. If this arrangement is agreeable to all, it becomes a functioning system but tends to be an unstable one over time as grandmother ages.

In this approach the therapist does not go directly from the malfunctioning structure to the functioning one but as a first step creates a different malfunctioning system. This system is only partially different, however, since the grandmother is asked to take charge when she has already been taking charge. However, she is put *fully* in charge. If the therapist attempts to go to the more normal system first, by having the mother take full charge, usually the grandmother will continue to intrude, demonstrating that the mother is not adequate to the task.

The Parental Child. One working mother called and reported to a therapist (Braulio Montalvo) that her eight-year-old daughter had set a fire in their apartment. An appointment was set and the whole family came for the first interview. It was a low-income black family containing a twelve-year-old boy, the eight-year-old problem girl, and three smaller children. There was no father in the home. The incident that precipitated the crisis was a fire in a mattress set by the small girl. The older boy, who was responsible for the children, managed to get the mattress into the bathroom and put the fire out. He did not call the mother because he did not wish to disturb her at work. When asked about the fire, the girl only cried. It became apparent in the first interview that the older boy was a parental child. In the room he hovered over the problem girl, answering questions she was asked, and seemed to be more motherly with the child than the mother was.

The first step in this type of case can be to create an abnormal situation by making the mother central, with all communication going through her. This step is abnormal insofar as it does not allow organizational hierarchy among the children, which is necessary in families, particularly in a family with a working mother, where an older child is needed to take charge at times. To make this step, it is necessary to block off the parental child and make the mother central.

Both in the room and in the directive for a task at home, the therapist blocked off the parental child and forced the mother to talk to her daughter about what had happened. When the older boy intruded, the therapist quieted him and physically moved the boy over beside himself. He placed mother and daughter side by side to talk.

The therapist gave the mother and daughter a task to do at home. He defined the task as something only for this girl and her mother, not for the other children, who were put temporarily in the charge of the parental child. The mother was to spend five minutes, timed with an egg timer, teaching the little girl how to use matches. At this point in the session, the parental child wished to demonstrate how he could use matches, but he was blocked off.

In the following session, the therapist had the daughter demonstrate that she could safely use matches by lighting a small fire in an ashtray. He then had her teach a younger sister how to do it, showing how the mother had taught her, while the mother observed. By this second session, the mother was blocking off the parental child from intruding into her activities with the daughter, so that the therapist no longer needed to do so.

At this point it was necessary to reorganize the family in a more normal way. Rather than have him be overburdened as a parent when only a child, the twelve-year-old boy was moved out as the only pathway of communication between the mother and the children. He was therefore delegated responsibility for the children when the mother was away, but the therapist emphasized that mother was in charge and that the boy was not a fellow parent. The boy was also encouraged to go out with peers, and the therapist worked to overcome the mother's reluctance to give him freedom because of evil companions on the street. Making friends outside the family weakened his parental child position within the family.

The mother was also encouraged toward activities outside the home so that she was not sacrificing her personal life for her children. The fire setting vanished with the change in organization.

The Two-Generation Problem

When there is a child problem, the therapist can focus on the child or on the unit of parent and child or on the triangle of mother, father, and child. When the focus is on the parents and child, it is a two-generation problem, in contrast to defining the problem as multigenerational. The therapist can enter the triangle of child and both parents in various ways. There are also different consequences for the family, depending on the approach the therapist chooses.

A classic family therapy way of conceptualizing this triangle is to view it as a structure in which one parent, usually the mother but sometimes the father, is extremely involved with the child. The other parent is more peripheral. The involved parent knows all the details of the child's symptom, if not of the child's whole life, and the more peripheral parent sometimes doesn't even agree that the child has a problem that merits therapy. This type of structure is created by a repeating sequence. The mother and child interact intensely, and as the child increases problem behavior, the mother calls on the father for assistance. When the father steps in to deal with the child, the mother reacts against him, saying that he really doesn't understand the child as she does. The father withdraws, not wanting to upset the mother and jeopardize their marriage. Mother and child join together again, and when the child increases the problem behavior, the sequence repeats itself. This sequence can occur for many years, since it is not determined by age. Sometimes it is the father who is intensely involved with the child and the mother who is more peripheral; the sequence continues with that structure.

If one views the child problem in this way, it is possible for the therapist to choose different ways to intervene. The therapist might direct the peripheral parent to take more charge of the child, holding that parent in that task when the other parent objects. This is a a classic family therapy procedure. The therapist might also enter this triangle by encouraging the intensely involved parent to be more involved and take more charge, while the peripheral parent remains peripheral.* One might also not put either parent in charge of the problem but ask the parents to jointly agree on what is to be done and to carry it out. Finally, it is possible to enter the triangle through the child, by having the child join the other children in giving the parents a task that would make their lives happier, such as going out together to a place they enjoy.†

These different approaches to the family triangle will be described with illustrations. One should keep in mind that the triangle of mother, father, and child can exist even if the parents are separated or divorced. As parents, they continue to deal with each other in sequences that continue the problem unresolved.

Approach 1: Entering Through the Peripheral Person. The most traditional approach that has developed in family therapy is to enter the triangle through the disengaged parent. Whether to use this approach will be determined by the unique situation of each family and by the therapist's judgment of how workable a relationship he or she can establish with the peripheral parent (usually the father). In the sequence of this type, the father usually has attempted to deal with the child and has met opposition from the mother as she reclaimed the child from him, often protesting that he does not understand the child. Often, too, the father has criticized the mother for her overprotection of the child, antagonizing her and convincing her that he does not understand either her or the child. Therefore, to activate the father to intervene between mother and child may require skillful persuasion.

---

*See C. Madanes, *Strategic Family Therapy* (San Francisco: Jossey-Bass, 1981).
†For a discussion of putting the children in charge, see C. Madanes, *Behind the One-Way Mirror: Advances in the Practice of Strategic Therapy* (San Francisco: Jossey-Bass, 1984), p. 91.

In using this approach, one must be careful not to imply that the father is being brought into the situation because the mother has failed. Such an indictment of the mother may not only antagonize her and risk her taking the family out of treatment but also exacerbate the bad feeling between the mother and father. The child may thus be freed from the intense involvement with the mother, but bringing the parents together may be made more difficult.

There are different ways of making the situation acceptable to the mother. For example, if the problem is a male child, the therapist can say that the child has now reached an age where he should be more involved with men and therefore the father and son must do certain activities together. In this way the overprotection by the mother in the past is not condemned; the child has just reached an age where, according to an expert, different behavior is appropriate. If the problem is a female child, the mother can be convinced that she has an obligation to see that her daughter understands men, and therefore the girl must be encouraged to be involved with her father as part of her education.

If this approach is used, there are three stages before the goal is achieved. In the first stage, father, son, and therapist become involved in an activity while mother is shifted to the periphery. This stage creates a new abnormal organization. In the second stage, mother, father, and therapist are intensely involved while the child drops out of the adult struggle and is free to join his peers. He may or may not need guidance into peer activity. In the third stage, the therapist must disengage and get out, leaving the parents involved with each other and the boy involved with friends.

When the therapy goes well, these stages flow logically one to another. For example, when the mother is excluded at the first stage, she is motivated to become involved. As she is blocked off from being involved with the child, she becomes involved with the father. This change occurs naturally when she objects to the way the father is dealing with the child. When the therapist focuses the parents on each other and excludes the child, the second stage is under way. The therapist must then disengage, entering the final stage, ensuring that the child will not be brought back to replace him or her.

A typical case that illustrates these stages is presented in detail in the Case Report at the end of this book. A variation of this approach can be illustrated with a case in which the parents were divorced and yet the same type of intervention was used. A thirteen-year-old boy sexually molested an eight-year-old neighbor girl. The boy lived alone with his mother and saw his father, who was married again, only occasionally. He was arrested for his act and put in court-ordered individual therapy; he was also given group therapy with a heavy emphasis on sex education. After a year of therapy the youth was released as cured of the problem. Two years later the young man, now sixteen, required another small girl to perform oral sex with him. Again he was arrested and the court ordered therapy. He was referred to a family-oriented institute. The therapist, Walda Furst, required the father to come to the first session even though the couple were divorced and he had remarried. He had not even known of the first offense but had learned of this second offense because he was a policeman and had been informed by friends on the vice squad.

At the first interview it was learned that the mother and son lived alone together and were quite intensely involved; they seemed to function more as peers than as mother and son. Rather than repeat the approach of doing therapy with the boy individually, with occasional involvement of the mother, it was decided to introduce the father into a whole-family approach. The father was given the task of dealing with the youth about sex of all kinds and all relations with girls. Mother was to continue to supervise his school and household behavior but not deal with him about sex or females. Father accepted the task, talked with the boy about sex and his own sex life, read with him a book on male sexuality, and became more involved in positive ways with the youth. After several interviews, the boy revealed that he himself had been sexually molested by an adolescent when he was younger. His mother received this report angrily, since he had not revealed this in the previous therapy or even when the judge had insisted that he admit whether he had ever been sexually abused (since it is not uncommon for a sexual abuser to have been abused). However, the boy talked about the incident only after the structure of his relationship with his parents changed. The therapy continued for a period of months with irregular follow-ups to be sure the sexual problem was resolved. It should be noted that when the father was put in charge, the mother responded as if she had been criticized. This took the form of her asking whether perhaps being divorced and being a single parent might have caused the problem. The therapist reassured her that this was not so.

Obviously not all families change easily, and families may become stuck at different stages. Sometimes the peripheral parent just cannot become involved successfully with the child or retreats precipitously if a conflict with the spouse occurs. At times the therapist cannot become disengaged but continues treatment when it is no longer necessary, preventing the final change that frees the child. All therapy works best if the therapist can become intensely involved and then rapidly disengages, being willing to give credit to the family for improvement.

An important finding of the last decade has been the discovery that the way the therapist enters the family can create problems—which the therapist will then believe are part of the structure, if overlooking his or her own involvement. When the therapist puts the peripheral parent in charge, the involved spouse reacts, and there is a stage of parental conflict, if not marital conflict. The therapist often sees the parents alone at this time. This set of stages has become almost taken for granted. The idea was at least partly based on the observation that there is often a spouse conflict as a child improves—*when the approach through the peripheral parent is used.* However, it has recently been noted that if one uses the approach of putting the more involved parent even more in charge, often there is not a stage of parental or marital conflict. It is not yet clear whether this is an observation based on a small sample or whether the stage of marital conflict in family therapy of a child problem is a consequence of the particular way of entering the triangle—through the peripheral parent. That is, it is possible that the therapist is producing the data that are then used to theorize that there is a marital problem "behind" a child problem. If it is true that less conflict between the parents occurs if the more involved parent is put in charge, then that would seem to be the approach of choice—unless one believes there should be conflict because salvation comes through suffering.

There is another aspect of this choice to consider, however. It has often been observed that a possible function of a symptom in a child is to involve the peripheral parent more, often the father. For example, a child might set fires and so force a busy father to be more involved with him. At times such a situation can be resolved by having the father involved with the boy in a positive way so that symptomatic behavior is not necessary.* This strategy requires involving the peripheral parent in dealing with the child.

When one considers a therapist's theory as possibly based on data the therapist has engineered, it alerts us all to becoming more aware of the effects of our actions on our data. Years ago it was said that families containing a schizophrenic communicated in peculiar ways; they were vague, amorphous, double-binding, and not clear and straightforward. In recent years, at least with some therapists, such families typically do not behave in that way. Granted that some of them communicate in strange ways, they are not routinely that way. It is possible that they have changed, but it seems more likely that the therapeutic situation has changed. We can now observe that in those days a therapist was typically vague, amorphous, double-binding, and not clear and straightforward. If a family member asked at a first family interview, "Why are we here?" the therapist would not answer directly but would say something like "Why do you suppose you are here?" or "I wonder, why do you ask that?" Faced with ambiguous and confusing therapists, families often began to behave strangely. In recent years it has been assumed that with such families the therapist should say what he or she has in mind in the first interview. Why the family are called together, what is hoped for from the interview, and what are the goals of therapy are laid out clearly so the family can agree or disagree with them.

*See C. Madanes, *Behind the One-Way Mirror: Advances in the Practice of Strategic Therapy* (San Francisco: Jossey-Bass, 1984).

Of course, the discovery that a therapist produces much of the data he or she theorizes about is not new; it was noted years ago that patients in Freudian analysis had different, sexier dreams than patients in Jungian analysis. Each analyst was puzzled why there were different theories when the data for the theory were evident right there.

Approach 2: Entering Through the More Involved Parent. Another way of entering the problem situation is to focus on the parent and child who are more involved, placing the more peripheral parent in an advisory and supportive position. There are a variety of ways to intervene between a parent and child, usually a mother and child, when that relationship is intense. One gets the most cooperation from a mother in this situation if no interpretations are made to her about how she overprotects the child. Usually such interpretations merely antagonize her and prevent change. A successful way is to guide the mother in helping her toward activities more appropriate than hovering over her child. In situations where her husband is providing her with little satisfaction, this diversion may be difficult, because what little satisfaction she receives is from the child. Sometimes a program of work, education, or community action outside the home can divert her, particularly if this change is accompanied by arranging activities for the child that require his association with peers and not with adults in some natural activity (rather than an artificial activity like group therapy).* As mother and child become occupied in different directions, they become less involved with each other.

A quite different approach is to provide a task that appears to encourage the mother's helpful protection but in actuality disrupts the relationship because it is unbearable to continue in the same way. The following case example illustrates such a task.

Erickson reports a case† that provides an example of entering the family through the overinvolved dyad. A twelve-year-

*Getting the mother involved with her own mother or with other members of her family network is a procedure advocated by Murray Bowen and can be seen as another way of disengaging her.

†J. Haley, *Uncommon Therapy: The Psychiatric Techniques of Milton H. Erickson, M.D.* (New York: Norton, 1973), pp. 207–208.

old boy was wetting the bed every night, and his mother was
excessively concerned about him. The father was not concerned
and did not think the boy should be treated for the problem.
The therapist interviewed the father, found him a difficult and
uncooperative man, set him aside, and focused on mother and
child. Erickson reports:

> As I sized up the situation with mother and
> the boy, it was apparent that Johnny was utterly
> hostile toward his mother about this bedwetting.
> He was angry and in a struggle with her about it.
> I told Johnny that I had a remedy for him that he
> wouldn't like. It would be an effective remedy, ab-
> solutely helpful, absolutely certain to get him over
> the problem, yet he would not like it—but his *mother*
> would *dislike* it more. Now what could Johnny do?
> If his mother would dislike it more than he did, that
> would be fine. He could put up with anything that
> made his mother suffer more.
>
> I proposed to Johnny that his mother could
> get up at four or five a.m. in the morning, and if
> his bed was wet she could rouse him. She didn't
> have to wake him up if the bed was dry. However,
> if his bed was wet and she roused him, he could
> get up and sit down at his desk and copy so many
> pages from any book he chose. He could put in the
> time from four to seven o'clock or from five to seven
> o'clock, copying material. His mother could watch
> him do that and watch him learning to improve his
> script. The boy's handwriting was really terrible
> and needed improvement.
>
> To Johnny it sounded horrible to get up at
> four or five in the morning—but Mother had to
> get up first. It sounded unpleasant to have mother
> sit there watching him improve his script, yet he
> only had to do that on mornings when his bed was
> wet. Nothing more disagreeable than getting up
> at that hour of the morning—to improve your hand-
> writing.

They began this procedure, and it wasn't long before Johnny didn't have a wet bed every morning. He began skipping mornings. Pretty soon he had a wet bed only twice a week. Then a wet bed every ten days. Mother still had to get up every morning and check.

Finally it was a wet bed once a month, and then Johnny reoriented himself entirely. He developed the first friendships he had. It was during the summer and the kids came over to play with him, he went over to play with the kids. His marks in school that following September were greatly improved. His first real achievement.

Now that was playing mother against son and son against mother. It's the simple approach of "I've got a remedy for you, but you won't like it." Then I digress to the fact that mother will hate it even more. Johnny wants me to come to the point of what is the remedy? Then he's all for it. Improvement in handwriting becomes the primary goal, a dry bed becomes an incidental, more or less accepted thing. It's no longer the dominant, threatening issue at hand.

Mother, watching her son improve his handwriting, could take pride in her son's accomplishment. The son could take pride in it. When the two of them brought the handwriting to show me, it was just an eager boy and an eager mother showing me this beautiful handwriting. I could go through it page after page and point out this letter "n," this letter "g," this letter "t," and discuss the beauty of the script.

Since Johnny has a dry bed, his father has played ball with him—coming home early from the office. The father's response when the boy stopped wetting the bed was surprisingly complimentary. He told the boy, "You learned to have a dry bed faster than I did, must be you're a lot smarter than me." He could afford to be generous, since he felt it wasn't the psychiatrist who solved this problem, but the superior brain power he had bequeathed to his son. In the family it became a joint achievement which was blessed by the father, and the boy got recognition and acceptance for his accomplishment.

When a therapist is dealing with a problem child, with two parents involved, there are choices to be made about how to deal with the family triangle. As an example, a thirteen-year-old boy was diagnosed as depressed and had refused to go to school for six weeks. The parents had tried to persuade him to go to school and had threatened to force him to go. When threatened, the boy called the family pediatrician, who advised the parents not to act. The boy was also in therapy with a therapist who believed that depression in young people was a result of being under pressure and who, along with the pediatrician, insisted that the parents not take any action to make the boy go to school. Meanwhile he was sitting at home getting more depressed. At a hospital consultation, the boy was given a family interview by Michael Fox, M.D., who was supervised in a training program by Cloé Madanes.* The therapeutic plan decided upon was to have the boy go back to school as soon as possible, preferably the next morning. Since he declined to go, the parents would have to make him go. The therapist needed to persuade the parents to take this action. It was assumed that not going to school was abnormal, and if the boy was in an abnormal situation he would feel and behave abnormally. Getting him back to school and so in a normal situation would either resolve the problem or clarify just what the problem was.

After an hour interview the parents were in agreement that the boy should go to school, and the therapist had found out that the school was safe and the boy had friends there and teachers who liked him. His insistence on staying home was not because of a problem at school. The supervisor's hypothesis was that the boy's staying at home had a function in relation to the parents and the home.

*For a more detailed description of this case, see C. Madanes, *Strategic Family Therapy* (San Francisco: Jossey-Bass, 1981), p. 103.

The mother was extremely involved with the boy, talking at length about his problem and knowing every detail of his difficulties. The father was more peripheral, seeming puzzled over why the boy wouldn't go to school and attending the session out of duty. The situation could be described as an involved mother and a peripheral father. When Madanes had the therapist ask who was more sensitive to the boy and most understanding of his concerns, which is a way of asking which parent had similar symptoms, the mother raised her hand and said that she was coming out of a depression and so she understood the boy's depression. A choice to be made was how to get the boy back to school. The therapist might choose to put the peripheral father in charge of getting the boy to school, or put the more involved mother in charge, or put the parents jointly in charge, or let the boy decide, as was being done by his individual therapist.

If the more peripheral father were put in charge, a reaction could be expected. If the father insisted that the boy go to school the next morning, the boy would likely get upset, perhaps say he was ill or even vomit, and refuse to go. As father insisted, mother would get upset and intervene to save the boy from father. Conflict would develop between mother and father, the father would likely back off from the task, and the boy would remain at home. If the father held to his position at the therapist's insistence and got the boy to school, there would expectably be a conflict between mother and father, which would be the next stage of therapy.

Instead, in this case Madanes had the mother put in charge of getting the boy to school, since she was the "expert on coming out of a depression." She was to take the boy to school, and since he might be anxious and try to leave, she should sit with him in each class, including gym. An adolescent is really not enthusiastic about having his mother sit in class with him, and so this was no minor threat.

The parents survived arguments and threats from the boy all evening. The next morning he went off to school, and he continued to do so. He also came out of his depression. It might be hypothesized that when the boy was sure his mother was all right, he was willing to go to school. He would know she was all right when she insisted that he go to school and required that of him.

In this approach with the more involved parent, there was no stage of parental or marital conflict after the boy was in school. One or two sessions helped the family organize the household and the other children so that mother had less difficulty, but there was no problem between the parents that appeared and needed to be dealt with. This result is not unusual when the involved parent is put in charge of solving the problem.

Approach 3: Entering Through the Parents Conjointly. A therapist may decide that neither father nor mother should be the one put in charge of solving the problem of a problem child. Instead, the parents should conjointly take action. This approach is usually best when the problem of the offspring is severe. When there is a violent youth, psychotic behavior, drug abuse, or suicidal threats, usually the parents are equally involved. One parent might appear to be more involved than the other, but the therapist will find out that the seemingly peripheral parent is very much involved with the child. When the problem is extreme in this way, it is best to have the parents reach agreement on what is to be done with the child. Sometimes this involves patient encouragement of discussion and the testing out of implicit disagreements that are there. Often when the child is most disturbed, the parents say they have no disagreements about him. Yet as plans are made about what is to be done, disagreements appear and can be resolved.

This type of interview is typically done when an offspring is in custody in a mental hospital or a juvenile hall. The therapist plans with the whole family how things are going to be when the youth gets home. Usually the youth has been out of control and the community was called upon to do something about him or her. Now as the youth is coming home, the family must take charge so that the community does not have to be involved again in the future. Having the parents plan the homecoming, with the rules and consequences, helps work out the disagreements between the parents so that they pull together to deal with a difficult child.*

*For a discussion of this approach to severe problems, see J. Haley, *Leaving Home* (New York: McGraw-Hill, 1980).

Paradoxical Approaches

At times the therapeutic approach is not a straightforward request that one or both parents resolve the problems of a child. Other approaches can be used, and sometimes when an indirect approach is used the structure resolves itself in the same way as it would if a parent were put in charge. In the following example, a peripheral father took charge without being directly requested to do so by the therapist.

A family arrived for treatment with a five-year-old boy who had never been toilet-trained and who several times a day had a bowel movement in his pants. He had never gone to the toilet. His younger brother was properly toilet-trained. The family was seen for three diagnostic interviews by a child psychiatrist who focused on the child. After evaluation, the family was transferred to Curtis Adams, M.D., for treatment. Adams was participating in a strategy seminar, and the members of the seminar decided to treat this family by doing only one thing—restraining the family from improving. Adams would adopt the posture of being benevolently concerned about what would happen to the family if the child became normal and would not do anything else.

The family was interviewed as a whole family in the first interview. The parents were a young, middle-class couple very concerned that they might do the wrong thing with their child. The boy was quite bright and articulate, saying such things as ''I poopy in my pants, and sometimes I get into my pajamas and I poopy in my pajamas.'' He was also able to talk with wonderful imagery if a therapist was interested in exploring that. The mother was an attractive, nervous young woman who was keenly alert to what the therapist thought of her. She was over-involved with the child and benevolently exasperated with him. The father was an engineer who often worked or studied at night and who stayed on the periphery. However, when he was home, he helped the mother clean up the child.

At the end of the first interview, the therapist asked the parents what consequences there would be if the child began to go to the toilet normally. They replied that it would be wonderful.

He expressed doubt and suggested they go home and think about
what changes would occur in their lives if their child became
normal and they were normal parents. The therapist's attitude
expressed the idea that he could do something about the problem they presented but that he would rather not until he was
sure of the consequences for the whole family.

When the family returned the following week, the parents
had not been able to think of any adverse consequences if the
boy were to go to the toilet normally. This reaction is typical
for such a directive. The therapist himself had listed thirteen
or fourteen consequences, but in the treatment he needed to
use only three or four. He first approached the dyad of mother
and child, raising the question whether the mother could tolerate
being a mother who successfully solved her child's problem. He
pointed out that some women can tolerate success, while other
women cannot.

Although the therapist planned to do only one thing—
restrain the family from improving—it is clear that there are
multiple messages involved in any one act. To raise the question whether the mother can tolerate being successful is to restrain her from changing. However, no woman likes to think
she cannot tolerate being successful, and so a second message
is involved. There is also a framework, deliberately established
by the therapist, that he thinks she can tolerate success but that
he wants to be sure. In this way the woman is not merely condemned as someone who cannot stand being successful—she is
supported in the idea that she *can* stand it, while being motivated
to *prove* it. Each of these consequences emphasized by the therapist has the following levels: (1) that he thinks the person can
tolerate success, (2) a benevolent concern about the person, and
(3) a suggestion that the person finds intolerable.

The mother responded by indicating that she thought she
could stand being a successful mother. She seemed uncertain
whether the therapist was joking or not, as did her husband,
but the therapist gave no indication. He asked whether becoming successful might not make her more successful as a mother
than her own mother, and perhaps she could not tolerate that.
The woman replied that she could certainly stand being more

successful than her own mother and began to discuss her difficulties with her mother and her alcoholic father. She also discussed her mother's feelings about her not having the boy toilet-trained. (In this approach, the family members usually bring up more relevant material than they do if interpretations and inquiries are made. The problem for the therapist here was how gracefully to turn off the mother on issues of her history with her mother.)

The therapist shifted to the question of what the mother would do with herself during the day if the boy were over the problem. Much of the mother's time was occupied washing the boy's clothes, putting him on the toilet without success, and keeping him near her rather than outside so that he would not be playing with his pants fouled. It was revealed that the mother kept the boy on the toilet many hours a day, even putting the television in the bathroom so that he might happen to have a bowel movement in the toilet while distracted. Clearly, she would have much more time to herself if the boy were over the problem, and she considered seriously what she would do with that time and what she would think about if she did not have the problem to worry about.

After exploring the mother/child dyad, the therapist shifted to the similar consequences if father were a successful father. Then he dealt with the consequences between the couple if they became a normal married couple. Because of the child's problem, they had never had a babysitter and gone out together. Where would they go if they could go out, and who would decide? This approach was not emphasized as a way of exploring their struggle but as a new decision area they would have to work out. The father thought they could tolerate going out together if they just had the chance. So did mother, mentioning how often she had wanted to go out but never did.

A similar discussion of consequences was centered on what the couple would talk about in the evening if they did not have this problem to discuss. Each evening there was a report on the mother's difficult day with the problem. At the dinner table the focus was on the boy, since he would get a faraway look in his eye and leave the table, and they would rush to put him on the toilet—without effect. Husband and wife decided they could find something to talk about besides the child's bowel movements.

This discussion of consequences is in a framework of benevolent concern, which makes it difficult for the family to get angry at the therapist. Yet from their point of view the therapist is a successful husband and father who can tolerate being normal, and he is suggesting that possibly they cannot. It is a provoking situation for the family. Typically, they become highly motivated to solve their problem to prove that they can tolerate being normal.

Another aspect of this restraining technique should be emphasized. When the therapist talked with the couple about having a normal husband/wife relationship and being able to tolerate going out together, he was provoking them about their ability to be attractive to each other. In the process he could be said to be establishing a pseudo-courtship relationship with the wife that was provoking the peripheral husband to reclaim her.

On the day of the third scheduled interview, the mother called and said they would rather not come. They boy had gone to the toilet properly the day before and they did not want to "rock the boat." Whereas previously the mother had talked in a helpless way, this time she was quite firm and assertive in her statement.

The family returned the following week at the scheduled time and reported that the boy was now regularly using the toilet every day and had not had a bowel movement in his pants again. The mother mentioned that she was able to enjoy the time to do other things with herself. Both husband and wife talked about having gone out together and enjoyed it. They indicated to the therapist, without explicitly saying so, that they could tolerate being normal.

They mentioned, almost in passing, that the change had occurred after father sat down and had a serious talk with the boy. He told him he had to poopy in the toilet, and if he did not the father would have to give him a laxative and make him sit there until he did. He explained what a laxative was. Apparently the boy took his father seriously, and the mother did not interfere with the father's intervention.

The therapist began his disengagement process by saying that he was puzzled that the problem had resolved itself and that he was pleased they had done so well. Credit was given to the family for the change. An appointment was set for two weeks later to be sure everything was all right. In two weeks the family returned, reporting that all was well. The therapist deliberately shifted from a helping relationship to a social one in a brief interview. His task was to shift to a peer relationship with the parents and move out of the expert/client relationship. Such a shift can be calculatedly achieved in brief therapy.

This restraining approach can be used as a main therapeutic approach or as a different type of intervention when therapy is not going well. It can also be used when there is competition between a therapist and a parent and directives are not being followed. The following case illustrates the use of this technique when a mother and a female therapist are approaching an impasse.

A family presented the problem of a fifteen-year-old girl who was defying the mother, refusing to do what she asked, answering back rudely, and so on. The mother was a stepmother to this girl and to her eight- and nine-year-old sisters. She also had a two-month-old baby who was her only child with this father.

In the first interview, the daughter cried and would hardly talk, the stepmother was angry and complaining, and the father was busy explaining that the daughter had suffered a miserable childhood with an alcoholic mother. It had taken the father years to finally separate from his first wife, and he felt guilty about what the girl had experienced.

In the first interview, the therapist attempted several tasks for the family that would involve mother and daughter in some way. The mother objected to every single task and refused to do anything with the daughter. Her attitude was that she had had enough of the girl and the clinic could take her or give her to somebody else who would straighten her out.

The interview was supervised "live" by Cloé Madanes, who began to believe that the problem was the relationship between the mother and the therapist. Both were in their early twenties, and it appeared that the mother was refusing to accept instructions from a female therapist of the same age who obviously had little experience but who was a professional person while the mother was not.

Having suggested previous tasks and watched them fail, Madanes called the therapist out of the room and suggested to her that she use an approach of restraining the family from changing. When the therapist returned to the family, she said she could probably help them solve the problem with the daughter, but she was not sure she should, because she was concerned about what consequences there would be if the problem were solved. When the family said there would be only positive consequences, the therapist pointed out that the father had been very close to his daughter through very difficult times, and he was also close to his wife. If mother and daughter became close to each other, father might feel excluded and jealous and be unable to tolerate such feelings. Father assured the therapist that he could tolerate his wife and daughter being closer. The therapist also pointed out that the two little girls might become jealous, and she ended the interview suggesting that the family think about the consequences for the next time.

During the week, the therapist and supervisor prepared a list of possible consequences, which the therapist memorized. When the family returned, the therapist pointed out that a possible consequence would be that the mother would be a better mother than her own mother if she solved this difficult problem of three stepdaughters and a new baby. She suggested that some mothers could not tolerate being better mothers than their own mothers. The mother said she could certainly tolerate that. The therapist mentioned a few other consequences, such as the reaction of the mother's mother and how the change would affect the new baby. The family denied there would be any problem. The daughter began to talk a little. A week later mother and daughter came in reporting they had gone shopping together. The mother had bought a miniskirt for the daughter against the father's wishes. The daughter had cleaned the house and done all the laundry. The therapist pointed out that the mother was siding with the daughter against father over the miniskirt issue and that this was an example of what the therapist feared. Perhaps the father could not tolerate this change. The father said he certainly could. The therapist suggested that the relationship between mother and daughter had not really changed, because although they were doing their duty toward each other, there was no real friendliness and no real pleasure in each other. Therefore it was important that for the next week they still think about the consequences of a change.

The next week the family reported that the father had been on a night shift and that the mother and daughter spent the evenings together playing Monopoly and card games and enjoying themselves. They were getting along well together. The therapist expressed her pleasure with this situation and apologized because she had not been able to help the family but the problem had somehow disappeared. The therapist apologized in a rather embarrassed way, and the mother reassured her in a rather patronizing way that she had done her best. They separated with the agreement that the therapist would call in a few weeks to see how they were doing, and the family would consult if another problem came up. A follow-up several months later showed they were doing well and there were no other problems.

This approach, restraining the family from changing, is effective with sensitive, overconcerned middle-class parents but is not as effective with working-class or poor families. The family must be keenly attuned to the therapist's opinion of them.

In summary, the process from the beginning point at which one parent is overinvolved with a child to the end point at which the adults are involved with each other and the child is attached to peers cannot be made in one leap. There is a series of stages that will be determined by the approach. If the approach is through the peripheral person, there will be a stage of coalition among therapist, peripheral person, and child; then a stage of involvement between therapist and adults; and finally a stage of the therapist disengaging from the adults. If the approach is through the overinvolved person and the child, there is a stage of intense involvement between that adult, therapist, and child, followed by a disengagement of therapist from both of them.

When families are treated from this point of view, certain rules will make the therapist more effective. He or she should not oppose or confront the family members with what they are doing wrong but should "accept" what they are doing and within that framework make a change. The therapist should not make interpretations to help them understand why or how they are behaving but should use interpretations tactically to motivate them to do what can be done. The therapist should not explore the past but should focus on the present situation and organize the family to change what is happening. The therapist should not seek long-term involvement but brief, intensive intervention and rapid disengagement.

6

Marriage Therapy as a Triangle

≋≋≋≋≋≋≋≋≋≋≋≋≋≋≋

All clinicians must deal with marriages in some way, because everyone is either married, planning to be married, or avoiding marriage. Since marriage is so important in human life, one would think that a therapy focused on marriage would produce new ideas about human beings. That does not seem to have happened in the history of marital therapy, or marriage counseling, as it was called for many years. It was not a type of therapy with a high reputation for innovations in technique or for a theoretical contribution to the field. Instead, marriage therapy tended to follow the current ideas developed in other therapies. When psychodynamic theory was popular, marriage counselors tended to see spouses individually and to explore the influence of their pasts on their present marriages. During this period, mate selection was explained as a "neurotic choice of partners," suggesting that a man chose a wife who was like his mother (despite the possibility that his family, particularly his mother, chose his wife, which would be a different explanation of mate selection).

When behavior therapy ideas became prominent in the individual therapy field, marriage therapists began to change toward encouraging positive reinforcements and became more concerned with current behavior rather than the past. When family therapy became popular, marriage therapists began to see spouses together and to think of a marriage as part of a larger system. During this period therapists were trying to break free of individual descriptions. Couples were viewed as interacting systems, as rule-governed entities, or as conditioning systems in which what one person did reinforced what the other did. It was observed that couples followed sequences of behavior that they could not seem to change when they tried, as if they had interpersonal reflexes. An example of how a couple follows rules is in the way the two persons deal with an issue by maximizing and minimizing it. When some partners talk together, they will tend to balance each other out. Whatever they are talking about, whether work or sex or problems with children, one of them will say the problem is serious and the other will say it is not. As one spouse minimizes a problem, the other spouse must maximize it to compensate. This compensation, in turn, requires the first to minimize even more in response to an exaggeration. If a therapist believes that making partners aware of their rules will cause change, he or she can point out what they are doing. Often in such a case the wife will agree that it is a serious problem that they follow that rule, while the husband will say it really is not a problem. Should the therapist use directives, one spouse is likely to take the directive seriously and the other spouse will not. As therapists discovered the interpersonal power of rule-governed behavior, they found themselves with increasing doubts about free will. Often clinicians would behave as if they believed people could choose their acts while privately suspecting that it was not so. For therapeutic effectiveness, it is often best to expect people to choose what to do, but a research view tends to be more deterministic.

When therapists observed that what one spouse did provoked the other, who provoked the first in turn, they began to see that a dyad was unstable and that it required a third person to prevent a "runaway." For example, if two spouses competed over who was more ill, total collapse could only be prevented by pulling in a third party. Rivalrous quarrels that amplified in intensity required someone outside the dyad to intervene and stabilize it.* If a third person is regularly activated to stabilize a dyad, the unit is in fact not dyadic but is at least a triad. With this view, the unit becomes a unit of three persons. Similarly, if a husband and wife regularly communicate to each other through a third person, the unit is three persons instead of a married "couple."

Thinking in this way, it is possible to see different stages of marriages. For example, a therapist may observe that the husband and wife spend the early part of their marriage differentiating from their parents. As this task is accomplished, they produce children that become part of the marriage. At no point do they form a distinct dyad. Of course, the issue is one of definition. If one is thinking in units of three persons, a marriage does not exist as an independent entity. The description must include an observer, a therapist, a friend, parent, child, or some other third person.

At this time many clinicians are learning to think in the unit of three or more and giving up the dyadic unit even when doing marriage therapy.† Sometimes one must seek out the larger unit, but at times it is obvious. As an example, a husband lived separately from his wife when they came in for marital therapy. He lived separately because his ninety-year-old mother-in-law would not allow him in the house where his wife lived. Resolving their problem required a larger focus than their dyad. Similarly, there were two spouses who, for over twenty years, each had an ongoing affair with someone else. They came into therapy when the wife's lover died and the quadrad became unstable. That marriage was never a dyad. Another couple in their seventies had a forty-year-old son who had continually been in trouble all his life and they could not resolve their parenting difficulties enough to deal with marital difficulties. A more

---

*For a description of this issue in a native culture, see G. Bateson, *Naven* (Palo Alto, Calif.: Stanford University Press, 1958).
†I have written about marital therapy largely from a dyadic view in *Strategies of Psychotherapy* (Orlando, Fla.: Grune & Stratton, 1963). I have also presented the different stages of marriage over the life cycle in *Uncommon Therapy* (New York: Norton, 1973).

unusual, one can hope, situation occurred with a woman who married and immediately went into psychoanalysis. Eighteen years later she was still in analysis. At that time she divorced her husband and also quit her analysis. A question can be raised whether she ever had a relationship that could be described as dyadic with her husband. These situations might appear exceptional, but with each of them many therapists would have focused on the individuals or on dyads. It is a matter of what the clinician chooses as the best way to think to bring about change.

Goals of Marital Therapy

A special problem in marriage therapy has been deciding what the goal is. When a therapist sits down with a couple, what can be thought of as a successful outcome? In the past there was an idea that a therapist knew how a marriage should be. There was an "ideal" marriage, or at least a "normal" marriage, and the therapist's task was to achieve that. Yet there was never an agreement about the ideal, and ideas about it have varied with time and fashion. For a period, for example, it was thought that a normal marriage was conflict-free. Therapists focused on conflict resolution techniques to create a more tranquil marriage. At another period an ideal marriage was based on "healthy conflict." Marriage therapists focused on bringing out bad feelings and even taught spouses how to fight.

It seems more obvious now that there is not an ideal marriage that can be the goal of a therapist. There is simply too much diversity. One cannot force couples of different cultures or of different classes into the same type of marriage. A new marriage also has to be different from a marriage that has lasted fifty years. There are also arranged marriages as well as romantic ones, and we must also include homosexual marriages in our descriptions. There are even couples getting marital therapy after they have divorced and continued to live together. No simple ideas about how a marriage should be can provide a map for the therapist today. There must be great tolerance of all the different ways couples find to live together or apart. A more sensible focus would seem to be on the particular problem a couple

are having within their type of marriage. The nature of the marriage might not be changed at the end of therapy, but ideally
there will be a change in the problems they came in with that
were distressing them.

There is one new concern that therapists have today that
they had less of in the past. Divorce is so easy and so frequent
now that one cannot assume the marriages will continue. Marriage has always had, and apparently needed, an outside force
to maintain it. The church and state made divorce difficult.
Today that is not so. It would seem that if divorce is too difficult, people must stay together in misery. If divorce is too easy,
they separate over a quarrel they could have resolved. Marriage
therapy is becoming one of the forces that help people stay
together.

It can be said that there is no single marital therapy, in
the sense that the approach differs depending on how the problem is brought to the therapist. The three main ways that couples
arrive to present a problem are through a symptom of an individual, through a child problem, and through a direct request
for marital counseling. Each situation requires a different therapeutic approach.

Symptoms as Presenting Problems

It is possible to think of marriage therapy as a way of dealing with an individual symptom or to think of symptoms as part
of a marriage arrangement. It is more common today to bring
in a spouse when a severe symptom is presented rather than
seeing the person individually. With an eating disorder such
as bulimia, for example, a directive given to the married couple
is more likely to be followed than one given only to the individual. The spouse can also help a therapist resolve an individual's problems in ways the therapist might not have thought of.

The other way to think about symptoms is to assume they
are part of a marriage contract. When symptoms are dealt with
effectively, the therapist necessarily becomes involved in marital
issues. If a wife has anxiety spells that incapacitate her regularly, a therapist is interested in the function of such spells in

her marriage and concerned with what will happen if the symptom is resolved. The therapist may find that such a wife is anxious whenever her husband wants her to do something that she would rather not do. Or perhaps the wife becomes anxious whenever her husband becomes depressed and he comes out of his depression to help her when she is anxious. Some therapists will try to persuade the couple that the real problem is a marital one. Others will continue to focus on the symptom while dealing with the marital problem. After an improvement, these latter therapists may make a new contract to deal with the marriage.

Whenever a married person has a severe symptom, it inevitably has a function in the marriage, and there will be consequences in the marriage when a symptom is cured. For example, if a wife has headaches that incapacitate her several days a week and if those headaches are cured, she and her husband will face a different marital relationship than before. The man who cannot do certain things because of an exaggerated fear of some kind usually has a wife who both benefits from this problem and is exasperated by it. To resolve the "fear," it is best to deal with the marriage. Treating an individual for symptoms is like assuming a stick has one end.

Often there are symptoms that can be resolved most easily with couples therapy. Agoraphobia, for example, in which a wife cannot leave the house except in the presence of her husband (or sometimes another adult), is a difficult problem in individual therapy. If one assumes the wife is partly protecting the husband by staying at home, it is sensible to put the husband in charge of helping his wife leave the house step by step. Under the therapist's guidance, the husband helps the wife go farther by herself each day, and she will go as far as a husband can tolerate. In such an approach, one does not point out to the couple any benefit of the symptom for the husband but merely helps the couple resolve the problems that make the symptom functional as improvement occurs. When it is assumed that a symptom is protective of someone else, then putting that someone else in charge of helping the person over the symptom seems to be an obvious approach.

A Child as the Presenting Problem

Some married couples appear to be able to have savage battles without involving their children, while others center the marital struggle on the child. When a therapist helps parents exclude a child from their struggle, often they will exclude the in-laws from their marital struggles. Similarly, if a mother-in-law problem can be resolved, the parents seem to deal with each other without triangulating with the child. That is, if the married pair draw a generation line in one direction by holding together in relation to the children, they also seem to hold together in relation to the in-laws.

It should be emphasized that a child may be part of a marital struggle even after divorce: the war can still continue through the child. When a divorced mother offers a child as the problem, it is essential to inquire into the involvement of the divorced father. Dealing with the divorced couple to have them reach agreement about the child is not marital counseling but postdivorce counseling, which usually requires that the therapist decline to deal with any issues except the child.

When the child is an adolescent or young adult and has reached the age of leaving home, the parents are actually entering on a new marital contract. The therapist faced with that kind of problem must assist them in working out a new set of issues.

Another way therapists find themselves dealing with marriage is when the presenting problem is a family crisis. When there are threats of violence, suicide, or family behavior that arouse the community, a therapist is often called on to do something. The approach to marital issues at this time requires action rather than reflection, and the therapist must often take responsibility and make decisions for people who are in no state of mind to do so themselves.

Some family crises happen only once. But there are also marriages in which a crisis happens regularly, as part of a cycle. There may be threats of beating or suicide, and then amiable behavior, and then beatings and suicide threats erupting again. The marital therapist needs to bring the partners together and change that eruption cycle or to help them really separate without an unfortunate consequence. Typically, the therapist tries to bring them together. If that does not work, one must move decisively to separate them. Such a move requires dealing with one's own uncertainties about how and whether one should have such influence on the lives of people. When there are threats of violence or suicide, the therapist too faces risks.

It is in crisis times that the most can be done with a couple and that the most is asked of the therapist. A crisis means instability, and working with a couple at such a time can be emotionally upsetting for the therapist but most beneficial to the couple. Using medication to tranquilize partners when they are upset may prevent change and delay the resolution of issues until the next crisis.

The Marriage as the Presenting Problem

When a couple present a marital problem, the therapist's views may depend on who is interviewed. If the therapist sees the wife alone, he or she may sympathize with her for having such a problem husband. When such an interview is followed by an interview with the husband alone, the therapist usually discovers that there were a number of things the wife neglected to mention and that the husband has a justified point of view too. When seeing them together, the therapist discovers patterns of action between them that show the marriage to be quite different from what either spouse described. With experiences of this kind, the therapist learns not to naively take sides with one spouse against the other and learns the value of seeing how people actually deal with each other rather than listening to their reports about how they do. When the couple is seen within the larger family group, a different understanding of the marriage is added because it is seen in context.

Usually a couple present a marital problem as an attempt to stay together. Otherwise, the couple would not come together to present the problem. Sometimes one of the spouses is determined to separate but has not revealed this decision to the other. For example, a husband may want a separation but not want to upset his wife. Therefore he will appear in marital counseling supposedly to work out problems but actually to arrange an amiable divorce. This intent can be learned only by seeing the spouses alone, since it will not be revealed in the conjoint interview. In addition, sometimes the only way to learn certain kinds of information (such as an involvement in an extramarital affair) is through an individual interview.

When the spouses describe their marital problems, they sometimes characterize each other as being mean, vicious, hostile, and so on. It is better if the therapist does not think of their actions in that way. Underlying most marital problems is a protectiveness that keeps the problem going. It is the benevolence that is often most difficult to change. The wife who viciously insults her husband can be seen as a villainess, but one can also think of her behavior as a way of helping her husband. If he is in despair and she provokes him, he comes out of his unfortunate state and becomes angry at her, thereby feeling better. Similarly, a love affair can be seen as a betrayal and a way of attacking a spouse, but it can also be seen as a way of protecting a spouse by helping him or her to avoid sex or to maintain a safer distance. Whatever is being said, there are always things not said because they would be too harmful.

When one examines a presenting marital problem, it is evident that the couple is following habitual rules of behavior and that the problem is at the level of those rules. For example, the wife may say the problem is that her husband is irresponsible with money and does not do what he should. The husband may protest that his wife is too prudish and never wants to enjoy herself, so he seeks his pleasure elsewhere. From the therapist's viewpoint, the couple is following a number of rules that make this kind of behavior appropriate. One rule may be that the wife is to behave responsibly and the husband irresponsibly. Why they have that rule or how long they have had it is probably unknowable. Changing the rule requires the therapist to intervene in such a way that they cannot continue with such behavior.

Whatever rules a couple is following, the therapist is part of the rules. For example, a couple with a rule about responsibility will follow it in therapy. The husband will behave irresponsibly about the therapy and the marriage, be reluctant

to come, miss appointments, and so on. The wife will responsibly bring the husband to the therapy, insist on bringing out
all the issues, and so on. The therapeutic leverage comes in the
way the therapist changes that rule as it is used in relation to
him or her (not by objectively commenting on it to the couple).

One should also keep in mind that when rules are followed,
the participants are sometimes replaceable parts. For example,
when the wife is responsible and the husband irresponsible, a
shift can sometimes take place so that the wife becomes irresponsible and the husband takes on the responsible position. The
marriage relationship has not changed—the positions have just
reversed.

In the complexity of the millions of messages exchanged
by a married couple from moment to moment, there are multiple rules at multiple levels. There are not only rules about how
to behave with each other, how to relate to outsiders, and so
on; there are also rules about how to negotiate rules, and rules
about who is to establish the rules. Much of a marriage therapist's time may be spent patiently negotiating agreements over
specific issues that can generalize to the larger situation of the
couple. Given the nature of therapy, the therapist must be
simplistic and focus on issues that seem crude compared with
the complex richness of conceptualization involved in a research
investigation of a marriage.

One of the ways to think about marital difficulties is in
terms of flexibility. When the rules of a marriage are too rigid,
the partners are distressed because they cannot adapt to changes.
In a successful marriage, it appears that the two spouses are
able to be equals in some areas and the wife can also take care
of the husband and he of her. A couple that is limited in range
can follow only one pattern. For example, the wife may be able
to take care of the husband, but they cannot shift, allowing the
husband to take care of her. Therefore, if the wife becomes ill,
the husband must become more ill so that she can continue to
take care of him, since that is the only behavior pattern they
have. Or the two persons may take care of each other, but being equals is against the rules. Therefore, the partners can never
function as peers, and so decisions made by equals are not part

of their repertoire. One of the functions of marital therapy is
to enlarge the possibilities of the two partners so they have a
wider range of behavior. Just as one way to see the goal of all
therapy is to introduce complexity, so in marital therapy the
opportunities of the partners are greater if their relationship has
more complex possibilities.

When doing therapy with a couple, it is best for the therapist to consider that whatever the partners do in relation to
each other is also in relation to the therapist. That is, the therapist should consider the triad whether he or she explains that
context to the couple or not. If the therapist is male, he is in
one set of coalitions that are different from those of a female
therapist. If the therapist is older, the response of a young couple
or an older couple will be different in his presence. If the male
therapist is admiring of the wife, he must accept the fact that
the husband will have a response to that. Should the therapist
side with the husband, he must take into account what consequences this coalition will have for his relationship with the wife.
There are no "objective" data in marriage therapy. A comment by the therapist is not merely a comment but also a coalition with one spouse in relation to the other or with the unit
against a larger group.

Where the coalition becomes most important as an issue
is with those therapists who are "growth" oriented and primarily
concerned about the individual. Often the therapist may feel
that the wife outgrew the husband and it is therefore appropriate
that she divorce him, or that the husband "outgrew" the wife,
who is "only a housewife." Sometimes therapists who are supporting a feminist position encourage a wife to assert herself
whether she wants to or not. Or a therapist may feel that one
spouse is willing to work on the problems and the other is not
and so separation should take place. A fundamental assumption should be that if the couple separate while in therapy and
did not come in with separation as the presenting problem, the
therapist is part of that separation and has contributed to it by
coalition behavior.

Although a therapist need not take the position that separation and divorce should never occur—obviously such a position

is not sound—the issue is whether the therapist is being responsible. A therapist who thinks in threes will not naively break up a marriage because of ignorance about being involved.

One further note on separation. Sometimes a couple wish to live separately while "working on" their marriage. To do therapy on the marriage of a separated couple is often a waste of time, in my experience. There are too many forces leading them apart when living separately, and the sessions tend to be conversations about problems rather than attempts to solve those problems. It is best to force the issue by requiring them to live together if marriage therapy is to be done.

When working with a couple, the therapist should organize what is said and done so that the therapy has specific destinations. As a therapist intervenes, he or she finds that a philosophy of life and marriage is necessary as a guide. The therapist must think through the issues of separation and divorce as well as responsibilities within the family group. Simply not giving advice to a couple will not avoid the issue, since what the therapist thinks will be communicated somehow. It is preferable to clarify one's own thinking so that the marital problem of a couple does not meet an expert too confused and uncertain to be helpful.

Often a marital therapist may feel like a labor negotiator or a diplomat involved in conflictual issues. If the therapist joins one side against the other, he or she becomes part of the problem rather than part of the solution. Yet inevitably the therapist is personally involved in whatever the issues may be; and so one may find oneself taking sides, like it or not. What is so appealing, and yet so stressful, about marital counseling is the way the action draws on the feelings of the therapist. One's own biases about men and women and one's own attitude about marriage are forced out into the open as one struggles with the marital issues. Usually a therapist's own marriage undergoes changes in response to his or her experience with couples. Sometimes these changes are unpredictable. While helping a couple clarify some positions, obscure others, and negotiate compromises, the therapist also tries to stabilize the beneficial changes with the couple—while in his or her own life there may be changes not so beneficial, which must not interfere with the therapist's work. Yet if successful therapy is defined as solving specific problems so that there is more variety and complexity in the life of an individual, the opportunity for the therapist to achieve that goal in his or her own personal life is extended more through marital therapy than any other type.

Guidelines for the Therapy

How the therapist approaches a marital problem will be determined by many factors. What to do will be determined by the unique nature of the particular situation, although one can apply a few general rules. One way to approach the issue here is to emphasize what not to do as a way of presenting common difficulties. The following discussion points out some things to avoid when dealing with a marital couple.

The therapist should *avoid minimizing problems*. Whatever the issues between the couple, in the beginning of therapy the therapist should not try to soften the problem by minimizing it. The couple might respond politely, but they will feel he does not understand the severity of their situation. If the wife does not feel her husband treats her with respect, the therapist should explore that issue in detail. If the husband thinks his wife acts bored with his friends, the therapist should emphasize that as an important problem. A problem may seem trivial but will represent a larger issue. Dismissing it will dismiss the larger problem. A small problem may be an analogue for a large one.

The therapist should *avoid abstractions*. It is better, whenever possible, to require the couple to focus on specific behaviors rather than on larger issues. The intellectual wife who is protesting about the rights of women may hesitate to state her objection to picking up her husband's underwear, but that situation may be where the larger issue manifests itself. The husband who protests that his wife is not affectionate can be focused on how he wishes to be received when he comes home from work. The therapist needs to search for specific behavior so that he or she can devise a directive that will lead to change.

A good therapist will *avoid consistently being in a coalition*. Although at times a therapist will side with a wife and at times with a husband, the art of therapy is to avoid the consistent coalition. One should join a spouse against the other spouse only in a calculated way for a specific purpose. If a man says he will not allow his wife to work and the therapist is female, she may find herself wanting to save the wife from that villain of a male. Such an approach will lose. The therapist's problem is how to keep her own biases from intruding into the changes sought by the couple. Similarly, if a husband is giving up a fine career opportunity because his wife will not move away from her family, the therapist should not automatically side with the husband because he thinks he needs to join him against the wife on this issue. A therapist must always find ways to monitor his or her behavior to determine whether a covert coalition has happened. A colleague placed behind a one-way mirror is a help, if available.

To avoid coalitions, it helps to keep in mind that one can be trapped by a spouse by either seductive or provoking behavior. It is not just happenstance that issues important to the therapist come out, because the spouses will test what is important to that therapist. One should also not assume a simple situation but expect more complex issues. A husband who "won't allow" his wife to work may have reasons the therapist does not know about. For example, the therapist may not know that the wife has arranged that the husband say just that.

Insofar as the therapist is an expert, he or she is higher in the hierarchy than either spouse, and joining one spouse against the other means crossing generation lines and possibly causing the problems one is trying to change. As a general rule, when one is caught in such a coalition, it is best to interview alone the spouse one has been joining against. Whenever one sees a person alone, the tendency is to join that person against others. For example, if a therapist is siding with a wife against a husband, seeing the husband alone can help. However, one must balance the situation by seeing that the other spouse is not neglected.

Another solution is to bring in more people at that time— either a colleague behind the mirror or the couple's children or parents. A larger group will shift coalition patterns.

The idea of bringing in extended kin should always be considered when the therapist is unable to resolve a problem with a couple. A discovery made with the family orientation was that a problem in one part of the family may reflect issues in another part. For example, a couple might be having a sex problem, which could be seen as an intimate problem between them and so focused upon. However, it can be that the bad feeling causing the sex problem is actually the result of an unresolved in-law problem. To improve the sex life, the therapist needs to do something about the extended family situation.

In certain situations a therapist might want to *unstabilize* a marriage to produce change. Sometimes a marriage is stable but miserable. An effective way to unstabilize the marriage is to join one spouse against the other and simply hold that position. Whatever is said, the therapist sides with one spouse and defines the other as wrong. It can be either spouse. The therapist must appear to be intending to hold to his coalition permanently, even though he or she may intend to switch later. This procedure, perhaps best developed by Minuchin, will bring out emotions and action in a stable couple. However, it requires skill and should not be used lightly by the average therapist.

The therapist should also *avoid debates about life*. Some couples will wish to discuss the meaning of life with a therapist; they should do that with other people. When philosophical issues come up, the therapist should shift the couple to more concrete issues. The task of the therapy is not for the couple to persuade the therapist to change his or her ideology or for the therapist to educate the couple about life; it is to have the two partners deal with each other in more productive ways.

It is a good idea to *avoid the past*. It has become a cliché to say one should focus on the present rather than the past in therapy, yet many therapists continue in different ways to involve themselves in past issues. This problem is greater with a marital couple than with other types of client situations because marital partners are experts at debating past issues. They often see their situation as a product of what has previously happened, may quarrel about who was right about what, and may end with bad feelings and no resolution. They can then blame the therapist for letting the quarrel happen. No matter how interested a therapist is in how people got to the point where they are, it is necessary to restrain oneself from such explorations.

Sometimes, of course, something about the past can be used to motivate a couple in the present—for example, by finding some time in the past when they were getting along fine. Past ways of solving problems can also sometimes be used again. However, when there are unforgivable things in the past, the therapist should not explore that past but should find something to do in the present that allows forgiveness, so the couple can move on to better times. A task that is an ordeal for a couple can sometimes help them go beyond a bitter experience. For example, a Puerto Rican faith healer may resolve the problem of a wife's having had an affair by taking the two steps often used by traditional marriage therapists with this problem. First, he persuades the couple that the wife was not really responsible for the affair, it was the ghost of another woman (other therapists might say the wife is not responsible because of an unconcious acting out). He sends the couple a long distance to a remote place, to a particular tree, to perform a specific ceremony to exorcise the ghost. Such an ordeal provides a ritual for ending the issue and gives both partners an investment in its ending. (A similar ordeal can be paying for expensive individual or marriage therapy.)

In a first interview with a married couple, some exploration of the past may be necessary, but by the end of it the therapist should have shifted to the present context. Various ways of dropping the past must be developed. A "fresh start" is a phrasing that is appealing; and it is always best to start the couple on a new agreement that they will attempt a change. In extreme cases it might be necessary to simply forbid a couple to discuss anything that happened before a week ago. However, one should try to avoid arguing with a couple about dismissing the past and simply shift the topic to the present and future.

Another way of thinking about the past is possible. People describe the past differently, and remember it differently, depending on their present circumstances. For example, when an individual or a couple says the past was a time of misery, this can be understood as a statement reflecting the present. At another time, the same individual or couple might describe that past quite differently—and, more important, will recall it quite differently.

The therapist should also *avoid thinking that problems are identical*. It is disrespectful to believe that a problem enjoyed by a married couple is the same as the therapist's own problem, even when it appears to be. If, for example, a couple never go out together, and neither do the therapist and his or her spouse, these are not the same problem. Just as each snowflake is different, why one couple do not go out and what to do about it is different from why another couple do not go out, because their ecology is different.

A therapist who is young should not try to appear wiser than he or she is. The beginning therapist is often young and even unmarried. Faced with a couple married for twenty-five years, the beginner may be tempted to act as if he or she understood that stage of marriage as well as they do. It is not so. Instead, the therapist should find a stance to work from that is acceptable to an older couple. For example, the beginner can say, "Obviously you know more about marriage than I do, since you've been married a long time, and certainly you know more about your own marriage than I do. But as an outsider, I can offer you an objective view of some of your problems."

A therapist should *avoid leaving goals unformulated.* It is often more difficult to formulate goals for marital problems than for other kinds. Yet out of negotiations with the couple should come goals. If a therapist does not have a destination, his or her path to get there is likely to meander. Whether in clarifying long-term goals or in talking about the present, it is helpful to have the emphasis on how the couple "should deal with the situation." For example, if they describe a fight that occurred the previous weekend, and the therapist allows them to describe that fight, they will reactivate the feelings of the fight and there will be bad feeling in the therapy room. It is better to say something like "Let's talk about the incident in terms of the way you should have dealt with it to be pleased with each other." When the incident is first framed that way, they then talk about the fight as a deviation from the way they should deal with such situations.

At times the therapist wishes couples to ask explicitly for what they want from each other, *but indirectness should also be allowed.* Directing a wife only to "ask your husband for what you want" may be asking her to do something she would rather not. She might feel that asking for something directly would be unwifely or might risk shaming her husband if he could not deliver. Sometimes it is better to request more indirection. For example, the therapist can say, "I want you to ask for what you want from your husband in such a way that it takes him a while to understand what you mean."

Multiple therapists can make the situation more difficult to change. One therapist can do therapy as successfully as two, and one is more economical. Usually cotherapy is set up for the sake of uncertain therapists, not for the case.

A problem occurs when one of the spouses is in individual therapy with someone else and also wants marriage therapy. Usually this combination is not wise. For example, a husband may be in therapy and the individual therapist may feel the therapy is not getting anywhere but does not wish to give up the patient. So he suggests adding marital therapy, hoping that might make some kind of change. The marriage therapist then starts under a handicap. The husband is talking to his individual therapist about what happens in the marital sessions, thus livening up his therapist. But the wife has only the marital therapist and no one to talk with about the situation who is exclusively on her side. Usually she insists at some point on individual therapy for herself. At that point either the couple drop the marital therapy or else each has an ally outside the marital therapy. This coalition structure makes change in the marriage more difficult. It is better not to combine couple and individual therapy. Even at the risk of antagonizing a referring therapist who wants to hold his or her patient, it is better to suggest that for the period of the marital therapy the couple only have therapy together and recess the individual therapy.

Finally, the therapist should *avoid allowing irreversible positions*. Although at times it may be necessary to force a situation where there is no turning back, in most situations it is extremely important to keep a husband or wife from stating a position he or she cannot change. The therapy should not allow free expression by the couple but only expression that will achieve a purpose. If a husband is saying something that the therapist can see will make the man look like a sap or will force him to defend an indefensible position, the therapist should intervene and not allow it. If the wife is going to state something she will not be able to undo, then the therapist should distract her. The goal should be to allow room for change, negotiation, and flexible alternatives in the life of the couple.

In summary, the marital therapist must take problems seriously, focus on specific issues, form deliberate coalitions to tip balances, not allow free expression of ideas that might cause irreversible harm, formulate goals, and not always require that couples talk explicitly about problems. Most important, the marital therapist should not assume that one couple or one problem is identical with another.

A Case Example

Although every couple is different and every therapist is different, an example can be useful to show both specific and general ideas about the process of beginning marital therapy. The therapist in this case was Richard Belson, D.S.W., raconteur, author, and associate professor of social work at Adelphi University. I was the supervisor. It was a colleague and not a trainee supervision, as Dr. Belson had been a supervisor himself for a number of years. It was "live" in that there were plans made before the session, telephone calls with suggestions during it, and a recess for discussion behind the mirror about how to end the interview and what directives to give. The interview was video-recorded, and the dialogue presented here is verbatim. The problem presented was a couple married for twenty-seven years who wanted marital therapy because they were in conflict and were about to separate. They were both employed and had three children, aged fourteen to twenty-two. A respectable middle-class husband and wife in their fifties, they were quite solemn. The therapist began by asking them about themselves. "Could you tell me a little bit about who you are and what you do? Let me begin with your wife. What kind of work do you do?"

The wife, a tall woman with a silk bow at her throat, explained that she worked as a secretary in a university and also attended university classes.

"Why the class?" asked the therapist. "Are you trying to form a new career, or is it just your own interest in an education?"

She said it was just for her own interest, and when asked what class she was taking, she said, "Calculus."

The therapist laughed and said, "So you're an advanced mathematician."

"No, only second semester."

"I was taking some math in my college career," said the therapist, "but when I came to calculus, I knew I was in the wrong field."

The therapist learned more about where the wife was working and then turned to the husband, who told him he was an electrical engineer and worked for a utility company.

"So both of you," said the therapist, "have this mathematical thing in common. I don't think it's the basis for a happy marriage, but it's rather remarkable. I don't know many people in math, and least of all do I know a couple that both knew anything about math except to fight over the checks."

"Well," said the husband, "she possibly knows more about math than I do."

"No kidding. So you're being very gracious as a husband that is about to get divorced. Which I want to ask you about. Are you interested in changing your marriage, or what is the change you would like from your wife that we can help you with?"

In this casual way the therapist slides from a social discussion into the issue of why they are there. The husband struggles with a reply. "Well, my wife has, evidently, a great deal of difficulty talking to me. I detect that she doesn't tell me some things. She won't talk to me about some things. She is acting like she's afraid to talk to me, or she's hostile, or something. There's some hostility there. It is uncomfortable and she would like me to move out."

"Why is she here today? What is it she wants from you?"

When beginning therapy with a couple, one usually finds that they have a list of complaints about each other. Sometimes they have rehearsed in their minds what they will say before they arrive. If a therapist asks each of them to say what the problem is, they can go on at length attacking the other. When that is done, the situation looks hopeless. It is sometimes best not to allow those speeches. One way to do that is to ask the husband, "If I asked your wife what the problem is, what would she say?" Then one does the same with the wife. Each then has to say what the other's complaints are. In this case, the therapist used a modified version of this approach by asking the husband what it is that the wife wants.

"Well," said the husband, "she said she would like me to come in for a couple of sessions, and I agreed to do this. I personally would like to see the marriage continue, but I think that she's getting very uncomfortable over the past few weeks, and I've become uncomfortable too."

"Well, when things start to get bad, it's hardly enjoyable. What is it your wife wants you to do that you're not doing? Could you be just a little bit more specific?"

"Well, I have a temper."

"You, an electrical engineer, have a temper?"

"I get mad at the kids sometimes."

"I see. So she would like you to control your temper with the children." The therapist continues, "What is it she would like for herself from you?"

"Well, other than not yelling at the kids, I don't know exactly what she wants from me. She won't tell me."

"Well, let's just guess and then we'll ask her. What do you think she would say if I asked her what it is that she wants?"

"Well, I think she would want me to control my temper, but other than that, I don't know." He added, "I think there are probably other things, but I don't know what they are."

"Well, we'll find out very soon. Do you hit her?"

"I haven't for quite a few years."

"I see. Did you used to hit her badly?"

"Well, I hit her a couple of times."

"How long ago was that?"

"About twelve or fifteen years ago."

"So it was a long time ago. Has she hit you recently?"

"No."

The therapist has easily and quickly learned whether there is abuse in this family. In this approach there is no history taking to begin with, since that biases the therapy in a historical and information-gathering direction rather than one of change. Relevant aspects of the problem are sought and brought up as the first interview is conducted. The information gathered is then in context, not a sociological-historical review.

The therapist asked more about what the wife wanted, and the husband said she would like him to read less and get involved in more hobbies.

"What are these hobbies that you used to do that she wants you to do? Make love to her?"

Again, in a casual way, the therapist slides in an important issue.

"Well," said the husband, "that is something she definitely does not want me to do now. She used to not feel that way."

"Was there a time that was a hobby she liked?"

"I would say yes."

When discussing the cost of hobbies, the therapist asks, "Is money an issue between you?"

"I think it probably is."

"She thinks you make too much?"

"She thinks I don't make enough."

"How much money do you make?"

"Before taxes, about $42,000."

"How much does she make?"

"Around $12,000."

"So you make more or less fifty thousand dollars a year. Is it enough to cover your costs? I notice you have three children."

The therapist has straightforwardly asked about the couple's income, just as he did about sex, as a therapist should with a couple.

In the discussion of the children, it turned out that one daughter had just graduated from college at the early age of nineteen. They had a son who was, as the father put it, "moving along toward getting a degree. Slowly." They agreed he could be doing better, but it turned out the father never saw his grades. The therapist asked why not.

"Because he doesn't choose to show me," said the husband.

"You're the father," said the therapist. "Where does he get the nerve to talk that way to you?"

"I'm encouraged not to inquire," said the husband, indicating his wife.

"Really," said the therapist. "So there is some issue going on there too." When he asked who was paying for the son's education, it turned out the wife was doing so. "How did you make this arrangement between the two of you that the wife pays for the tuition? I mean it's an interesting idea. It's a new idea."

The husband explained that when he had said he didn't have the money to send the son to college, the wife had gone to work to earn the money to pay his tuition. Apparently this couple quarreled over the years about this particular son. When the wife went to work to help the son, she benefited herself by becoming a more independent woman. Previously the husband had controlled all the money; when she went to work, she had money of her own. A problem for the couple was that the son was about to graduate from college, and they did not have his problems to communicate with each other about. That was when they began to have more trouble in the marriage. This couple could be thought of as at the stage where a child who was an issue between them leaves home; then they must communicate with each other more directly. That situation can cause difficulties or even a separation, which was threatened here.

The therapist turned to the wife and said, "What if I asked your husband what he wants from you, what would he say?"

"Someone to wash the clothes and buy the food and prepare it and clean the house and run the errands and quit running up high bills." When asked about the bills, she said, "It seems that whenever a bill comes in, there is a confrontation over it." She mocked his voice: "You've overspent the clothing category again. You are not to spend any more money for clothing."

"So what you're saying is that you work together well around the money."

"It's just easier not to say anything to him. We fight less if we don't say anything at all."

"So you're like passing ships. You wave to each other occasionally that you still exist?"

"Nope. Don't even wave," said the wife.

When the therapist asked how long this had been going on, the wife said for years and years. "This trouble about money," said the therapist, "is one of the major issues. Is that it?"

"The struggle about money is a power struggle, not a money struggle," said the wife.

"Sometimes in marriage people struggle about power," said the therapist. "Are there any happy years you had together?"

Often with a couple in severe difficulty it is good to go to a time in the past when they got along well. That marks that period as a baseline and establishes the possibility that they can get along well again. In this case, the wife did not imply that they had ever got along better. She said, "There were years where we fought less."

The wife described how they had been to several counselors over a period of years, sometimes in relation to their son and sometimes in relation to each other. She found it helpful. Her husband did not.

To the husband the therapist said, "What didn't you like about them? I don't want to make the same mistakes."

The husband replied that he did not see any change in the marriage.

"So that must make you a little bit cautious about whether or not this therapy is going to be helpful."

"Well," said the husband, "I have serious doubts that it will be helpful. I think her mind is made up and she wants a separation. If that's true, this counseling is not going to prevent that."

The therapist asked whether he thought his wife had the slightest interest in seeing what could still be done. "You know, a lot of things turn around even when they've reached a very bad point."

"Well, that's the reason I agreed to come in at all."

"Yes," said the therapist. "You've had a lot of experience in your life that sometimes when things look very black, they start to get better."

The therapist emphasizes that a positive change is possible in their marriage, and he also begins to explore their plans for separation. Sometimes one can take a couple through a hypothetical separation and get rid of it. That is, they may find they will still be financially entangled, they will still be parents of the children together, and so on. The husband in this case says he would live nearby if they separated, and he would have to support the wife and children. He would also visit the children.

"I think it would be a financial hardship on both of us," said the husband, "but I don't contribute much to the house."

"You mean emotionally, spiritually, sexually, or financially?"

"Oh, the tasks I do aren't much." He described doing the dishes and doing a little work around the house. He added that the wife would probably find the four-bedroom house too big for the one child left at home.

When asked her view of the possible future separation, the wife said that the house was too big. When asked whether she would stay in touch and speak to her husband, she said, "Arguing on a false premise, I honestly don't know."

"A false premise?"

"That he is not at home."

This comment was the first suggestion by the wife that she was not assuming, and perhaps did not want, a separation.

"I was just hypothesizing," said the therapist. "How it would be if you moved in this direction. I'm not saying a separation is going to take place."

The wife said she would assume she would see her husband occasionally and talk to him if they separated. When the therapist asked whether the wife had another man in her life at present, the husband said, "Not that I know of."

"Let's ask her if she does," said the therapist. "Just take a second."

"Do you have another man in your life?" the husband asked his wife.

"Sexually, no."

"That sounds ominous," said the therapist.

The husband pointed out that she worked with a group of people she liked and they went to concerts where one of the men—a married man—sang.

"They say you can't trust a person that sings," said the therapist. "You never know what his sexual life is about." He continued, "Are you jealous of the relationship?" and the husband said he was not particularly. He didn't think she was in love with any of that group, but she liked them.

"Do you mind if I spend a few minutes talking with your wife alone and then with you?"

It is important in a first interview to see each spouse for a while alone. This allows each one to say what he or she might not say in the other's presence. It also gives the therapist more power, since he knows what each spouse has said and the other spouse does not. Whoever has more information has more power.

Sometimes therapists are concerned about learning some confidential information that they could not share with the other spouse. It is usually better to have that information. How confidentiality is dealt with should be up to the therapist. If a spouse seems to be trying to set a trap by emphasizing private information, the therapist should say that he or she will take responsibility for deciding whether to protect confidentiality or not, and so the spouse should not say anything that should not be passed on. Usually, however, there is not a problem, and much is gained seeing spouses alone.

In this case the wife talked more frankly when alone about her difficulty with her husband. Not only was there a power struggle over money, but "for a long time it was as though he was the daddy and I was the little girl. If I was good, he would say, 'You have been good,' and if I were bad, he would say I had been bad. I would straighten up and behave. He doled out the money according to how he thought it should be doled out." She added, "I had been brought up to be very obedient, and he would tell me what to do and I would try to be obedient. Then I began to question some of his wisdom, and when we saw counselors he would not speak to them."

It became more evident that this was a woman experiencing what many women had experienced over the last few decades. She had moved from being an obedient and subservient wife to being an independent woman. Her husband was struggling to adapt to that change and faced counselors who supported his wife in her endeavor and not him.

"Is there anything that didn't come out of the discussion so far," asked the therapist, "that I should know? Any secret you've never told?"

"That covers a lot of territory."

"Sure. Why not?"

The wife said that her husband threatened regularly to leave, and this time when he threatened she said perhaps it was a good idea. "Well, it evidently really pulled the rug from under him," she said, "and he agreed to go to counseling."

This is not an unusual situation. Typically the spouse who can leave, or threaten to leave, has the most power in a marriage. The other will give in on an issue rather than separate. Sometimes the other spouse says, "Well, all right, then leave," instead of giving in on an issue. That change precipitates instability, and the couple seeks therapy.

She talked about how her husband now didn't have the power of threatening to leave or power with money since she was employed.

"Does he have any power left if he doesn't have the money?"

"I think he sees it as very powerless. Money is power."

The therapist asked, "Has this affected your sexual life with him?"

"Since I asked him to leave, which was about three weeks ago, yes."

"Did it get better or worse?"

"It stopped."

When asked how it had been before that, she said, "It varied a lot. It depended entirely on me. If it were up to him, it would be at least once a night year-round."

"And if it were up to you, it would be twice a night year-round?"

"There are times when I am more inclined than others. If we've been fighting bitterly, I'm just not inclined."

When he interviewed the husband alone, the therapist

said, "Your wife is interested to try and see if the marriage can be turned around. Would you object to that?"

"No, I would not object to that."

"Would you mind if things got better?"

"No, I wouldn't mind."

"Could you tolerate happiness after so many years of in-between?" asked the therapist, and when the husband replied that he could, the therapist said, "Would you feel resentful if we helped you here and you didn't figure it out for yourself?"

"No," said the husband. "I go to the doctor when I'm sick and he figures out things that I can't figure out. He cures me. I'm not resentful of being cured or being helped."

Before bringing the couple back together, the therapist consulted with the supervisor behind the mirror on what might be done. It seemed evident that the couple wanted to stay together and that they needed some task to take home with them. Since this was a dramatic moment in their lives, the possible breakup of a quarter-century marriage, any task should be a dramatic one. A minor task would not do in a major crisis situation. The directive should not only be dramatic and extreme, but it should deal with the particular problems they were most concerned about. A directive was decided on, and the therapist returned to the interview room with the couple. The ways he motivated the couple and presented the task are an excellent example of directive therapy.

The therapist said, "Your husband is interested to see if your marriage can be turned around. He's interested in coming here to do that, as a conservative approach. I think it's always possible you still may separate, but if that should happen, it's good if you separate with better feeling, so that if you go your separate ways, it is with pleasant memories rather than bitter memories about how it ended." He began with the directive by saying, "I would like to give you a specific suggestion. I suppose that you have heard that the way we work is, instead of just talking, we like to make some suggestions for people to follow. You were aware of that?"

By saying "the way we work," the therapist is including the institute as backing for his directive. It is not merely an idea of his, but a respectable procedure by an institution. He also dismisses mere talk as not productive, as the husband thinks. He adds, "You know, the usual kind of psychology in therapy is talking and talking. People go on for years and years, but if you don't have any results or any action, what good is it? So I would like to make a suggestion that I would encourage you to follow. Would you agree to do it? Then when you come back, we can find out how it worked itself out. Because if you don't do it, it would be just like a waste of time. If you're going to get any change after all these years, clearly, you know, just to say to you, 'Why don't you be nice to each other,' that's going to be a fruitless and thankless kind of undertaking. Because the usual kind of common sense isn't going to help you much. Would you agree to that? That you know already, right? I mean, what am I going to tell you that you don't know? So I'd like you to make some changes that will make some changes. Would that be all right?"

The couple nodded their heads in response, and the therapist continued, "All right, now I'd like you both to be a little bit flexible. Would you be willing to be flexible and to show some open-mindedness?" The husband nodded agreement, and the therapist said to the wife, "And you?" She too nodded. Neither could admit to not wanting to be flexible. "We have to do something that will be of help," continued the therapist, "otherwise you're going to end up in the same position of not talking to each other, and so forth." To the husband he said, "I would like you to do something that would be absolutely a remarkable move toward your wife. And," he said to the wife, "I would like you to do something remarkable, enduring, and courageous back to him. I want that to be in response to what he is going to do for you. I will ask you what it is that you will do, and I don't think it should be a small thing. If you're going to go, you might as well go for it. I mean, at this point in your life, with the kids getting older and things falling apart, you might as well put out your chips and play for the big numbers. Okay? So what I want you to do," he said to the husband, "in the next five weeks—just for the next five weeks. I'm not asking you to do it for six weeks or for seven weeks or for eight weeks, only for five weeks."

Often a client will do a task if it is time-limited, when he might not do it if it is forever. In this case the therapist picks the specific number "five" because he will not be able to see the couple for five weeks because of scheduling problems. He wants the task to be continued until he sees them again.

Continuing, he said, "I would like you to take your paycheck and put it in your wife's hands for the next five weeks. She will do with it whatever she pleases. Okay?" The husband stared at him, not responding. "That would be an extraordinary move on your part. Since your husband has agreed to that," he turned to the wife, accepting the husband's nonresponse as an agreement, "what would be your extraordinary response to this for the next five weeks? What would you be willing to do yourself? Just before you respond, you understand you would do with the money whatever you want. However you want to spend it, you would have the complete responsibility. That's what your husband has agreed to. So I would like your response to be as courageous and dramatic and extraordinary as his proposal and his commitment."

"You've told him what he is to do," said the wife, "and you've left it up to me what I'm to do."

"Right."

"Wow. That's pretty heavy."

"Well, it's a heavy thing that he got."

"What I have to do is something that I would consider nice, or something that he would consider nice?"

"It would be an extraordinary move on your part. Similar to the extraordinary move on his part of giving you all his money for five weeks and leaving it to you to decide how you want to spend it, including its responsibilities."

The wife discussed different possibilities, such as giving her husband the money to get their car fixed to sell. The therapist said, "I could mention one thing, but I don't want it to be the thing that you want, because your idea might be more dramatic than mine. You could agree to sit down and talk to him and pour out your heart for ten minutes every night. But I don't want to suggest something that would be too timid."

This suggestion was an inadequate one, by design. Often

if the therapist suggests something that isn't satisfactory, the client will come up with a better suggestion.

"That would bore him," said the wife.

"It should be something," said the therapist, "that would deal with some area of conflict, just as his following this directive will end the struggling over money for five weeks."

"The easiest thing for me to do would be to have sex with him."

"Would that be extraordinary?"

"No."

"How many times a day were you thinking about?"

"Once," said the wife.

"Well, you could make it extraordinary by doing it five times or twice."

"I'd need some cooperation."

"Of course." To the husband he said, "Could you cooperate with that for the five weeks?"

"Not more than once a day," said the husband, "my circulation is to the point . . ."

The therapist said, "Did you ever think that it could improve your circulation and break up the sugar deposits? Okay. Does that sound like an adequate response to what you are doing?"

The husband nodded, and the therapist accepted that as an agreement.

By requiring a task of the husband and asking the wife to volunteer some action in return, the therapist leaves it up to the wife to choose whatever she might prefer. If she chose some action in the area of sexual relations, it would be an idea of hers, not an idea of the therapist's, so she would not be having a sexual action imposed on her. (In this case, even though the task was supposedly for the husband, there were indications that the wife enjoyed sex more than he did, and so this was not exactly an ordeal.)

The therapist continued, "You understand this is a dead serious thing that we're doing. It's not to be taken as just empty talk. To get results, you have to work for results. As soon as you walk out the door, it begins. You have to immediately transfer all your money to her. Not tomorrow, or the next day, or a week from now.''

When a task is given, it should be done as soon as possible. If the couple delays beginning the task, they might find reasons for not doing it, or they might quarrel and forget the task. The therapist continues, ''I think if you end up separating, it's best if you have been nice to each other and you remember doing nice things together. So I want to suggest that if you start to be nasty with each other, just go into separate rooms and cool off. In five weeks we'll review how it has been. Now, what are you going to do when you get into the car?''

''Well,'' said the husband, ''we're in two different cars.''

''What are you going to do before you get in the two different cars?''

''Well, my paycheck is in my car. I don't have it on my person.''

''Are your two cars near each other?''

''No, hers is out there, and mine is four blocks away.''

''Okay, the first thing you can do is to arrange for your cars to draw alongside each other. That will indicate symbolically an equal relationship.'' He turned to the wife, ''And you can think about what allowance to give him.'' By putting it that way, he dramatized how completely she was to take over the money.

''An allowance to give him?''

''Yes,'' said the therapist. ''You're in charge of the money. He ought to have a few dollars in case he runs out of gas. Or if he wants to buy a newspaper. Okay?''

The couple left, looking serious and thoughtful.

This beginning stage of the therapy involved gathering information about the problems, joining the couple in a plan to do something about them, and giving tasks specifically related to the particular issues. These tasks were relevant to this particular couple, and they might or might not be appropriate for some other couple. The directive must be designed for the particular situation.

This couple continued for three more interviews, spaced a month apart, and then terminated because they were getting along well and had decided to stay together. At the second interview they reported that the wife had dealt with the money and the husband had accepted that. They found that the husband could have authority in the home without controlling the money (control of money is a weak power position to be entirely dependent upon). The sexual agreement lasted two weeks and ended in a quarrel. When the therapist, at the second interview, emphasized that they were people who restrained their passions, they were pleased with that explanation of their restraint with each other. They began to change that, and they also negotiated a number of changes around the issues between them. By the third interview, the wife was complaining about the responsibilities of handling the money. At the fourth interview they came in cheerfully and reported they were getting along well. The therapy appeared successful after these four months and in a later follow-up continued to be so.

The way the therapist terminated was to be puzzled and surprised at the rapidity of improvement in their relationship. This was partly calculated. If an individual or a couple improves rapidly in therapy, it can be a problem. After all, the clients have been trying to solve their problems for a long time, and if they change in a few interviews, it gives the therapist too much power. There is an imbalance that must be corrected. One danger is that they will relapse to correct the balance by showing the therapist he is not all that powerful and influential. One way to avoid this is to have the therapist puzzled by the improvement, so that it appears he did not arrange it. Another procedure is for the therapist to encourage a relapse. The couple can demonstrate their power in the situation and correct the imbalance by not relapsing.

7

Problems in Training Therapists

Until quite recently a therapist could graduate from a clinical training program and be considered trained even though none of his or her teachers had observed the student doing therapy or even conducting a single interview. It was also possible that a student never watched anyone do therapy in order to see how it might be done. Even more curious, the student's success or failure with cases was never examined because therapy outcome research was not part of a clinical curriculum. It is perhaps not surprising that the average therapist, whose work is unobserved and whose results are unexamined, is not particularly skillful according to therapy evaluation studies.

With the introduction of one-way mirror rooms and video-tape equipment, clinical training is changing. Many programs now focus sharply on training in interview skill. They also examine outcome. However, therapy training changes only when theories of how to do therapy change, not because of technical advances. One-way mirrors and audiotape have been available since the 1950s. Yet many clinical programs continue unchanged as if a need for observation had not been suggested. Entirely new approaches to therapy, such as therapy with a family orientation, have even been introduced into the field, and yet the training continues in a traditional manner.

As clinical training programs change, it is being discovered that a theory of therapy and a theory of training are often synonymous. Teachers who believe that insight causes therapeutic change will train student therapists by giving the students insight into themselves and their personal problems. Therapists who think that change occurs because of an increase in positive reinforcements will train therapy students with positive reinforcement procedures. Some of the parallels between the premises of therapy and the premises of training will be offered here as current training issues.

Selecting an Orientation

Any therapy training program must make choices about what therapy *is* and how it should be done. Sometimes there are no choices because traditional procedures continue unexamined or because the setting determines the training. For example, psychologists find it difficult to learn how to do family-oriented therapy if they have only undergraduate college students as clients, because training thus takes place in universities isolated from cities. Psychiatric residents may learn little about therapy if they are forced into a framework of medication and custody because they function as agents of social control in mental hospitals.

Within the limitations imposed by a setting, the faculty of a clinical training program operates on basic premises about the nature of therapy. These premises will be offered here in terms of polar extremes, one labeled Orientation A and the opposite extreme Z. It is recognized, of course, that many teachers of therapy try to be liberal and eclectic and therefore waver between the extremes.

Spontaneous Versus Planned Change. Within Orientation A, the responsibility for therapeutic change resides with the patient. At this extreme, the responsibility of the therapist is not to produce change but to help people change themselves. The therapist is a reflector, a consultant, or an adviser, but he or she is not an enforcer of change. Usually, in this approach, the therapist helps clients understand themselves and their situation; what happens then is up to them. Should therapy fail, that failure rests with the client and only partly, if at all, with the therapist.

At the other extreme, in Orientation Z, the responsibility for change belongs to the therapist. He or she is expected to plan a strategy of change to bring about what the patient is paying money to achieve. If change does not occur, the therapist is a failure. Blaming the client for not changing is not allowed.

Although these opposite premises are general orientations to therapy, they become evident as the basis of operations in a single interview. In Orientation A, what is to happen between therapist and patient in the next interview is unpredictable; it is a happening and cannot be planned, since the therapist must wait to see what the patient offers. The therapist is a responder and must wait to comment on or interpret what the client initiates.

In Orientation Z, the therapist is expected to make a strategic plan that takes into account what is to happen in the next interview. He or she initiates the action. For example, it is the therapist's job to provide a reinforcement program or a directive for the client to follow.

In the clinical training programs of Orientation A, the teacher or supervisor is an adviser or consultant to the therapist. The teacher is not responsible for the success or failure of the case. If a case is going disastrously, the supervisor may intervene, but generally supervisors do not consider a failure to be their fault. What happens between student and supervisor is spontaneous and unplanned. Supervisors must wait to see what their students bring them, and failures are on the heads of the students. If supervisors have helped the students understand themselves and the dynamics of their cases, they have done their job.

In Orientation Z, the supervisor is responsible for what happens with a case and is expected to plan with the therapist what is to happen. In facilities where there is "live" supervision, the teacher is placed behind a one-way mirror watching the student work. She is expected to telephone the student during the interview and guide him, if necessary, or bring him out and discuss what is happening. In this arrangement, if change is not taking place, the supervisor is a failure. Not only is it her job to protect a client from a beginning therapist, but also she must help a student in difficulty. If a client is provoking a student and so preventing change, the supervisor's job is to find a way to help the student solve that problem. Just as the therapist is expected to find a way to change the client if the client's life is going badly, so is it the supervisor's job to find a way to change the student if the student's therapy is going badly.

A Growth Versus a Problem Orientation. One can think of the goal of therapy either as the expansion of the life of a human being or as the solution of specific problems. Orientation A is based on the premise that the goal is to help people develop themselves, and so the therapist's task is essentially an educational one. He wishes to focus on enriching people's lives. If a family presents a child as a problem because he sets fires, the therapist has as his goal the development of the child or family. The fire setting is thus "only a symptom."

At the opposite extreme, in Orientation Z, the therapist is a problem solver. It is his job to clarify and get people over the specific problems they bring to him. If a child is presented as a problem because he sets fires, the goal of the therapist is to arrange that the child no longer sets fires. In the process of solving the fire setting, organizational changes may be made that allow the child and parents to grow and develop, but the focus is on the symptom.

These two orientations produce different therapeutic action. Orientation A tends to leave the details of symptoms unexamined and to focus instead on the general background of the client. Directives are not used to bring about a change. Instead, the approach is interpretive or experiential. Often the therapist attempts to persuade the clients that what they really want is something other than a solution to the complaint they offer. For example, parents who present a child as the problem may be influenced to see the marriage as the "real" problem. Or a therapist may describe a child as "scapegoated" and may feel his or her task is to point out other children in the family who are problems, to get the problem child out of the scapegoat role. In contrast, Orientation Z accepts what the client offers as the problem and focuses on that. If a symptom is offered, the therapist engineers change through the symptom. If a child is offered as the problem, the therapist accepts the description and only later may shift to other children or marital issues.

Training a student therapist can be conceived of as providing him with a rich philosophical life and helping him grow as an individual, or it can be conceived of as teaching specific skills. In Orientation A, there is a trend toward helping the young therapist grow and develop himself. Instead of being taught interview skills, he is encouraged to enter therapy himself so that he can discover from his own experience what the human mind is about. It is assumed that the clinical program and his personal therapy will help him become a mature and developed individual and also an expert therapist. At the other extreme, in Orientation Z, it is assumed that a therapist grows with success in his work and the first task is to train him to do his work well. The focus is on helping him solve the problems he meets in therapy, not helping him enrich his personal life. For example, if a therapist has difficulty dealing with an authority figure, such as a grandfather, in therapy, the two training programs would have different emphases. In Orientation A, the therapist would be encouraged to understand how he feels about authority figures and to resolve that personal problem. In Orientation Z, the training program would be expected to train the therapist in specific ways to deal with grandfathers.

To put the matter another way, according to Orientation A the client should welcome therapy because it is good for people and will make them part of a special elite who have had a unique experience. In Orientation Z, therapy is for handicapped people who wish to get back to normal.

Understanding Versus Action as a Cause of Change. Orientation A includes therapists who assume that people should be more self-aware. They think that if a client understands what she is doing and why, she will not do it anymore. Thus the therapist's job is to help the person understand herself both cognitively and experientially. The approach may be to lift repression by making conscious the unconscious, within the transference framework, or it may be to make interpretations about communication to help people understand how they are dealing with one another. This approach sometimes includes the idea that if a person expresses her emotions she will change, and so it emphasizes the honest and open expression of "real" feelings. Within this orientation, a case conference tends to focus on individual dynamics, including the past history that led up to the problem. Or, if the conference expresses a family orientation, it tends to focus on interaction process and dynamics. The conference will involve discussion of the ways family members interact in both verbal and nonverbal ways. Such discussions do not usually emphasize what to do to bring about change.

In Orientation Z, it is assumed that neither understanding nor the expression of emotion causes change. Therefore the therapy will not involve interpretation or uncovering. Instead, the therapist must plan a strategy and devise directives requiring new behavior. These directives may be types of behavior programs for an individual or directives for a family. The conference will involve little discussion of dynamics and a great deal of discussion of what to do in the therapy and how to do it.

Within Orientation Z, it is expected that a symptom cannot be resolved or a problem solved by merely talking about it. Therefore both therapy and training will emphasize bringing the problem into the therapy room. If a child has temper tantrums and bangs his head, only having a discussion about this behavior is not likely to lead to change. What is required is action—the head banging should happen in the therapy room. If a couple have a problem of fighting, they should have a controlled fight in the room. Of course, some problems cannot be brought into the room, but those that can be should be put into action.

Because of the emphasis on self-awareness and individual experience, therapists in Orientation A are willing to bring clients together in group therapy. Since the emphasis is on changing the individuals, it does not matter whether they are interacting with strangers or with a "pretend" family. Therapists with this view will also bring several families together in a large group, usually assuming that the members will learn from one another and, by thus understanding their own families differently, will change.

In Orientation Z, it is the behavior within a natural group that must change, because the therapist is trying to change repeating sequences involving several persons habitually together. A man may understand how he relates to women in a group therapy setting, but that does not mean he will change his relationship with his wife. To change in relation to his wife, he must be interviewed with the wife, not with other women.

Finally, the emphasis on understanding often leads therapists within Orientation A to help clients notice how they are treating the therapist. "Have you noticed that you are resisting me as if I were an authority figure?" says the authority-figure therapist. Or "The way you are behaving is making me angry." It is assumed that if clients know how they are treating the therapist, they will not do that anymore. Orientation Z assumes that how the therapist feels is his or her own problem and need not be pointed out to clients in the hope they will stop doing what they are doing. It also assumes that the therapist must behave differently if clients are resisting and must not comment on that resistance.

Training within these two approaches tends to reflect the basic orientations. One approach assumes that a therapist learns by understanding himself and supervision therefore consists of conversation about his conduct with a case. The other approach assumes that the problems of the student therapist must appear in action before the supervisor.

Within Orientation A, it is sometimes assumed that if a therapist understands his own personal involvement with his patients, he or she will be a competent therapist. The teacher's talk is intended to make students aware of their biases and to change their way of thinking. If students are cleared of their own neuroses and fully understand their involvement with their own families, they will be good therapists. Given this assumption, therapists are persuaded to enter personal therapy or to have encounter experiences in groups. One premise carried over into the training is the idea that since patients are expected to confess everything themselves, therapists are also expected to confess all. In family therapy training programs within Orientation A, therapists may be expected to go through simulated family exercises revealing their ideas and feelings about their own families. They may also be assigned the task of contacting all their relatives to activate their extended kin networks and to help them understand their involvement in their wider families.

Orientation Z does not assume that therapists will be more effective if they understand themselves or freely express their emotions. Instead, it assumes that they will improve as therapists only by doing therapy under supervision and improving their skills. Instead of helping students understand their feelings or their transference involvement in a case, the teacher will offer active ways to resolve the difficulties in the case. The teacher must teach the student ways to use himself or herself to bring about change. It will be assumed that the student will change with action, not reflection about himself. Just as the families treated by this approach are not expected to confess all, neither are the student therapists. In this approach, group exercises involving students having experiences together or sculpting their own family problems would not be done, since that would distract the student from the real issue, which is how to change a family.

Self-Report Versus Observation. The therapist within Orientation A tends to consider the ideas and fantasies of a person more relevant to therapy than the person's real life situation. Therefore such a therapist often does not feel it is necessary to bring in the patient's intimates for observation but accepts the patient's self-report about them as adequate data. If the therapist interviews the whole family, action among the family members is not encouraged. Instead, each family member is asked about what happens in the family and reports about it to the therapist.

In Orientation Z there is grave doubt about the reliability of self-report. The primary concern is what is actually happening rather than the person's ideas about what is happening. The difference between observation and self-report was discovered a number of years ago, when therapists began to bring in whole families because they discovered that what a person said about his or her marriage or family and what could be observed were markedly different. When the whole family is brought in, the members are asked to deal with each other so that the therapist can see how they do that rather than listen to them describe how they do that.

As training is reflected within these two opposite orientations, the difference centers on the supervisor's data. Within Orientation A, the supervisor tends to accept the self-report of the therapist. The therapist makes notes and takes them to the supervisor, who tries to guess what might have happened from that self-report. Lacking any other observable data, the supervisor naturally tends to discuss the therapist's ideas and fantasies about the case.

In Orientation Z, the supervisor observes the therapist in action with the family either live, through a one-way mirror, or on videotape or audiotape. The supervisor does not believe that the therapist can accurately report what happened, just as a family member cannot accurately report what happens in his or her family. Supervisors want the action in front of them so they can observe it. When supervisors learned that what a student therapist said about a session and what could be observed in the session were quite different, teaching began to focus on what really happens in the interview and therefore on interview skills. The training program is concerned with hierarchy and organization, not with the content of students' fantasies, just as in the therapy.*

Procedures Lead to Theory

Although some people think that a theory is created and then procedures are designed to carry it out, quite the opposite can occur. Procedures develop and then theories are created to rationalize them. It is also possible for a new procedure to develop that leads to a new theory, but the training of practitioners

---

*Although it may appear modern to have a supervisor watch the actual therapy of a student, this is an old-fashioned procedure. In the nineteenth century, when therapists were commonly using hypnosis, they were trained by someone who watched them work. It would have been thought absurd to think a hypnotist could learn his art by reading about it and—never having watched anyone be hypnotized—go off alone into a room and hypnotize someone and return to tell his teacher how he felt about the experience. As hypnosis was abandoned, therapy was taught by people who apparently thought therapy did not require as much skill as being a hypnotist. Therefore a student could learn to do therapy without watching anyone do it or being guided by an observer. When Freud discarded hypnosis, he also discarded the training in interpersonal skill that went with it and offered as a poor substitute a didactic analysis in which the student could make biased observations of one analyst at work on one case.

then suffers a time lag. The training operates on an old theory while the procedures suggest a new one. There are clearly parallels in the clinical field between a theory of change and a theory of training. But new theories of change may develop while traditional training methods continue.

There does not appear to be a single research study showing that therapists who have had therapy themselves, or who understand their involvement with their own families, have better outcomes in their therapy. Yet that assumption remains the center of some clinical training. Even teachers of family therapy continue to emphasize the personality and personal problems of a therapist when they would not emphasize the personality and personal problems of a family member in therapy. Some family therapists have only shifted from a one-to-one focus on the personal problems of the therapist to a group focus on the personal problems of the therapist. The students are brought together and asked to simulate families not only as a way of learning about family relationships but as a way of understanding themselves better. Encounter techniques and family sculpting techniques are used. In some cases these groups constitute the entire training process—a supervisor *never* watches a student do actual therapy. Perhaps the cause of this emphasis is a cultural lag. Many teachers of family therapy underwent individual therapy as a training procedure and so carry those ideas into their own training of family therapists. Others give brief workshops, in which supervision of real therapy is not possible.

Some of the conditioning therapists seem to train therapists on the basis of conditioning therapy, but others do not. Supervisors will use systematic positive reinforcements with a student if that is their theory of change, but therapists who use aversive therapy with patients do not seem to train their students by aversive reinforcements. The student therapist who shocks a client incorrectly is not himself shocked to improve his skill.

Attempting Consistency

It should be possible to train a therapist in a theoretical framework consistent with the approach to therapy. What will be outlined here is a training program based on a theory most like Orientation Z in the premise system previously described. The task is to teach therapy as a skill.*

Selecting Students. If one is doing a therapy that stresses problems in the real world, it is best to choose students with experience in that world. Therefore, mature students who have been married and have children will be easier to train than young people just starting out on courtship.

Besides a modicum of intelligence, the student should have a wide range of behavior so that he or she can adapt to a wide range of therapeutic approaches. At times a therapist must be authoritarian, at times playful, at times flirtatious, at times grim and serious, at times helpless, and so on. A student lacking skills in different kinds of social behavior will be more difficult to train than one who has had a range of experience.

One of the most necessary factors in training, and the one most difficult to achieve, is cutting student therapists off from other teachers of therapy at the time they are in training. If students are in a training program part-time, while also receiving input from teachers at other settings, they will be receiving conflicting ideas about how to do therapy and will be less likely to learn easily and successfully. When other teachers are influencing them, they screen what they know in terms of what other teachers say and can end up being so eclectic that they believe everything is so or nothing is so. At times they are pawns in ideological struggles between schools of therapy, and so their training time is wasted with irrelevant distractions.†

*Credit has already been given to others for many of the ideas in this book but should be especially emphasized here. The training approach described developed in the Institute of Family Counseling of the Philadelphia Child Guidance Clinic. Within that institute many ideas about training were generated by the faculty and by the students. When training a group for forty hours a week over two years, one learns a great deal from them. The faculty included the late Jerome Ford and the late Rae Weiner, who served as administrative directors at different times. Later Marianne Walters took over that task. Included as teachers were Braulio Montalvo, Cloé Madanes, Lydia Linan-Gervacio, and Mariano Barragan. The clinic director, Salvador Minuchin, not only helped work out the training ideas but also made a controversial program administratively possible.
†The therapy and training issues are similar. Rather than have several therapists involved with a family either as cotherapists or as individual therapists with different members, it is better to have one therapist. This approach avoids trapping

Learning by Doing. The kind of therapy emphasized here cannot be learned by reading about it, by hearing lectures about it, or by having discussions. It cannot even be learned by watching others do it, although watching is valuable at certain points in the training. Therapy is a personal encounter, and a therapist can learn how to do it only by doing it. All other training activity is peripheral, if not irrelevant. Ideally the therapist learns to do therapy by doing it while guided by a supervisor at the moment the therapy is happening.

With this approach, training starts when the therapist enters the room with a client, preferably a client family. Up to that point all that can help the therapist is some practice interviewing with simulated families so that he or she can learn how to do a first interview. Students can practice saying hello to people, asking them about their problems, getting them to talk with each other if it is a family interview, and clarifying exactly what the problem is and what the goals of the therapy are to be. They should also practice any special techniques before they are used. Practice not only helps the beginner know what to do and how to do it, but it protects the client from a total novice.

Sharing. The most economical way to train is in a group. In the traditional one-to-one supervision, the wisdom of a supervisor was available only to that one student. If a group of eight students are taught together, a variety of benefits accrue. First of all, the group observation from behind a one-way mirror multiplies the number of clients seen. If each student has seen four cases, they have seen thirty-two cases altogether. In this way they are exposed rapidly to a wide range of problems.

What a supervisor offers a student dealing with a case is observed by all the students and becomes available to all. It is also possible for a supervisor to watch a student doing therapy from behind the one-way mirror with the remainder of the group and to lecture while watching so that the group is guided through the interview.

---

the client in a struggle between therapists, just as one avoids trapping the student therapist in a struggle between teachers of different schools.

When the group is studying a case together, many more ideas about what to do are available to everyone. Each student can make a contribution to the strategic planning so that each student has input not only from a supervisor but also from peers.

The group provides a base of helpful support when a particular student is dealing with a difficult case. However, this support is helpful only if the supervisor deals with the group in a way consistent with the therapy. The group will have high morale if no psychiatric interpretations or group-therapy-style interpretations of one another are allowed, and so no innuendos about a student's personal problems. It is best if the rule is laid down that no one may criticize the work of anyone else unless he or she can offer a positive alternative. This rule prevents destructive comments as a way of trying to impress a teacher.

Show and Tell. With this approach, the goal is not to produce theoreticians but to produce practitioners. A student will, it is hoped, have developed a clear ideology after training, but the goal is that the student be able to offer effective therapy. Examinations, if there are any, should be therapy sessions, not discussions of therapy.

However, even with this emphasis on action, it is necessary for the therapist to think through what he or she is doing and also be able to explain it to others. As a means to this end, it is helpful to have students present videotapes of their work to one another and, later, to outsiders. By having to guide a group through an interview and to explain why he did what he did, the student learns to think tactically and learns to be articulate about his work.

As students learn skills as therapists, reading seminars may be appropriate so they can fit what they are doing into a broader model of the field. In this orientation, theory grows out of action, not action out of theory, and therefore reading of theories should come as the student does therapy and has an idea of what he or she needs to know.

Motivating Students. Just as therapy works best when clients are involved and interested, so does clinical training. If students are given a client within a few weeks of beginning their training, they are eager to learn because they feel so uncertain what to do. Similarly, if they are taught about a problem only when it comes up in therapy, they are interested because they are dealing with that problem. For example, if lectures are given first and readings offered in seminars about different types of abnormalities, the students learn about them as part of a duty. Later, if they meet a particular abnormality when doing therapy, they must recall the time they heard or read about that abnormality in their training. However, if a student is first faced with a problem, such as a withdrawn child, in therapy, then at that moment the student will be most receptive to learning about withdrawn children. When he or she is part of a group in which each student is meeting new problems that the whole group observes, then the whole group are motivated to learn about those problems because they are face to face with them. The motivation of the student is maximized. Teaching this way is the reverse of traditional training. Having a problem arise in therapy and generalizing from it is quite different from first generalizing and later having the student meet such a problem. Similarly, in therapy it is best to deal with an issue when it arises and then generalize from that issue rather than generalize first and hope that later the client will recall the ideas when an issue arises.

How to Tell Someone What to Do. Action therapy involves telling clients what to do whether inside the therapy room or outside. The clinician trained only in the traditional nondirective style is given no instructions in giving directives. After training he can only reflect, interpret, or offer advice as skillfully as the average layperson. Skills in offering directives are not part of the curriculum and are even objected to, so that a therapist trained in that way gives directives badly as well as reluctantly. He may say to a client, "I wonder if you have considered the possibility of perhaps under certain conditions thinking about talking to your wife in a different manner." Only with a premise that a therapist must take responsibility for change can a therapist tell someone, "I want you to do this." He gives a vague and confused directive only for a tactical purpose.

A training program in directive therapy must include teaching students how to motivate people to do what they are told, how to give directives, how to clarify whether they have been understood, how to anticipate reluctance to follow them, and how to check to see whether they have been followed. The training must include practice in giving directives. Simulated situations are used to develop skills in offering instructions to people. The student should learn to give straightforward directives as well as subtle, indirect, and metaphoric ones. One of the best ways to train a student therapist in the skillful use of directives is to give training in hypnosis.

An essential aspect of giving directives is learning what directives to give. Students must be taught to think strategically; they must develop skills in diagnosing a sequence and structure; and they must be able to design directives that will produce the changes they want.

Fitting Therapeutic Problems to Students. Therapy should have a problem rather than a method orientation—a therapist should vary what he or she does depending on the problem. Similarly, the training of a student therapist should vary depending on the needs of a particular student. While watching a student, a supervisor can observe deficits in his or her range of skills and can select future clients to fill out the operational skills of the student. For example, a student who seems to improve markedly with success should be presented with a series of cases where a successful outcome is most probable and only later have more difficult cases. Other students thrive on difficulty and should begin with cases of that kind. A student therapist should meet, planned in his training, the range of problems he will meet on the job. He should deal with children, with young people, with couples, with older people, with the poor, with the upper class, and so on. Since most clinicians are expected to deal with whatever comes in the door, their training should touch upon issues they will be forced to solve. Learning to cure a psychotic is as essential as learning to cure a bedwetter. Later in training, students may specialize in types of patients or particular social classes, but they first need the exposure to a range of problems. This range is needed not only for the particular skills in dealing with those issues but also for maximizing the flexibility of the student. Just as the therapist should design a therapy for a particular client, supervisors should design a training program for a particular student.

An essential part of the flexibility learned by the student is an ability to work in different contexts. A student should have experience working in the home, in the school, at work, and in the neighborhood as well as in the office. As therapy becomes more and more defined as working with people at the interfaces of conflicting groups, such as between home and school, a therapist must learn to work where the problem is when it is impossible to bring the problem into the office.

Checking Outcome. After a few months in a training program, every therapy student should be required to bring back the clients he or she has worked with and terminated to see whether the therapy has produced a change. When students work in a group, they can be taught to do follow-up interviews with one another's cases. They should learn how to inquire of a family whether they were satisfied with the therapy, how to determine whether the changes sought have taken place, and how to think about the biases of both therapist and family in reporting on changes. The purpose is not to produce therapists who can do outcome research but to produce therapists who think about the outcome they want as it will appear months or years from now. Focusing on outcome forces the therapist to orient toward change, to formulate problems that can be changed, and to think about how the people she is assisting now will manage without her in the future. It also helps a therapist think experimentally. If her outcome is not good, she can change her procedures to do better.

Choosing a Place for Training

Many apprentice therapists face the problem of selecting somewhere to train. Often they have minimal information about such places, and yet their whole career can be affected by the choice. A few points can be made specifically about training settings.

Where one trains should be determined by the nature of the future work planned as well as by the training opportunities available. If the apprentice plans to enter a peaceful private practice, he should train where he can find Orientation A as described here. The idea that change takes a long time and the initiative belongs with the patient is best for private work. Private practice is most easy and lucrative when clients come several hours a week for many years. An active therapy approach requires three times as many referrals and many inconveniences. The place chosen to train for private practice should offer the advantage of meeting respectable people who will ultimately make referrals of well-to-do patients. Since most long-term therapy in private practice is now didactic, the apprentice therapist who has that goal should fit himself into an academic situation where future therapists can, if not must, come to him for personal therapy to improve their chances for future referrals.

If one is inclined toward Orientation Z and so wishes to train to be a therapist who takes the initiative for change and brings it about, the training opportunities are fewer and more difficult to find. Some students choose a place that is not especially good and use it as a base of operations while traveling to sample different approaches and experts over a wide geographic area. Often the situation is deceptive because many places appear to offer the right kind of training but in fact do not. Certain indicators can be suggested here. First one can list negative characteristics of training establishments as indicators for avoiding them.

1. One should avoid institutions where the emphasis is placed on the personality and personal problems of the therapist rather than on skills to bring about change. Similarly, if an emphasis is placed on using a group of students either as a form of group therapy or as an experiential focus "to loosen the student up," the setting should be avoided. When the focus is placed on the student's personal life, usually the teachers do not know how to teach how to do therapy. (This warning does not mean that students should not have a pleasant and stable personal life. The quality of one's work is always partly a product of one's intimate sources of support. A person's personal life is too important to be tampered with by teachers.)

2. One should avoid training in a place where only one class of people or ethnic group is available. For example, a university setting out in the wilds with only middle-class students

as clients is a limited way to learn unless work placement opportunities offer variety.

3. One should avoid training in a clinic where the rules
of the place are too rigid to allow experimentation in therapeutic
approaches.

4. Generally, if the institution puts great emphasis on
diagnostic skills, one can expect to learn little about how to do
therapy.

5. One should avoid inpatient settings. These environ-
ments exist for purposes of social control. Therapy tends to make
for trouble and instability because it encourages diversity and
new alternatives. Social control, in contrast, has the task of reducing diversity and forcing conformity on people who are out
of control. It is difficult to learn to bring about change in places
that seek to reduce instability.

Since inpatient settings are so common in the training
of clinicians, the issue should be elaborated further. It was once
thought that people could be changed by plucking them from
their natural situations, reforming them, and then sending them
back transformed. Therefore, people were plucked out of their
communities and put in hospitals or juvenile halls. This system
has failed and has adverse effects when compared with crisis
work, which contains the person in his or her situation and
changes that situation. Whether a person is mad, delinquent,
or retarded, the first goal is to arrange that the family and the
community solve the problem. Therapists should be trained to
achieve that goal. If the family continually uses the state to
restrain a problem person, the family and the state begin a collaboration which leads to a cycle of in and out of custody, so
that nothing gets resolved. If the problem cannot be solved in
the community, as a last resort one can always custodize.

Certain handicaps are difficult to overcome when doing
training within an inpatient institution. First, there are the im-
permeable walls. Most inpatient settings are of such a nature
that the therapist does not control going in or going out. Besides,
they are often placed outside the community and are not easily
accessible to families. I once taught a seminar on therapy for a

group of psychologists in a Veterans Administration hospital. After a while I stopped, because there was no way to teach how to do therapy in that situation. The psychology interns did not control discharge and so had no power to influence the hospital career of the patient. They could not control medication and so had little influence over what was put into a patient. The hospital site had been chosen for political purposes and not for convenience and so was far from the families and communities of most patients. Therefore, families could not easily visit, nor could the patient easily visit home, and the therapist could do few home visits. Besides this handicap, the government paid the patients disability pay for being incapacitated, so that they lost money if they improved. The psychologist could not change that system. All an intern could do was pass the time of day on a ward with a group, or sit alone with a patient listening to him ramble on. In the old days, when it was thought that sitting and having a conversation with a patient inside a hospital would transform him, this arrangement was considered therapy.

Another example can illustrate how the thinking and affect of therapists become disordered when therapists find themselves in a bureaucracy of a mental hospital. I recall two social workers in a state mental hospital who were dealing with a family in which the mother had become upset and was hospitalized when her mother-in-law moved into her home. The mother-in-law moved out two weeks later, and the woman was ready to go back to her husband and children. The therapists were not focusing on her going home but were bringing her husband and children into the hospital to help the family "clarify communication," whatever that means. When I asked whether they had the power to discharge the woman so her communication could be improved at home, they replied that they did not and had not thought about it. They listed at least four members of the administration who would have to approve discharge. They themselves had no say in the matter at all. Meanwhile the woman was being integrated into a variety of hospital programs, and her family was learning to function without her. When a therapist cannot easily move a patient in and out of an institution, he may forget about the goals of therapy and think about working on communication or about therapeutic communities instead of changing people.

Second, inpatient settings emphasize diagnosis. Psychiatric residents often have the misfortune of training on psychiatric wards, even though few of them will become hospital psychiatrists. Usually, such a setting fixes their views and ways of working so that it is difficult for them to change later, particularly if they later meet anyone who has gone mad. Within the hospital, residents learn to spend their time in conferences on diagnosis and on the effects of different kinds of medication. They learn little or nothing about therapy. When a psychiatrist trained in this way meets someone defined as psychotic, he is incapacitated as a therapist. He cannot think of what to do with the family and the social situation to change it. He can only think about whether the presenting problem is schizophrenia or an affect disorder or the manic phase of a manic-depressive cycle, and so on. Such questions are irrelevant to therapy and handicap the therapist in his thinking about what to do. All he has learned to do is diagnose, medicate, offer some insight, and pray. If the psychiatric resident begins his training in outpatient settings and *later* works on a psychiatric ward, he learns to see people less as medical entities and more as people with real human dilemmas.

A student therapist should avoid inpatient institutions unless the following conditions exist:

1. The therapist has control over discharge, whether from a mental institution or a juvenile hall. He or she must time the move back into the community to the needs of the therapy, not to the needs of the institution.

2. The therapist has control over medication if psychosis is involved. The therapist must either be a physician and take that responsibility or have an agreement with the doctor in charge that medication will not be adjusted without the permission of the therapist on the case.

3. The therapist should have control over visits home and visits of family and friends from the community to the institution.

4. The therapist should control other forms of therapy

given the patient in the institution to avoid being in conflict with other staff members over the approach to the problem.

Clinicians have had many years of experience failing when individual therapy is carried on with people defined as schizophrenic in institutions and almost as many years failing with family therapy when families are brought to the institution to pass the time of day with a member. Only if the therapy focuses on prompt discharge and its consequences is there a chance of forcing the family issues enough to bring about change. To achieve this focus, the therapist must control the exits and entrances. Since it is unlikely that a student therapist will be given sufficient power within an institution, a student should avoid custody settings and should instead work in community clinics.

Some of the positive characteristics to look for in a training setting are the following:

1. It is possible to observe therapists at work because there are one-way mirrors and they are used.

2. Students can be observed at work and given "live" supervision so that they can be guided while in the act of doing therapy.

3. Videotaping of sessions is easily and routinely done so that a student can go over the videotape with a supervisor at leisure.

4. It is assumed that students need to learn a variety of therapy techniques so that they can choose the one for a particular problem. The place should be one where whole families are interviewed as well as individuals.

5. The presenting problem is emphasized and taken seriously.

6. Outcome is emphasized, so that case discussions are guided by the destination of therapy, not merely by the process of the journey.

Live Supervision

When estimating a place to work, as well as to train, the therapist should look into whether supervision is taken seriously enough to be taught. Not every competent therapist is a competent supervisor or teacher. Such skills must be taught just as one must be taught how to do therapy. A clinic program should include supervisory training.

The most effective form of supervision, and the most expensive for a training institution or clinic, is live supervision, in which the therapist is observed from behind a one-way mirror and so coached during the interview. Several criteria can be used to judge the procedure.

The supervisor's unit is the family *and* the therapist, not merely one or the other. If therapist and family get into a repetitive cycle, the supervisor must intervene to make a change. To do so properly, therapist and supervisor must agree on how this intervention is to be done. First of all, situations will differ depending on whether the supervisor is supervising only this one case or the therapist's whole caseload. Situations also vary depending on whether they are part of training students, staff development, or merely assisting a colleague. Before the interview, the supervisor and therapist need to clarify just what their relationship is and what the purpose of the supervision is. The supervisor must be able to adapt to a relationship with an experienced colleague, to a student who is experienced but not in a particular approach being taught, or to a student who has never done any therapy at all.

A contract should be made between supervisor and therapist before the interview takes place. There should be agreement on at least the following points:

1. The supervisor will call reluctantly and will not interfere with the interview unless it seems essential. (It is better to use a telephone rather than a "bug in the ear." As the therapist listens to the bug, his eyes glaze and he is trying to attend to two different conversations at once and is not sufficiently involved in the therapy. Such a device also makes it too easy for the supervisor to interrupt, and so the supervisor tends to talk to the student too often and too much. To sit in the room and guide the student is less effective as a training device because it involves the supervisor in the therapy and prevents private collaboration and strategy planning between therapist and supervisor.)

2. In a call, the supervisor should usually present only one idea. When a therapist is involved with a family, remembering a series of things can be difficult.

3. The supervisor should present the idea concisely so that telephone conversation is brief and to the point.

4. If the suggestion is more involved, or if the student wishes more clarification than can be offered on the telephone, the student should leave the room to discuss the issue. The student should be taught ways to leave the room gracefully, and outside the room the conversation should be as brief as possible.

5. The general strategy of a case can be discussed before the interview, and larger issues can be dealt with when student and supervisor go over the videotape of the interview later. What is crucial during live supervision is brief interventions by the supervisor that make the interview go well and also teach the student some aspect of therapeutic skill.

6. A student should not deny that the family is being observed when it is or that she is being given suggestions when she is. Students will find that if they become comfortable with this arrangement, the family usually does not mind at all. In fact, many families welcome the idea that more than one person is involved in their problem.

7. Perhaps the most important rule is that supervisor and therapist should agree that any suggestion is *only* a suggestion, since the therapist in the room has more information than the supervisor behind a one-way mirror. Behind the mirror one misses many empathic aspects of the interview. However, if the supervisor is responsible for the outcome of the therapy, when the supervisor says the therapist "has to do" something, that is not merely a suggestion—it must be done. Such a directive should be used only when the therapy will otherwise be ruined or when people must be protected.

It should be clear that the supervisor's task is not only to make the therapy go well in this case and to teach a student therapist but also to protect the family from a beginner's incompetence. Equally important, the family needs protection from intrusion into private areas that are not the therapist's business. For example, a therapist should ask about how husband and wife get along with each other only if the therapist can indicate how this information is related to the problem to be solved. At times a therapist may be exploring and therefore inquire without a clear contract about the relevance of the inquiry, but the supervisor should judge when the invasion of privacy is greater than is proper. Two examples may illustrate different aspects of this problem.

Once a student therapist was talking to a mother about a problem child. The mother mentioned something about her sex life with her husband. The student encouraged her to say more about that topic, and the supervisor behind the mirror allowed the discussion to go on. The woman did not return for the next interview; apparently she was ashamed of how much she had revealed to the student when it was not clear to her how this information was necessary or relevant. The supervisor should have intervened.

In another case a school counselor was brought in for a session with the family, and the therapist began by asking the family about their week. The mother began to talk about the family problems. The supervisor called and asked the student to deal with the school issues and then send the school counselor out before dealing with the personal problems of the family that need not be revealed before the counselor.

Observing therapists at work will lead a teacher to realize the inadequacy of the former supervision model, in which all that was revealed about a session was what the therapist chose to tell someone about. We have progressed, over the last twenty years, from a supervisory model in which a student made notes and took them to a supervisor, who tried to guess what happened from those comments. After that we had audiotapes so that a supervisor could at least know what was said. Then came videotapes, so that both the words and the movement could be observed and commented on. Yet in none of those procedures could there be any help and guidance at the time the student most needed it—when he or she was in the act of interviewing. With live supervision we finally are able to protect the clients from incompetence and overintrusion and also to teach how to do therapy at the moment when the therapist is doing just that.

8

Ethical Issues in Therapy

‖‖⌐⌐‖‖⌐⌐‖‖⌐⌐‖

The main ethical issues in the field of therapy tend to fall either within the area of fair exchange, which involves issues common to any business or profession, or within the area of the control of information, which is especially important in the therapy enterprise. Fair exchange is a balance between what one receives and what one gives. In therapy the ethical issue arises because therapists are humanitarians helping people who need them, while they are also making money on that help. The therapist is paid by a sufferer, or by some advocate of the sufferer, to be helpful. The question of fair exchange inevitably arises because to accept money and not give proper service in return is unethical, just as it is unethical to gain some personal advantage and not return sufficient compensation to the client. When we acknowledge that different ways of doing therapy can produce more or less income for the therapist or for his or her agency, the ethical issue becomes tied to questions about therapy technique.

It can be argued that *good* in human relations is an equal balance of rewards and that *evil* is unfair exchange. After therapy, if either client or therapist has given more than he or she has received, this imbalance indicates an ethical problem. What complicates the issue for many therapists is the obscurity of the therapeutic goal and therefore an uncertainty whether fair exchange has occurred. Therapists who have the goal of removing symptoms or solving problems, and who do so, have done their job and earned their pay. Therapists who have the goal of helping people "grow," or of providing a "human" experience, or of giving self-understanding to the client, have a more difficult ethical problem. They are uncertain whether or not they have succeeded. And they may feel they have offered fair exchange for their pay even if at termination the client still has the problems that he or she sought therapy to have cured. Clinical ideology, as well as technique, is inextricably mixed with the ethical issue.

One further aspect of fair exchange has become an issue in recent years. Despite its humanitarian nature, the clinical field is also an important arm of social control in society. Governments pay therapists to quiet segments of the population and keep them from making trouble. When the poor riot, mental health clinics proliferate in the slums. The ethical dilemma for many therapists is that they wish to help the poor and so welcome the government funds, but they do not wish to be used by the establishment to keep the peace and prevent basic social change. Each therapist must decide whether the impoverished client receiving therapy truly gets a fair exchange for the money his government is providing.

A similar problem exists when therapists function as agents of social control in relation to people who are defined as psychotic and who make trouble but not enough trouble to be legally put in jail. Does someone who is put in custody for bizarre behavior receive a fair exchange for what the therapist receives for custodizing and quieting the person in an institution? The difference between therapy and social control hinges on who benefits from the procedures.

Controlling Information

The observation that a therapist functions at the boundary of conflicting groups makes it possible to define the ethical issue in terms of how the flow of information between those groups is controlled. When a therapist keeps something confidential, that is controlling information. It is possible to describe the groups involved from the smallest to the largest in the network.

The smallest unit could be considered to be the individual (although it is impossible for an "individual" to exist, since even the act of observing an individual creates a dyadic group). If we arbitrarily suppose that an individual could be an independent entity, the issue of information control involves flow from outside awareness, or the "unconscious," to the "conscious." When the theory of repression was rampant, the obligation of the therapist was to bring ideas from the patient's unconscious into consciousness. An ethical issue thus centered on how quickly to reveal unconscious ideas so that the patient was not overwhelmed with anxiety. To help patients permanently conceal ideas from themselves would have been considered antitherapeutic, if not unethical.

In recent years it has become more accepted to help people conceal ideas from themselves not only for temporary periods but also permanently. We appreciate the value of natural amnesia more now, as we begin to realize that we forget things and overlook matters for sound reasons. In fact, a person with total awareness, if such awareness were possible, would be a strange and deviant individual. We seem to function best if many aspects of our lives continue outside awareness. (I recall Gregory Bateson once saying that it did not puzzle him that people had an unconscious mind but it did that they had a conscious.)

If it may do harm to make a person aware, then the therapist is involved in an ethical problem. For example, should a therapist help people conceal from themselves ideas that might upset them? Suppose that a client became anxious at being successful. Would it be wise to help her avoid realizing that she was successful? These issues arise when one accepts the idea that total awareness is not an ideal state. Some therapists may consider it patronizing, if not harmful, to help a person conceal an idea from herself. From another view, helping a person avoid facing more, whether shame or power or success, than she wishes to face is an act of respect by a responsible person. Respecting the boundary within individuals can be considered as important as respecting the boundaries between people. From that view, the skillful control of amnesia becomes an essential part of therapy.*

Of course, the individual exists only in relation to someone else, and so the unit of the dyad is actually the smallest unit. The ethical issue of helping a person conceal from himself is inseparable from the issue of allowing the patient to conceal information from the therapist. How much will the therapist require that the patient reveal of himself? And how much of his own ideas and operations will he reveal to the client? Some therapists argue that there must be no concealment between therapist and client because concealment prevents intimacy and sharing. Yet the same therapists often emphasize the importance of helping the client toward "individuation." It can be argued that individuation and total sharing of information are incompatible. The act of concealment between therapist and client defines a boundary between them and so individuates them.

Another dyadic unit the therapist deals with is the boundary between a married couple. Should the therapist reveal to a husband what the wife has told the therapist in private? To withhold information is to draw a boundary between the couple and to say that their interests may conflict. Favoring entirely "open" information between husband and wife amounts to saying they are "one." The act of concealing or revealing information is not only an ethical one but a definition of marriage.

The next larger unit is the nuclear family, with the therapist functioning at the boundary between parents and children— the generation line. Should a therapist conceal or reveal to the parents information received from a child? Revealing what the child has said may be betraying a confidence and so behaving "unethically." Yet what if the child is three years old and the therapist feels the parents should know what is on the child's mind?

A larger unit is the nuclear family and the extended kin, with the therapist functioning at the boundary between them. Should the therapist conceal from the nuclear family what the grandparents have said, or vice versa? As a gatekeeper of infor-

*J. Haley, *Uncommon Therapy: The Psychiatric Techniques of Milton H. Erickson, M.D.* (New York: Norton, 1973).

mation, the therapist may consider it unethical to pass information about a family's troubles to the wider kin network.

The largest unit is the family in relation to the community. It is generally accepted that it is unethical for a therapist to reveal to the agents of the community what has been told him or her in confidence in the family. By concealing information, the therapist defines family and society as separate entities with conflicts of interest (while a therapist in a socialist state might not). Most therapists consider it ethical to conceal information from the community, but ethical issues arise when a therapist learns that a family member has murdered and plans to murder again. Less dramatically, a therapist sometimes knows that something he learned in confidence about a family would help a teacher in school deal with a child. But should he reveal that information?

Although there are many ethical issues at the boundary between these various subsystems, the emphasis here will be placed largely on the boundary between the therapist and client. Is it unethical for therapists to conceal their operations from their clients?

Manipulation and the Therapist

Whether therapists are "honest" with their clients or are "manipulating" them has been a source of controversy. It is now accepted that one cannot do therapy without manipulating people in the sense of influencing them to change, since change is the purpose of therapy. The pretense that sitting with a deadpan expression and responding in monosyllables would not influence a patient's life decisions has been recognized as only a pretense. The question remains how much of the therapist's maneuvering should be done outside the patient's awareness, either by concealing information about one's strategy or by using distraction techniques.

As actual therapy has been examined on videotapes and film in recent years, it has become increasingly clear how complex the interchange is between a therapist and one or more persons. Every minute hundreds of thousands of bits of information are exchanged in words and with body movement and vocal intonation. Both client and therapist may be conscious only of small amounts of so complex an interchange. A therapist may, for example, indicate displeasure with a topic by slightly averting his head. If he averts his head deliberately to block off the continuation of that topic, he is said to be a manipulator. If he makes this indication without realizing it, he is said not to be manipulative. One might say that the ignorant therapist is not a manipulator because he does not know what he is doing. But the issue is more complex than that.

If we deal with the concealment and revealing of information across the therapist/client boundary, and if we include the dimension of awareness or consciousness, we fall into an almost unresearchable bog. When a therapist does X with a patient and we wish to know whether he was aware that he did it, we must inquire. Not only may the therapist have a variety of reasons for not telling us the truth or for offering biased information, but he may not have been aware of the act until the inquiry. Then he becomes aware that he was aware, even though he might not have been without that inquiry. If we wish to find out whether the patient was aware that the therapist did X, we have the same problem. The issue is one familiar to researchers in hypnosis, in which testing an amnesia may lift the amnesia. Not only are there many ways, both subtle and obvious, to communicate with someone, but there are also multiple levels of awareness.

An example arose with Braulio Montalvo and Salvador Minuchin. Working on a film of a therapy session, Montalvo noted that Minuchin in a variety of ways joined an inadequate father throughout the session. At the beginning of the interview Minuchin walked into the room with the family, not knowing what they were like. He stumbled and fumbled and knocked over an ashtray. Montalvo argued (in a private exchange) that Minuchin sized up that situation immediately and "joined" the father by this behavior. He cited as evidence that in other interviews Minuchin did not behave in that way. Minuchin could have "deliberately" fumbled as he entered the room with a fumbling father as a way of sharing something with the man. If so, he was consciously manipulating. He could also have been,

as Montalvo suggested, deliberately unconscious of his act so
that he would not be consciously manipulating. If he "accidentally" and "unconsciously" fumbled when such behavior was
appropriate, was he manipulating? Questions of this kind are
probably unanswerable.

Conscious Manipulation

When we leave the issue of the therapist manipulating
outside his or her own awareness, we can focus on whether it
is ethical for a therapist to manipulate outside the patient's
awareness. This issue involves revealing and concealing information across the boundary line between therapist and client.
When the therapist plans a strategy or a set of tactics, is it ethical
to deceive a patient by giving false information? What about
deceiving a patient by concealing information?

As a general rule, it is unwise for a therapist to tell a
falsehood to a patient, not only because it is improper to lie but
also because it is naive to lie and believe that one will not be
found out. In a temporary relationship, lying may be successfully
carried out. But in any long-term relationship people learn to
read each other so well that false information is recognized even
though that fact may not be conceded.

It is said that one should not lie in therapy because it
teaches the patient that the therapist is untrustworthy. An equally
important issue is the fact that lying is usually patronizing toward
patients. It is treating them as if they were too dumb to recognize
a lie. Most therapists do not lie to clients to take advantage of
them but to "help" them. The deceit has a benevolent motive.
Yet even the small white lie risks being patronizing when offered by a therapist.

There are several areas where lying or not lying is not
so simple an issue. For example, it is unethical for a therapist
to reassure a patient by telling a lie about himself, such as saying, "I too have that kind of problem with my children," when
in fact the therapist does not. Yet there are times when the therapist says that something happened between him and his child
when it may or may not have actually happened but is so "in

character'' with this therapist that it does not really matter whether it actually did happen or not.

When it is obvious to both participants that a statement is a lie, it is not necessarily unethical to lie. For example, a psychiatrist was treating a woman and her family for a period of time. One day, when angry at him, the woman asked, ''Are you a doctor?'' The psychiatrist replied, ''No, I'm not.'' This statement was made for tactical reasons and was not a lie in the sense of a falsehood insofar as the context defined it explicitly as not true.

The lie as a joke is not quite a lie. For example, a mother was impatient with her child. The therapist said, ''I get angry with my child, and I feel like throwing him out the window, except I don't want to put a dent in the top of my car. He's eighteen months old and should behave better.'' The mother responded by saying he should have more patience with a child. What the therapist said was a lie, and yet the ''joke'' indicators clarified that it was not true.

When a complex situation is discussed and the therapist emphasizes or even exaggerates one aspect of it, she is not simply lying. For example, if a therapist says she felt like doing such and such when she had a multitude of feelings in that situation and is only emphasizing a minor one, that is not clearly a lie.

Therapeutic maneuvers involved in encouraging symptomatic behavior are not simple lies. For example, if a person is afraid in a certain situation and the therapist tells the person she wants him to be afraid in that situation, she is not telling the truth. In the larger context of the goal of therapy she does not want the person to be afraid, since she is curing him of fear. At that particular moment in that situation the therapist might actually want the person to be afraid so that the fear can be extinguished. However, often in using this approach the therapist does not want the person to be afraid but is only saying so to cure the fear. This statement is a benevolent lie and so must be approached with caution on both ethical and tactical grounds.

This type of situation arises by the nature of therapy where the goal of the therapist is to persuade a person to change ''spontaneously.'' The therapist does not want the person to change because she says so. She must *arrange* a situation so the patient *initiates* the change. One of the many ways to do this is to encourage the client to rebel against the therapist. When encouraging a symptom, the therapist is provoking the client to respond by not having the symptom. In this sense the ''lie'' of encouraging the symptom forces the person to take more responsibility for his behavior. The therapist is tricking the patient out of his problem, a method traditionally used by shamans.

The question in this situation is not so much a question of whether the therapist is telling a lie but whether she is behaving unethically. Even if she is deceiving the patient for his own good, is it ethical to deceive a patient? If it is essential for the cure that deceit be used, it might be justified on that basis. However, one must also be concerned about the long-term effect on a person of experiencing an expert as an untrustworthy person, which may be more harmful than the continuation of the symptom.

A more basic issue is raised by this approach. Is encouraging the symptom deceiving the client? It is a lie, but is not a lie like a joke? If so, there is no deceit involved. This issue can be clarified for a doubtful therapist by having him explain to a client what he is doing when he encourages a symptom. Usually this procedure still produces a change—as long as the therapist insists the patient go through with the symptomatic behavior. In fact, some patients will point out that ''reverse psychology'' is being used, or they will say, ''You don't really want me to have the problem.'' The therapist simply agrees, since such ''awareness'' is irrelevant as long as the directive is given and followed. In that sense, the ''deceit'' is not necessary to the cure, since the client is not being deceived, although less overt resistance is met if the ''awareness'' discussion is not held. Later one usually receives indications that the client knew all along what was happening.

The problem may be complicated if the therapist does not notice that he is encouraging a symptom. For example, a therapist may say to a complaining patient, ''It is important that you feel depressed right now so that you can learn to understand the lifelong pattern behind it.'' Some therapists say this sort of thing as a way of ending the depression—they are encouraging the symptom as a way of changing it. Other therapists may say the same thing but without intentionally being paradoxical or deceiving the client. They say it because they really do want the person to experience the depression and learn more about it. Similarly, one therapist may encourage anxiety as a way of getting rid of it while another may do the same as a way of providing less pressure for the patient, or of allowing him to notice what he really feels, or for some other reason. In one case, an expert is deceiving a patient as a way of tricking him into being cured, while in the other case, the therapist is not deceiving a patient, at least not deliberately. Once again, we have the problem that "deceit" may be a matter of the therapist's awareness or ignorance of what he is doing. It may be compared with a young person's coquetry in a courtship situation. Whether the coquetry is deliberate or is part of a natural response to the situation is difficult to determine. In either case, is it deceit? Equally important, is the therapeutic relationship comparable to normal relationships? Is "deceit" applicable in the therapeutic context?

Encouraging a symptom or being "tricky" with a client is sometimes said to be all right with adults but not with children, because it could "distort their perception" and so do harm. The idea seems to be that a child has more fragile perceptions than an adult. Some therapists will make interpretations to a small child about quite adult matters and consider that less harmful than encouraging a symptom.

Concealing Information

One can deceive by concealing information as well as by giving false information. Some therapists are concerned about the flow of information between therapist and client and feel that any restriction on information by the therapist is unethical. The therapist should reveal whatever he or she thinks to the client. Other therapists are less expansive and feel that the therapist should not simply free-associate but should "time" interpretations to the client, so that ultimately all information is revealed, but at different stages. The issue is not merely a tactical one but also an ethical one, if a therapist who conceals information from a client is said to be behaving unethically.

Whether a therapist should reveal all observations to a client is one of the most important controversies in the field of therapy. Upon this question hinges one's view of a human being as a rational as well as an ethical animal. A therapist who believes it is possible and proper to change a person outside that person's awareness is conceptualizing men and women differently from the therapist who believes that whatever he or she observes must be shared with the people being observed and that change comes about with their understanding of themselves.

In the past the therapist was said to be not responsible for what happened to a patient—he was only an adviser and a consultant. He was not influencing the life decisions of a patient, and he was not a judge of the patient or of his or her family but merely a responder who would reflect back the patient's own views. The therapist was not really involved and therefore not responsible for what happened. He was largely helping patients understand themselves and their situations so they would be free to make their own decisions. In this mythological view of therapy, ethical issues were minimized. Any therapist who actively intervened in a patient's life or changed a patient outside awareness was considered unethical not only in his or her acts but in the very fact of being so intrusive into the territory of another human being. Whether therapy cured people of their problems was considered less important than whether the therapist was behaving properly.

A major difference between the psychodynamic school of therapy, on the one hand, and the hypnotic approach, the conditioning methods, and other directive approaches, on the other hand, hinges on whether a therapist should help clients understand themselves by the use of interpretations. It is a question not only of whether insight is a cause of change but also of whether the therapist is obligated to explain to the client what he or she observes.

A new aspect of this question has been raised by the new research on the brain. Gazzaniga* has suggested that the brain is made up of a number of nodules that operate relatively independently of one another. One of these nodules is a "hypothesis-making nodule," which constantly makes hypotheses about what is happening with the person and why, and it cannot stop doing that. It is questionable whether this nodule influences behavior, but it cannot stop hypothesizing about why that behavior. Most therapy in the past might be said to be made up of the hypothesis-making nodule of the client and that of the therapist together speculating on why the person behaves as he or she does.†

Awareness and Ethics

It is now out of fashion to be an insight therapist, and therefore many therapists deny they operate with that theory. Yet often they continue with an insight approach while denying it. There are three basic types of interpretations used by an awareness therapist. One type involves insight interpretations that reveal to the patient some connection of the past with the present in a transference context. An example is to help a patient understand his response to authority figures by helping him connect his response to his boss and his father and the analyst. Another type involves past interpersonal interpretations in which the client is made aware that a relationship in the past is connected with one in the present. An example would be "Have you noticed that your fear about your heart came the same year your brother dropped dead of a heart attack?" The third type is the educational interpretation, which brings about enlightenment on an issue in the person's present life. This type involves educational comments such as "You're overprotective

*See M. Gazzaniga, *The Social Brain* (New York: Basic Books, 1985).
†For a discussion of therapy from this view, see J. Haley, "Towards a Rationalization for Directive Therapy," in *The Power Tactics of Jesus Christ* (Rockville, Md.: Triangle Press, 1986).

of your child" or "You seem afraid of your wife" or "Have you thought you might be provoking people to criticize you?"

All these types of interpretations assume that clients will change if they understand themselves and their situations better. Such interpretations are to be distinguished from strategic comments that the therapist uses to block off certain behavior and not to bring about self-understanding. For example, a therapist may point out to a wife that when she attacks her husband, she is actually helping him. He may say this as a way of preventing her from attacking her husband, but the comment may appear to be an awareness interpretation.

If we define the use of insight broadly, to include all education of patients, we can focus on the issue whether it is ethical to change people outside their awareness or whether one is obligated to help them understand what is happening in the therapy as well as in their lives.

At one extreme are the therapists who admit that they explain to patients what is going on only when they themselves do not know what to do and hope the patient will. At the other extreme are the therapists who believe that human beings are rational animals and that changing them outside their awareness denies their nature. Many therapists feel that sharing with a patient what they observe is treating the patient with respect and encouraging his or her autonomy. In concealing from the patient what one sees or making an intervention outside the patient's awareness, the therapist would be deceiving and manipulative. Some therapists with this view would even argue that whether the patient achieves the change she wants is less important than whether she has an honest, human experience with a therapist who is sharing understanding with her.

Disagreeing with such a view is rather like attacking home and mother. Yet several questions can be raised. First, we must accept the fact that the therapeutic situation is not an honest, human experience; it is a *paid* relationship. The therapist is receiving money to be human with a patient, which is rather inhuman. Second, it can be argued that no therapist of any school can share with a patient all of his or her observations and understanding. Third, it is doubtful that a patient can actually achieve autonomy when exposed to the understanding therapeutic approach. Finally, and most important, it is unlikely that an honest sharing of understanding within a paid relationship solves the problems the patient is paying money to recover from.

In discussing such issues, a major problem is the fact that what actually happens in therapy and what is supposed to happen are not necessarily the same. If one observes therapists who claim to reveal all and share understanding with a patient, it is evident that they are doing neither. The therapist is carrying out many unmentioned maneuvers that are concealed from the patient, often for benevolent reasons, and even, hypocritically, from the therapist. (One has only to observe how such a therapist talks with a colleague about a patient and how he or she talks to the patient to note the discrepancies between the therapist's theory of honesty and his or her practice of concealment.)

In no therapy is all the machinery of therapy revealed to the patient. There would be no problem of "timing" or deciding what "depth" of interpretation to make if the therapist immediately revealed every observation. While ostensibly proposing full disclosure, therapists actually conceal their observations from the patient until the patient is "ready" to receive them. One way therapists attempt to solve the ethical problem of being straightforward and honest while concealing is to develop a theory of resistance. By splitting the patient into a resistant side and a cooperative side, the therapist can conceal from the resistant side those interpretations that would not be effective at a particular time.

Therapists of the various conditioning schools face the concealment issue in different ways. Sometimes a learning therapist will "shape" a client's behavior by responding to the client with positive reinforcements whenever the "correct" behavior appears. The client might not be told this reinforcement is being given. If working with a marriage, such therapists may have a wife positively reinforce certain behavior of the husband's outside the husband's knowledge. In such cases the therapist is forming a coalition with the wife to reform the husband—which is another way of saying that information is shared between therapist and wife but not between therapist and husband. Moreover, although controversies have arisen over the use of aversive stimuli to condition patients out of their symptoms, the concealment involved in some of the conditioning approaches has received less attention. The issue has been obscured by the enthusiasm with which some conditioning therapists educate their clients about learning theory as a way of selling them on following the directives. Such therapists may appear to be revealing all by discussing theory, but in actuality they use many reinforcements, sometimes deliberately and sometimes not, that are not revealed to the clients.

One of the concerns about change outside patient awareness has been the idea that such an approach is incompatible with a major goal of therapy—helping a person achieve autonomy. Therapists often say they seek to have their patients achieve individuality and independence and make their own choices in life. Ostensibly, sharing one's observations with a client will help him understand his problem and its causes and will thus give him freedom of choice about changing. Yet patients who have experienced such therapy may have their free choice limited by the indirect imposition of the therapist's ideology.

Any therapist trained in a school of therapy is going to learn an ideology of explanation about why people do what they do. Insofar as any ideology is narrow and limited compared with all the ways of thinking about human life, an "understanding" therapist is going to impose a narrow view on his or her patients. The result will be patients who are limited in their ways of thinking and behaving. Their choices will be made within the framework of ideas that has been systematically inculcated in them over time.

If a therapist believes in his ideology, he is going to impose it on the patient (even if he tries not to) by words, body movement, vocal intonation, and instruction. The more hours therapist and patient spend together, and the more months and years the contract continues, the more the patient will be persuaded to accept the ideology of the therapist. The more interpretations are made and accepted, the less autonomous the patient will become, in the sense that he or she has less freedom to think differently from the therapist.

Furthermore, a therapist with a comprehensive ideology always has an ideal person against which he or she will judge the patient. For example, the therapist may have an ideal model of a person cleared of all internal conflicts and repressed emotions. This model was not drawn from observation of normal people, since that observation never occurred in training. Such standards are not maps of actual human beings but of schematized ideal ones, and the patient will always fall short of the ideal portrait. We also have the "ideal" family as a goal for many therapists. Both the "confronting" therapist who tries to bring out all emotions and the psychoanalyst who tries to lift repression with interpretations tend to have an ideal as a model. Another variation is the theory developed by Eric Berne, in which all behavior is to be explained according to a stereotyped schema of a "parent–adult–child" inside the client.

One aspect of the issue is whether the goal of therapy is to produce an ordinary person who is over his or her problem or a member of an elite who has been given special knowledge or experience that ordinary people do not have. All elite therapies have ideologies that the clients accept as part of the therapy. The clients try to fit themselves into the models of how human beings should be. While emphasizing freedom and autonomy (which is an ideal in itself), a therapist may shape a client to a narrow ideology, thus preventing the diversity that human beings naturally display. To put the matter simply, if the goal of therapy is to introduce more complexity, then imposing on clients a psychological explanation of their own and other people's behavior is antitherapeutic.

An example may clarify the issue of autonomy and illustrate how sharing understanding can prevent a good therapeutic outcome. A woman visits a therapist, brought by her husband, and says her problem is that she is afraid to go out of the house alone. If she tries to go out without an adult with her, she panics and has an anxiety spell.

A therapist trained in the theory of repression may try to relieve the woman's fears by bringing out her ideas and emotions. The technique used might be an experiential group in which she expresses her emotions through various group experiences with strangers. Or she might be seen alone by an interpretive therapist who empathizes with her and explores the causes of her fears. Such a therapist may help her understand how her past experiences have led to this state of being afraid to be autonomous. If she becomes a habitué of groups, or if she is seen in individual therapy over a period of years, the woman may be induced to think about herself in terms of inner guilts, anxiety, and so on. She may be taught a narrow explanation of why she cannot go out alone.

A more socially oriented therapist would relate the problem to the woman's marriage and her husband's response when she goes out alone. Should the therapist be interpretive, she would share with the couple her view of the husband's involvement. Since the partners would not have the problem if they could concede the marital problem, they do not accept the therapist's interpretations. Exposed to unacceptable ideas, the partners may either terminate or set out to demonstrate that the therapist is wrong by an increase in the wife's anxiety, intended to show that the problem is really all her own. The therapist has been ethical in that she has honestly shared her views. Yet she has done nothing to help the couple solve the problem because she has only talked about understanding it.

A directive therapist who views the problem as a marital one might ask the husband to help her cure the wife of her problem, without suggesting that the husband has a part in the problem. She might, for example, ask the husband to help the wife leave the house step by step under the husband's supervision. she may tell the husband to stand on the front porch while the wife walks alone to the sidewalk, then stand on the sidewalk while the wife walks alone to the corner, and so on. The therapist will assume the wife will go as far as the husband can tolerate, and she will be working with the husband to extend that limit. In the process, the therapist will be revising the marital contract and dealing with the conflicts the couple could not previously concede—such as where the wife will go when she goes out alone and whom she will be with. By dealing with the marriage without saying so, the therapist can effectively relieve this problem. Is this approach ethical? Obviously the therapist has concealed her views, and she has "manipulated" the couple to change without making them aware of her therapeutic plan.

Whether one sees this latter approach as unethical is partly determined by one's philosophical views. From the "sharing understanding" view, the approach shows a lack of respect for people, since the therapy is carried out outside their awareness. From the strategic view, such therapy is courtesy therapy. It is assumed that husband and wife know perfectly well that the wife's inability to leave the house is related to the husband and the marriage. They do not lack understanding but a way to resolve the problem. To force them to concede that the problem is a marital one is discourteous. Accepting their way of presenting the problem and offering a change within that framework shows respect for them. The crucial difference in point of view centers on whether the therapist thinks that patients need education and self-understanding. If the patient already understands, what she needs is a graceful way out of the problem.

In the same way, one can view either the presentation of a symptom or the presentation of a child as the problem. Just because the parents of a problem child have an evident marital problem does not mean the therapist needs to "make them aware" they have such a problem. Similarly, if a wife is "depressed" and one notes that her depression occurs whenever her husband avoids her sexually, it is naive to assume that she and her husband do not know the depression is related to the marriage.

Along with the interpersonal explanation of symptoms has come the idea that people do not have problems because of ignorance but because of their social situations. If a therapist conceals information from a client, he is usually concealing what the client already knows. The therapist is showing both courtesy and respect by that concealment. Granting that some clients, and some therapists, are dumb, it is a more respectful view of people to assume that they are aware of their difficulties and that they need a therapist who will make change as easy as possible.

When clinicians are unwilling to draw a boundary between themselves and their clients and insist on sharing all, they not only risk failure but even risk doing harm. Priests and medicine men have traditionally drawn a firm boundary between themselves and their clientele by keeping their views and techniques secret. They did not expose the machinery of their work to the public they were helping. A new initiate had to take vows of secrecy before he was exposed to the esoteric teachings. If the knowledge could not otherwise be kept secret, it was put in an obscure language, a code understood only by initiates. In the contemporary world that type of secrecy has been opposed. It is said that priests were concealing the fact that they had no special knowledge or skills but were exploiting the "faith" of the clients. It is also argued today that such secrecy is elitist and should be condemned as undemocratic. When clinicians adopt the total disclosure view, the person doing research in the field is put in an awkward position. For example, a researcher might suggest that a child's problem changes only if there is a change in the marriage of the parents. When this research is published, "awareness" clinicians who read it will immediately rush off and tell parents their marriage must change if they want the child to change. Parents who do not like that way of being confronted, and who would have gone to marriage therapy if they had wanted their marriage treated, will reject the therapy. The clinician is then likely to condemn them as uncooperative and resistant to the "truth." The idea that the researcher hoped would help the clinician is used in such a way that people in need of assistance are antagonized and will avoid therapy.

Researchers are thus tempted to avoid publishing what they learn about therapy. They may seek instead to return to the idea that knowledge should be kept secret and not shared with everyone. Yet such a return to past ways prevents scientific validation and prevents the advancement of knowledge. Since therapy is also a business, secrecy encourages rascals who benefit when people are ignorant of their operations. Not only may the researcher's knowledge be misused, but it may be trivialized and stereotyped and watered down until it is meaningless. The dilemma is a severe one for serious clinicians, for researchers, and for writers of books like this one.

An obvious solution is to encourage clinicians to be sensible and not share all with their clientele. When clinicians concede that they keep private views to themselves and offer their ideas to clients only with care and circumspection, then free presentation of ideas among clinicians will do less harm. It helps if clinicians admit, although few like to, that whatever they would tell the client is probably known already.

To emphasize the difference between an "awareness" and a "courtesy" approach, we can give an example showing how "awareness" can prevent change. A family enters therapy after the adolescent daughter took a dozen pills in an abortive suicide attempt. Parents and daughter are seen together the next day. The family shows the typical pattern of a child growing up to the age of leaving home. Often at such a time the parents' marriage is in difficulty. Not only is it a major change when children leave home, but often the parents have stabilized their marriage by communicating through a child, and now that child is leaving. The interview reveals that the parents have marital problems and that the father drinks to the point of being called alcoholic. The therapist views the girl's suicide attempt as a way of calling attention to the parental difficulty and the father's drinking so that the family can get help. Given that view, the therapist thinks it reasonable, at the end of the first interview, to say to the girl in the parent's presence, "You seemed to be trying to get your parents some help by what you did, and attempting suicide was the hard way to do that." The therapist probably views this comment as a way of helping the girl get out of the scapegoat role by making the parents and the girl "aware" of the "real" purpose of the act.

From the research point of view, this kind of explanation of why the girl has attempted suicide might be of interest. But to confuse research ideas and clinical operations can be disastrous. It is naive, if not idiotic, to impose this explanation of the suicide attempt on the family. Should this in fact be the reason that the girl attempted suicide, the therapist is even more wrong to announce it to the family. The daughter would arrange help in this indirect way only if it was necessary because the parents would not accept help when offered. (The parents conceded during the interview that they had avoided therapy despite long-standing problems.) By announcing that the daughter is getting help for the family by this act, the therapist has undermined and defeated the girl's attempt to take the blame for the problem on herself as a way of getting her parents to accept help. Shifting the blame away from her when she has put it on herself is demeaning to her and defeating the purpose of her act.

Let us suppose that the parents want to change in therapy after the situation is defined in this way by the therapist. Should the father now decide to quit drinking, this decision cannot be *his* contribution, because it has already been defined as caused by his daughter's attempt at suicide. In addition, the mother has tried for years to get her husband to quit drinking. If he stops now after his daughter's act is defined in this way, he is letting his daughter help him when he would not let his wife do so. Rather than put his wife down in this way, he may go on drinking. Should the parents improve their marriage, they would be conceding that this improvement was arranged by their daughter. If they are angry at their daughter and would rather not give her credit for their better life, they will avoid improving their marriage. The act of making the family "aware" of why the girl did what she did is an act that prevents change. The odds are against any change in the marriage once this "insight" has been shared with the family. Instead of therapy increasing complexity, it has decreased alternatives and rigidified the social situation. The "awareness" therapist will not conclude that *his* act caused this unfortunate situation. Instead, he will say the parents have deep-seated character problems and long-standing marriage difficulties and are unreachable.

Information and Larger Units. Although we have been emphasizing the boundary between therapist and client, a similar issue arises at each of the other boundaries where a therapist functions. Should a therapist reveal to a husband what he or she sees the wife doing and to the wife what he or she sees the husband doing? Just as some therapists argue that a therapist should share all her own operations with a client, so do they argue that if a wife is having an affair and secretly tells the therapist, she should reveal this information to the husband as part of an "honest" approach. A therapist who assumes that if a wife is having a continuing affair her husband knows it will focus on how to resolve it rather than whether to reveal the affair to the spouse.

At the boundary of the larger unit, the line between parents and children in the nuclear family, a therapist may feel required to reveal all she knows about the children's behavior to the parents and vice versa. In family sessions she may focus on total revelation and point out to parents and children how they are dealing with one another. Alternatively, she may assume that the problem is not sharing information but establishing rules for behavior. For example, a therapist might persuade parents to tell their adolescent children about their unhappy sex life. A more interpersonal therapist would assume the adolescent knows that a problem exists. For such a therapist, the therapeutic issue is the maintenance of a hierarchical line between the parents and the children rather than the sharing of information.

Information Theory and Communication Theory

When one views a therapist as gatekeeper of information between segments of society, a more general issue than therapy is involved. Implicit in this view is the idea that revealing or concealing information at a boundary between groups creates a boundary between groups. To not reveal to parents what their child has said is to draw a boundary between parents and child and define them as two separate groups. Information and boundary are synonymous.*

*An analogy is in order. James Clerk Maxwell once proposed a model for describing negative entropy. If one places a gas in a container, the molecules move at a rate determined by the temperature of the gas. The molecules *average* the same speed, even though some move faster and some slower. Maxwell proposed that temperature could change on the basis of selectivity or ordering. He suggested that if one could conceive of the container as divided in half with a gate at which a "demon" is making selections of molecules, the temperature in the two halves could be changed. If the demon opened the gate when the fast molecule came along and let it through, and he closed the gate against any slow molecules, he would take randomness away from the activity. Soon he would have fast molecules on one side and slow ones on the other, changing temperature by selection. It is evident that he created the boundary between the two halves of the container by the very act of being gatekeeper who selected what could pass through the boundary.
In a way, the therapist is a "Maxwell's demon" when he functions at the boundary between two segments of society. By selecting what information will be allowed to pass from one group to another, he is defining those groups as having a boundary between them (and he might also be changing the temperature of the groups). He is exhibiting preference and so "ordering" the two groups.

From this view, certain propositions follow: First, information and coalition are synonymous. The act of giving and withholding information across a boundary is an act of forming and dissolving coalitions. To conceal from parents what their child has said is to form a coalition with the child on that issue. Second, information and power are synonymous. To be in a position to reveal or conceal information between groups is to be in a *meta-*, or power, position in relation to those groups. And third, a therapist's position in a hierarchy is largely determined by his or her control of information—the ability to reveal or withhold information.

One problem posed by many theoreticians is the distinction between information theory and communication theory. While information theory has a more solid base, perhaps because it has practical uses, communication theory has remained undeveloped. How information is coded between a sender and a receiver has appeared to be a different question from how a learning animal forms a hierarchy by communicative acts. One may deal with what information a creature has received in terms of bits but not be able to connect that with a description of how the creature has formed a coalition against a rival. Observing a therapist, a change agent, functioning at the boundary between groups clarifies the relationship between information and hierarchy.

Given this view, it follows that a therapist who seeks power and influence over an individual or a group should establish himself as a gatekeeper of information between that group and a larger one. By actuality or illusion, he should be defined as the one who allows or prevents information to pass. Therefore, his power is enhanced if he is provided with secrets to be protected. The more an individual or group gives a therapist information it wishes concealed, the more power and status the therapist is given. Thus the ethical issues involved in the control of information are an essential aspect of therapy and so cannot be avoided or minimized.

It also follows that a therapist not only should see a whole family together but should also see members and factions alone. He must have, or appear to have, information that he controls at a boundary. If he only sees the whole family together, he can exchange covert information by innuendo and nonverbal communication, but the task of concealment is more difficult because everyone may receive the information.

There is a contradiction, or a tension, between the need of the therapist to have power and influence and his or her need to provide fair exchange. For example, if a therapist on the staff of a mental hospital sides with a patient against the remainder of the staff by not revealing something the patient has told her, she is disloyal to her fellow staff members. Yet if she does not persuade the patient to give her confidential information and then keep it concealed, she is not establishing a unique relationship or a sufficient coalition with the patient to make change possible. Although this dilemma is obvious in such a case, it is present in more subtle ways throughout therapeutic endeavors.

Let us suppose a therapist is treating a child and wishes to "reach" the child. He therefore encourages the child to reveal to him information he has not told others. As the child does so, the therapist conceals this information from the parents as a necessary factor in encouraging the child to trust him and reveal more information. Yet the therapist is also an adult and is in natural coalition with the parents by that fact. He is an agent of the parents insofar as they are paying him to cure their child. In that sense, he is in the position of the staff member of a mental hospital siding with a patient against the staff, because he is siding with the child against the parents. Yet if he does not side with the child by being gatekeeper at the boundary between child and parents, he will not be able to form a coalition with the child sufficient to bring about change.

One of the major points of organization theory is that consistently breaching power lines is pathological. If a staff member sides with a patient against other staff members and so crosses that hierarchical power line, the organization is in trouble. If a therapist sides with the child against the parents, he is like the grandmother siding with the child against the parents and is thus causing the difficulties he is trying to cure. At this point the paradoxical problem is evident. To gain power and influence in social systems, it is necessary for a therapist to conceal information between groups. Yet the act of concealing information from someone low in the hierarchy may force the therapist into a coalition across generation lines, which produces a disturbed system.

Let us take another example. It is often assumed that, when dealing with a marital couple, one should not side with either spouse against the other. Insofar as the therapist is an expert, he is higher in the hierarchy than husband or wife, and so siding with one against the other is violating a hierarchical line. Yet if the therapist is gatekeeper of information between them, he can be so only if he conceals (even temporarily) from one the information he has received from the other. In fact, that act not only makes him an "expert" higher in the hierarchy but also places him in coalition with one partner against another.

One requirement for the resolution of these apparent paradoxes seems self-evident. The therapist must follow the fundamental rule of not consistently siding with anyone against anyone else. He must provide fair exchange not only between himself and his clientele but also between the subsystems of clientele. If he uses concealment of information to side with child against parents, he must do the same to join parents against child. In this sense, the therapist must be *meta* to all the groups with whom he works. The problems posed by his membership in a group with interests that differ from those of his client must be resolved at a higher level. The staff member who sides with a patient against her staff must do so in a way that allows her ultimately also to side with the staff against the patient. She must distribute herself equally, even within the group of which she is a member.* In this sense she must represent both her client and the community, using whatever devices allow her to place her weight equally with both systems in the long run. Of course in the short run she might at any time be siding with one against the other as she tips the coalition balance in ways that can bring about change.

*Quite possibly there is an unresolvable paradox here that is central to therapy. One cannot be a member of a group and also be *meta* to the group. The same problem exists when an item is in a class and is also the class, as in the "class of classes" paradox of Russell and Whitehead. See A. N. Whitehead and B. Russell, *Principia Mathematica* (Cambridge: Cambridge University Press, 1910).

Many therapists feel that too much is expected of them if they must judge what is best in the variety of social situations and make decisions for their clients. They also feel that accepting the responsibility for changing people and keeping their knowledge of what is happening to themselves takes the wisdom of Solomon. Many therapists therefore choose to share their views with the client and push the responsibility for change onto him. Yet if the therapist is trained to be an expert, he or she should be willing to take responsibility and should know what should be done in many different situations. Often the therapist will not know, but that does not mean he or she should not. When therapy is seen from a social network point of view, the teachers of therapists clearly have more responsibility to do an effective job than they had when training therapists in the past.

In this brief review, many ethical issues have not been touched on. One crucial issue is whether it is ethical to take an experimental approach to therapy, tampering with people's lives with untried methods. Is it not more proper to use tested methods even if they have failed? The many social situations that appear in therapy force sudden ethical dilemmas on the clinician. With experience in the field, a therapist develops an ethical posture and learns to consider each situation on its merit. Practitioners who have done therapy for many years know what is ethical behavior and what is not. They may rationalize and try to deceive themselves and others about their own conduct, but they know.

Case Report:
A Modern "Little Hans"

This case report illustrates the approach to therapy described in this book. The specificity of the problem and the obvious nature of the family situation make the case useful for illustration. It is a child problem that is clearly defined, the stages of therapy occur as they should, different types of directives are given, including paradoxical ones, and the outcome is good.

The therapist in this case was Mariano Barragan, M.D., who was in training as a Child Psychiatric Fellow when this work was done. Although he had experience previously as a therapist, he did not have experience with this therapeutic approach. The supervision was "live," with the supervisor behind the one-way mirror. Also present at each planning session were colleagues involved in a strategic therapy seminar, and therefore many ideas about what to do came from the group.*

The case is called "A Modern Little Hans" because of its parallels with Freud's case in which a boy named Hans was afraid to go out on the street because of a fear of horses. This boy is afraid to go out because of a fear of dogs. In both cases, the therapist made use of the father/son relationship to produce a change.

*The group included Curtis Adams, M.D., Mariano Barragan, Joanna Chapen, Lee Milman, M.D., Braulio Montalvo, and Frances Ziegler.

This family was composed of a father, a mother, an eight-year-old boy, and a six-year-old girl. The presenting problem was the boy, who had never in his life been able to associate with dogs. He could not approach near a dog, could not enter a house where a dog was present, and was largely confined to his home because he avoided dogs on the street. He would even run from them into traffic, and so his parents were afraid to allow him out on the street alone and accompanied him wherever he went. Because of the severity of the problem, the parents placed the boy in therapy. After one year of individual child therapy, for what was called a "dog phobia" there was no improvement. The therapist left the city, referring the boy. The whole family were interviewed, and in the first session the family discussed the problem and their history. A treatment strategy was planned, and in the second interview with the family it began. The first step was to obtain a clear statement of the problem, particularly from the boy, since he had said little in the first interview. The boy discussed his fear, and then he began to minimize it, making it necessary for his mother to correct him.

The boy reported that when he got a dog, he thought that would mean the end "of me being afraid of them, but it wasn't."

"When you got a dog?" asked the therapist.

"Yes," said the boy, "it was a puppy."

"So what happened?"

"We gave it back because I was afraid of it." The boy continued to discuss his fear. "As for German shepherds, those are the dogs I am most afraid of."

The mother corrected him, "Now, be very honest. Princess or Bruce, they aren't German shepherds. When Bruce is outside, which is all the time now, and we all get out of the car, what happens? And he's not a German shepherd."

The presenting problem was apparently a difficult one to change, and yet if one looked at this family three weeks later, the boy had a puppy in the room and was petting it. What must have happened in three weeks that had not happened previously in the boy's life despite a year of therapy? How can we explain that he was touching a dog when he could not do so before?

Various explanations are possible: There might have been spontaneous remission. There could have been insight that re-

solved the problem. There might also have been a decondi-
tioning process in which the boy was brought closer and closer
to a dog until his anxiety was allayed and he could touch it.
In actuality, a quite different approach was used. It was assumed that the boy's avoidance of dogs has a function in the
family. If family relationships are changed, the boy will be
over the problem. It is not assumed that insight or understanding is necessary or a step-by-step conditioning process. Instead,
it is assumed that a therapist must intervene actively and di-
rectively in a series of stages to bring about changes in family
relationships. By the fourth family interview the change was
begun, but six more interviews were necessary to complete the
therapy.

In this particular family the mother was very involved
with the child and excessively concerned about his fears. The
father was more peripheral. He held down two jobs and so was
rarely home. His contacts with the boy were largely because
he had to take him places because of his fear of dogs. It does
not seem uncommon for a child to develop a symptom that requires a parent's company. The goal of therapy can be put
simply. It was to shift the relationships in the family so that
mother and father would be more intensely involved with each
other and the boy would be disengaged from them and more
involved with his peers, while having a more positive activity
with his father. Although the goal can be described simply, the
tactics to achieve that goal are complex and are determined by
the unique nature of each family. To change the family from
the beginning arrangement to the end point cannot be done
abruptly. The first step can be to change the relationship between involved parent and child. When a therapist enters the
family, he or she can take this first step in many different ways.
One particular way was used in this case. The parent who was
more peripheral was directed to become more involved with the
child. In this case, the mother was the authority on the child,
particularly on his fears. The therapist intervened to make father
an authority, thus bringing about more action between father
and boy and excluding the mother.

The intervention to achieve this first stage came about
in family interview number two, when the mother left the room

briefly. Use of the father as an authority on dogs was previously planned as part of the treatment strategy. To begin the intervention when the mother was absent was not planned.

The therapist said to the boy, "How much do you ask your father about dogs?"

"Very little."

"Do you know what—well, tell me, what is your father's job?"

"A letter carrier."

"Right. Do you know that letter carriers are supposed to be pretty good with dogs?"

"I know dogs don't like them. Most dogs don't," said the boy.

"All right, how many times has a dog bitten your father?"

"None."

"None. So that must mean that he is pretty good, because dogs don't like letter carriers. Right?"

"Right." The boy turned to his father. "Well, Dad, can I ask you a question?"

"Yeah," said the father.

"How do you get them away from you?"

The therapist said, "That's what I wanted to hear," and he sat back and watched father and son talk.

The boy said, "Like, I mean at Gerald's house, if the dog was loose, like that big white dog over there. If he got loose, how would you get the dog away from you, if he was a mean dog?"

"Holler, scream at him."

"Yeah, but what if he didn't go away then?"

"Well," said the father, "then you have to get ready to do something else. But whatever you do, you try not to run. If I had a coat on, I would try to take my coat off and put it in front of me."

"Why that?"

"Well, if the dog is gonna bite me, he's gonna bite the coat."

"Yeah, but what if you didn't have the coat and it was summertime?"

"Well, then the thing that I would be able to do to ward

off a dog, to fight a dog, probably you wouldn't be able to think of at the time. If you take your hat and you put it in front of a dog, and the dog grabs ahold of the hat, he's gonna grab the hat. He's not gonna pass the hat and grab your arm. He's gonna grab the hat, right?''

"Uh-huh.''

''You kick him under the chin, while he's grabbing hold of the hat.''

''You kick him under the chin?''

''Yeah,'' he said, showing a foot movement. ''It fits real nice, you see.''

The mother returned to the room with the daughter. The boy continued to talk with the father.

''So isn't that cruel?''

''If the dog is trying to bite you, nothing is cruel. Defending yourself is not cruel.''

The therapist pointed out, ''You see, I think maybe you haven't thought that you have an expert on dogs right at home.''

''I know,'' said the boy.

''Your father deals with dogs every day.''

The mother described some of the dogs the boy was afraid of, and the therapist shifted the conversation back to father and son. ''Think, Stu, have you ever seen your father handling a dog?''

''Yeah. I've seen you do it. You kicked that dog the other day, didn't you?''

The therapist points out, ''You know, your father has been dealing with dogs as a letter carrier. Maybe you can learn from him.''

The first step has been taken. Father and son are interacting over the issue of dogs in an area where father is the authority and mother is not. When mother mentions the boy's fears, the therapist neutralizes her words by emphasizing the father's knowledge of dogs.

The next step was to get a dog into the home. This step was necessary to continue the involvement of father and boy over a dog. It was also done to bring the boy into proximity with a dog so that changes in the family could be estimated.

That is, the boy's association with dogs becomes a measuring stick for change. The closer his contact with a dog, the more family relationships are changing. To introduce a dog into the home was difficult, since the family had tried to do so before and the boy had become frightened. When one gives a directive to do a task that has previously failed, it is necessary to make the situation a new one. The therapist made the addition of a dog a new kind of situation in interview number two.

The therapist said, "All right, Stu, so it sounds as though you have to learn a few things."

"Yes."

"You know what I want you to do? If it's agreeable to your parents." They nodded agreement in response. "I want you to go and adopt a dog. But you pick one who is afraid."

This is an example of good collaboration between supervisor and therapist. The supervisor had said a dog must be brought into the home, and it must be done in a new way because they had tried that before and it failed. The therapist had thought of this new way, which was acceptable to the family.

"Afraid of me?" asked the boy.

"I want you to pick a dog who you think might be afraid. I know there is no way of knowing that. You can't ask the dog."

"I know how to do that," said the boy.

"Do you?"

'Yeah, it would probably be a dog that was running, not running around and come back to me and stuff, that would be a dog that I wouldn't think would be afraid of me. It would like me. I would say a dog that would—like, go away."

"Okay. Then I want you to adopt a dog that you think is afraid, and I want you to cure this dog. With the help of your parents. You are all to get together and cure this little puppy, who is going to be a fearful puppy." He added to the parents, "Is that all right with you?"

"Yes, it's all right," said the mother.

"It will be all right," said the father, "if he goes to get it."

"That's what I had in mind," said the therapist.

"What do you mean, Dad?"

"Just like I told you all along," said the father. "I'll take

you and get a dog as long as you get the dog. You pick the dog
up and bring it home.''

"Yes, I know what you mean," said the therapist. "But
I want you to get together and—today is Friday, I want you
to get together and talk about the dog.'' Turning to the boy,
he added, "Then I want you to decide exactly what you have
to do, and then I want you to go and do it. But first I want
you to talk about it with your parents.''

That ended the second interview. The following week the
family had not obtained a dog, and the session was a general
one on family life. At the fourth family interview, the family
arrived with a puppy. The boy let it out of the box, avoiding
touching it.

"I hope he doesn't go to the bathroom," said the mother.
The dog did so, and the therapist and family laughed. The
therapist said to the boy, "What I want to see you do is—you
know that he is afraid, right?''

"Right," said the boy.

"Now, how are you going to do something about that?''

"You want me to do something? But how am I gonna
do it?''

"You know that you have to get this little puppy over
his fears, right?''

"Right.''

"I want to see some action.''

"What?''

"I don't know, you've got a problem.''

"Pick the dog up," said the father.

"I can't pick him up.''

"You held him.''

"There are a lot of people here helping you," said the
therapist. "You can ask your parents, you can ask your sister,
Sharon.''

"I held him," said the boy, and he added as his sister
went to pick up the puppy, "No, Sharon, no, no.''

The mother mentioned the boy had come a long way,
"but he just won't pick up the puppy and carry him.''

"I've seen him hold him," said the father.

When mother said she didn't remember that, the boy

pointed out that he had held him at his aunt's house. The mother recalled it then.

The therapist asked the father what he thought of the boy's progress, and the father said, "I think he's doing all right. Maybe it may not seem like that, but I think he's doing a whole lot better."

"I feel as though he's doing good too," said the mother, and she mentioned how he used to scream if *she* touched a puppy. The therapist, who did not want to review the past fears, said quickly, "So you agree with your husband."

"Yes," said the mother.

At this point the boy has improved sufficiently so the therapist can begin to shift to the next stage of therapy. There seemed to be a marital issue, and to deal with that before there is a change in the boy would be a mistake. There must be a step-by-step process. If there are marital issues, which is not always so, the therapist needs to shift to them. The way the therapist began the shift was by giving credit to the parents for improvement in the child. They deserved the credit for their cooperation, and giving it prepared for the ultimate disengagement of the therapist when he would have to leave the family system. It is easier to leave if the responsibility for the change has been placed within the family.

The therapist said, "What I want to say is whatever progress Stu has made has been basically because of you. I think it is not the time to be modest."

"I'm not trying to be modest," said the father.

"You see," said the therapist, "what I am trying to point out to you both, but especially to you," he added to the father, "that there are lots of things that you have done about Stuart's fears."

"Well," said the father, "answer this, why couldn't I or my wife do it by ourselves?"

"Well, first of all, you didn't think about the business of your being an expert on dogs. Which you are. I mean, let's face it, whether you admit it or not, it seems very easy for you nowadays, and as a matter of fact it was such a part of everyday life that you never knew about it."

"Uh-huh," said the father.

"But your being a letter carrier has helped Stuart."

The mother said, "I agree, I agree. But you put it in words, that mailmen are experts on dogs."

"What I'm trying to say is that you have done a lot in here to produce whatever change has happened."

"That makes you feel good, anyway," said the father.

The therapist moved the family to the next stage by asking the parents, as a reward for having done so well with their child, to go away for the weekend. This forced a focus on the marriage. The task also shifted the mother from engaging with the child to engaging with the father. This shift often takes the form of complaints about his neglect of her and requests for more from him, and at that point the child is left out of their struggle.

"I don't know how you feel about it," said the therapist, "but I think that what is important is that you get a reward for what you have done. I can think of several. For instance, how about a weekend away by yourselves?"

"Yes, that would be nice," said the mother, and both parents laughed.

"Would that be nice?" asked the therapist.

"Yes, that would be really nice," said the mother. "I don't know if Stuart heard that."

It is typical in this type of situation for the mother to bring the child into an issue between the parents. The therapist quickly moved him out, and father noticed that.

"Never mind Stuart," said the therapist. "This is a trip for you two." He then added, "It will be good for Stuart, anyway."

Talking of a weekend together, the father said, "Can you remember that far back?"

"That would be ideal in terms of his realizing that you are not so concerned about him. Which is what I am trying to do," said the therapist.

In the sixth interview, the parents had not gone out alone together and were not talking about any marital issue. The boy was still somewhat afraid of dogs. Because of a danger of a relapse at this point, the therapist avoided having the family shift back to the boy's fears by doing so himself. He encouraged the boy to have a relapse and asked the parents to cooperate. Such a move stabilizes the improvement and prevents the family from going back to old patterns. In a playful way, the therapist asked the boy to help the puppy by pretending to be afraid of him. The boy's response was a classical one to a paradoxical therapeutic maneuver.

"Stuart," said the therapist, "do you think that we can play a trick on that dog so that he will be all right?"

"Like what?"

"But you have to be pretty smart. And I'll show you the way in which you can measure how smart you are being. All right?"

"How are you gonna do it?" asked the boy.

"I will ask you to do something, and I'll ask your parents to participate in that. All right?"

"Like what?"

"See, actually we have to trick this little puppy into thinking that *you* are afraid of *him*."

"Make him think that *I'm* afraid?" The boy looked stunned, and he scratched his head in a puzzled way.

"Do you get the idea? See, I want the puppy to try to convince you not to be afraid of him. This is just make-believe. I know that you are not afraid of the puppy, are you?"

"No."

"All right. This is just tricking the little puppy into thinking that *you* are afraid of *him*. Do you get the idea?"

"But how are you gonna do that," said the boy, "after I've already been touching him and holding him and everything?"

"Well, somehow you have to give him the message that you are afraid of him. Like, you know, you have to kind of—"

When the therapist hesitated, the boy said, "Run from him? I think that would be mean to him."

"Show him that you are afraid of him."

"Like doing what? Chasing him away and everything?"

"You don't have to chase him away. You know, do you think that if you are afraid of me you are going to chase me away? No, you're just going to run from me. Right?" He added to the parents, "Do you think that you can help Stuart to get afraid of the puppy?"

"I'll try," said the mother.

"No, no, no that's not very enthusiastic."

"Help him to be afraid of the puppy?" The mother and father looked at each other, puzzled. They were responding to the paradoxical idea that the therapist who was attempting to get their child over a fear of dogs was now asking them to encourage the boy to be afraid of dogs.

"I'm very serious about this," said the therapist, "and I'm sure you get the idea. The idea is to get the puppy to think that Stuart is afraid of him. So that the little puppy will understand that it is his job to convince Stuart not to be afraid of him. Now we all know that he is not afraid of the puppy, but it is just tricking the puppy for the puppy's benefit."

"Well," said the boy, "I think he knows that I'm not afraid of him."

"I know that, that's why it is a trick. And you only have to do it for a couple of days. I'll tell you what. I want you to ask your parents what they think about it, how they think you can do it." As the boy looks solemn, he adds, "Look, you don't seem too happy about the idea."

"No," said the boy.

"Why not? Look, you are an expert on that. Weren't you afraid of dogs for a long time?"

"Yeah."

"Well?"

"I think I acted crazy," said the boy.

"You think you acted crazy, when you were afraid of dogs?"

"Uh-huh."

"All you have to do is the same things that you were doing before."

"It's gonna be hard."

"Oh, I know it's gonna be hard."

"After all this time, seven or eight years, almost eight years, I've been afraid of them, but now it's slipping off of me."

The paradoxical intervention was successful, and the boy

began to touch the dog. The parents had not succeeded in getting away for a weekend, but they had a pleasant evening at home, which was unusual for them. The therapist continued to insist that they get away together without the children. A marital difficulty appeared. After congratulating them on their parenting, the therapist said, "But you haven't taken care of each other."

"We don't see much of each other," said the mother.

"You don't like that, do you?"

"No."

"When was the last time you even talked about it?"

"We don't."

"You mean you don't talk about things that you dislike?"

"No, we don't."

"How come?" asked the therapist.

"Because, well, I guess that we can't talk about those kind of things really."

At this point the therapist could continue to focus on the child problem or he could explicitly make a contract to deal with the marriage, which was decided as the next step.

The mother continued, "That would lead to arguments, and rather than argue, we don't talk about some things. Right?" she said to her husband.

He replied, "I guess. I don't see why."

When the therapist saw that the father was reluctant to talk about this issue, the therapist said, "This is not my business, right?"

"Evidently it is part of the therapy," the father said.

"Let me speak very frankly with you. I feel very optimistic about Stuart's fear of dogs. That will be gone." He continued, "If you want to stop at the level of Stuart getting rid of the fear of dogs, we can do it, but what I really had intentions of asking you today is—do you want the whole thing? Or just to get rid of this?"

After a long pause, the father said, "Do the whole thing."

"Do I have your permission?" asked the therapist.

"Yes," said the father.

The therapist had them talk about their life together. The

mother said, "I do need to get out of the house, but you just
get tired of saying it. I know that in order to make a happy home,
it's not just the children, it's time together, going places together
so that when you come back you can appreciate being with them.
If I went away myself, the whole weekend, I'd be happy."

When the therapist asked the father what he thought about
his wife's sadness, he said that he had seen the "tiredness, the
look on her face, the droop, I know."

"I am tired, and it's against my nature to prolong things."

"I think you're lonely," said the therapist.

"I know that, I admit that." She turned to her husband.
"I've admitted that to you, haven't I?"

"Yes," said the husband.

The mother talked about her situation and said, "After
awhile you get the craving for the conversation of grown-ups,
and being a woman, not only just grown-ups but the male."

The therapist decided to deal with this impasse between
the spouses by paradoxically encouraging a relapse. He said,
"There is a very good way to settle this situation."

"What's that?" asked the mother.

"Why don't you both try—and I'll ask Stuart to help
you—try making him afraid of dogs."

"Make Stuart afraid of dogs?"

"Yes, just as afraid as he was when he walked in here,
and then we can get busy working on that and we won't have
to talk about this anymore."

"That's a nice waste of time," said the father. "Is that
what you're saying?"

The mother replied, "He's saying that maybe that will
be a mutual meeting ground—Stuart."

The father said, "We don't need to talk about the dog.
Stuart doesn't need the fear of the dog. And we don't need to
keep on talking about it. I mean, the way you say it, that's the
only time that my wife and I get to talk is about Stu, and if
we don't talk about the dog, we won't have anything to talk
about?"

The therapist agreed, saying, "You know, you are making me feel like a villain. I come into the picture and make you

work on the problem and you get the problem solved, and all of a sudden Stuart is not afraid of dogs. I get the feeling that you worked against yourselves because there you are left kind of empty." He added, "By being so worried about losing the love of these kids, you've lost sight of each other."

The therapist talked with them about taking each other for granted, and the wife agreed that she felt that way. She added that she did not take her husband for granted, and then she said, "I *have* taken him for granted, but I don't think I do now. I know I don't."

"What made you change?"

"That's a different story," she said, and she hesitated. "Just something that happened between us, which made me not take him for granted, but then I think that now he takes *me* for granted."

"Something that happened between both of you?"

"Right."

The therapist asked whether they wanted to talk about it, and they were unresponsive. In this situation there was obviously a problem in the past between these spouses. Exploring painful aspects of the past is not essential in this therapy. The problem is how to get past them and move on. The therapist handled this one in an unusual way. He said to them, "Why don't you *pretend* that you told me, and then go on."

"Pretend what?" asked the mother.

"That you told me about it."

"All right," said the mother. "I'll say that we had Stuart and I was on cloud nine because this was what I really wanted. Then something happened, and I think that I started realizing that I was too wrapped up in Stuart. I wasn't giving enough attention to Tom. Which caused what happened to happen. And I wanted to, you know, maybe give him more attention, but I don't know if he wanted it. So that's the way it happened."

"All right," said the therapist. "Well, you said it."

"I think we changed, Tom changed."

"How much resentment was left?"

"A lot."

"Is it still there? Is that 95 percent of this situation?"

"Yes," said the mother. "Because I think you put it into words, and it's something that I have just been thinking all along. That the kids were being used to, like, bridge the gap. It's like what we had in common. I've said this to you, though," she added to her husband. "Right?"

"Right," he said.

In actuality the therapist had not said that they had used the children to bridge a gap between them. Obviously people often understand their situation and do not need interpretations from therapists.

The therapist began to help the couple resolve their difficulty. First he changed the idea of who was the villain and who was the victim, making them mutual victims, and then he persuaded them to drop the issue by reducing it to absurdity and putting it into the past.

"Now you've been punished for how many years?" asked the therapist. The mother said it was six and a half years and added that she was being punished too. "My husband," she said, "is stubborn and will never say that you are right or that you are wrong." She added, "The time that we have to sneak a word in edgewise, there are some subjects that are taboo, that I can't talk about. Like for instance, to bring it all out, he'll keep—which he didn't used to do—job and home entirely separate. It's like my husband is living two lives. From the minute he walks out the door in the morning until he comes home, that's one life that I dare not even ask a question about. But he was never like that before. So there he is punishing *me*. He withholds."

The therapist talked about the problem as having receded into the past, and then he gave the father a directive that offered the couple an opportunity to have a fresh start. He said, "What I would like you to do is to do something that she wouldn't expect from you. You know her very well and you know what she wouldn't expect. Would you do something, anything?"

The husband agreed, and when the couple returned the following week, he had brought the wife flowers unexpectedly. The therapist began to move the family to finish the change and began his disengagement from them.

"How is the puppy coming along?" he asked.

"The puppy is getting bigger every day," said the father.

"Is the puppy getting over the fear?"

"Yes," said the mother, "and everybody else has to be afraid of *him*. He doesn't let anybody come in the house but the four of us. He's a very good watchdog."

The therapist turned toward the boy and said, "It sounds like you and your dad have done a pretty good job." He asked the parents about the husband's assignment, and the wife reported she was pleased with the flowers.

To continue the improvement and to disengage himself, the therapist recessed the family for three weeks, which suggested they could do without him. He also suggested that mother and father would have a major disagreement. He did this partly to prevent a fight, but more to the point, it would pull the couple together against him, since they wished to disagree with him about this.

"I get the feeling," said the therapist, "that you are getting a little closer to each other. Sometimes when this happens, people tend to have some kind of disagreement. Like a big fight."

"When they get closer, they have a fight?"

"Right."

The wife turned to her husband. "Are you ready for that?"

"Uh-huh," he said skeptically.

They both said they doubted it, and the therapist said, "Okay, let's do this: you will still have it even though you don't believe it. You are not going to have it because I say so. It will happen because of the way things are coming along, which is very good."

The mother laughed with her husband and said, "Well, suppose we don't have it, just to say you're wrong? You know we do those kinds of things. We are very good at proving the other person wrong."

"I don't think you're that kind of person," said the therapist.

"Oh, boy," said the mother, "we've proved a lot of them wrong."

The tenth and final session was a disengagement session.

The therapist did a review during it. He asked how the boy was doing with his fear of dogs, and the mother said, "The dog on the street that he was afraid of from the very beginning, Bruce. Well, him and Bruce are friends." The mother discussed the dogs in the neighborhood, and the problem of the fear of dogs was gone.

The therapist said to the boy, "That sounds great, I'm proud of you." He added to the parents, "He is all over it, what he came originally for, right?"

Later in the interview, the therapist talked to the parents alone. The mother reported about the boy, "He's changing, in fact, he's even gotten a little more aggressive, you know. Whereas before he might not have started anything with you, but now he's, you know, I think all of that was in with the dog bit. You know, he was afraid of dogs, so he was a little afraid of other things. Like even of certain kids. One day I saw him and he just walked right up into a mob of kids."

At the end of the interview, the therapist brought the boy back together with his parents and said to the boy, "You know, your dad and your mommy and I have agreed that you don't have a problem anymore, so from now on we're just gonna be friends, okay?"

"I guess so," said the boy. "I never saw how anybody could be friends and never see them again."

"Oh, that doesn't mean that you can't come over and visit me. You can come over any time."

"I don't know," said the boy.

"He's telling you that you can," said the mother.

"Oh," said the boy, pleased.

Later the boy invited the therapist to attend a birthday party and he went.

Two years later a follow-up interview was done. The parents reported that their daughter was doing well and their son Stuart was not restricted in his behavior by any avoidance of dogs.

The father said, "He walks down the street with me now, and he doesn't even pay them any attention. Like I mean, he used to come up in back of me, and come up to the side, and all that kind of stuff."

At the end of therapy there did not seem to be any major change in the marriage relationship except that the son was out of it. In the two-year follow-up there was an inquiry into the current marital situation.

When asked whether they minded talking about it, the mother said she did not mind because there wasn't "any problem now." She added that she thought that in her own mind anything she might have been doing wrong was solved because she had gone back to church. She also baptized the kids. She added, "Then we started having company, we have company a lot. Which we weren't doing at the time."

The father added that they were having card parties, and that was something they used to do when they first got married. The father also said he didn't work two jobs anymore and so was home more, and the therapist congratulated him. The wife said she didn't see him much more because of the competition with the kids.

When the therapist complimented them on looking so relaxed, the mother said, "Do you want me to tell you why? Because two years ago Tom got a bonus, just after we finished here, and we took it and went down to the shore. All of us went. And we went again this summer," she added. "Also Stuart went to camp last summer. He has so much to tell you. He's joined the Boy Scouts."

The problems had been resolved, and the results lasted.

Index

Mother, in generation conflicts, 116–118, 119–122. *See also* Parents
Motivation: approaches to, 62–65; and directives, 62–65; of student therapists, 206–207

N

Negotiations: to establish problem, 8, 38–39, 128; in task-setting, 84
Normality, 114–115

O

Obedience, as problem, 32
Observations: not sharing, 17, 28–31; in therapist training, 52–54, 201–202
Ordeal directives, 88, 176
Organization: family, 17, 36–37, 85; malfunctioning, 114, 115–116, 138–139, 140, 143; and power, 107–111; tasks to change, 85. *See also* Hierarchy; Sequences; Structure
Orientations: in therapy, 195–202; and training setting, 209–210
Outcome, checking, 209, 261
Overinvolved parent, 22–23, 121–122, 141–142, 147–152, 246

P

Paradoxes, in communication, 131
Paradoxical intervention: and abnormal situations, 128–129; dangers in, 78, 100; with family as whole, 77–79; and metaphor, 72–76, 100–101; with part of family, 79–80; and resistance, 76–77; and restraining technique, 153–159; stages of, 80–84
Paraprofessionals, and hierarchy, 120
Parental child: defined, 119; discovery of, 37; in family structure, 119–120, 124, 129, 139–141. *See also* Child
Parents: divorced, 142, 167; involvement of, 21–23; overinvolved, 22–23, 121–122, 141–142, 147–152, 246; peripheral, 22–23, 122, 141–147, 246; putting, in charge, 49–50, 122, 142, 145–146; in two-generation conflicts, 121–123, 124, 141–152

Past, and marriage therapy, 175–176, 257
Peripheral parent, 22–23, 122, 141–147, 246
Philadelphia Child Guidance Clinic, 204n
Philosophy, avoiding, 175
Pittman, F., 24n
Play, 92
Playthings, for child, 28
Power: and hierarchy, 21–22, 108–111, 240–242; and information, 186, 240–242; and organization, 107–111
Preciseness: in defining problem, 38, 39; in directives, 65
Presenting problem. *See* Problem
Presenting Symptom. *See* Symptom
Privacy: invasion of, 216–217; of students, 210
Problem: child as, in marriage, 167–168; defining, 1–4, 38–42; exploration of, 18–34; family crisis as, in marriage, 167–168; fitting, to student, 208–209; focusing on, 135; marriage as, 167–173; as metaphor, 97–99; minimizing, 173; negotiating to find solvable, 8, 38–39, 128; nonexistent, 41; number of persons in, 31–32; orientation toward, 197–198; redefining, 128–129; responsibility for, 29; and social unit, 2–7; symptoms as, in marriage, 165–166; and task design, 85, 88; therapist in, 2–4; uniqueness of, 177
Problem child: and crisis interview, 48–52; in first interview, 23–24, 25–26, 28, 31–34; and generational boundaries, 37, 88; and marital problems, 30, 75, 87, 122–123; as scapegoat, 40. *See also* Child
Problem stage, of first interview, 14, 18–34
Procedures, and theory, 195, 202–203, 206
Projective tests, 104
Psychoanalysis: and analogies, 93; model in, 233
Psychodynamic theory, and marriage therapy, 161
Psychotic family, 124

R

Reciprocal inhibition technique, 127
Referral, 12; compulsory, 12-13, 44-48
Relapse, encouraging, 78-79, 133, 193,
    252-253, 256. *See also* Paradoxical
    intervention
Resistance: behavior change through,
    76-84; client, 72, 200
Responsibility: for change, 195-197;
    and compulsory therapy, 48; and
    directives, 57-58
Restraining technique, 153-159
Review, task, 67
Ritual, 92, 176
Rosen, S., 95n
Rossi, E. L., 56n
Ruesch, J., 131n
Rule-governed behavior, 162, 169-171
Russell, B., 242n

S

Scapegoat, 40
Sculpting, 201, 203
Secrecy: in family, 19, 24; and therapy,
    236
Self-report, 10-11, 103-104, 105, 201-
    202
Separation, and marriage therapy,
    171-172
Sequences: change in, 61-62, 88, 111-
    112, 114, 124-126; and hierarchy,
    111-116, 130-134. *See also* Structure
Sequential order, 108n
Sharing: with clients, 17-18; in train-
    ing, 205-206
Social control, therapy and, 6-7, 51-
    52, 211, 219
Social stage, of first interview, 14-18
Social units: and information control,
    219-222, 238-239; in marriage ther-
    apy, 163-164; in therapeutic prob-
    lem, 2-7; therapist and client in, 2
Specificity, in first interview, 30-31
Spokesperson, for family, 24-25
Spontaneous change, 75, 78, 134, 195-
    197, 225-226
Stages: of first interview, 14-42; of
    marriages, 163; of paradoxical in-

tervention, 80-84; of therapy, 127-
    130, 137, 159-160, 246, 251, 252
Stampfl, T., 94, 100
Stepparent, in two-generation conflicts,
    123
Structure: change in, 88; defined, 111;
    family, 17, 36-37, 85; malfunction-
    ing, 114, 115-116, 138-139, 140,
    143. *See also* Hierarchy; Organiza-
    tion; Sequences
Suicide, threats/attempts, 50, 167-168
Supervisor: assistance of, 10-11, 14n,
    26; and evaluation of therapist, 52-
    54; in hierarchy conflicts, 118-119;
    intervention of, 196-197, 215-217;
    in systems, 132, 133; and training,
    196-197, 202, 205-206, 214-217
Symptoms: as communication, 99, 106;
    defined, 2; false, 97-103; focusing
    on, 135, 197-198; as function in
    relationship, 166, 246; information
    needed about, 39; in marriage ther-
    apy, 165-166; and social context,
    1-2
Systems, theory of, 130-133. *See also*
    Hierarchy; Sequences

T

Tasks. *See* Directives
Therapist: attitude in first interview,
    27; and client resistance, 72, 200; in
    coalitions, 5-6, 23, 126-127, 171,
    172, 173-174, 231-232, 242; disen-
    gagement of, 145, 157, 159, 193,
    251, 259; evaluating, 52-54, 201-
    202, 214-217; gender of, 23; in
    hierarchy conflicts, 118-119, 123-
    124, 174; ideology of, 232-233;
    manipulation by, 222-227; and
    marriage therapy, 169-170, 171,
    172-173, 231-232, 242; multiple,
    14n, 178, 204n; in therapeutic prob-
    lem, 2-4; responsibility for direc-
    tives, 57-59; and social issue, 4-7;
    and stress, 23-24. *See also* Training,
    of therapists
Therapy: and analogies, 93-99; com-
    munication in, 89-93, 239-243;
    compulsory, 12-13, 44-48; crisis,